The YWCA in China

Contemporary Chinese Studies

This series provides new scholarship and perspectives on modern and contemporary China, including China's contested borderlands and minority peoples; ongoing social, cultural, and political changes; and the varied histories that animate China today.

Ruoyun Bai, *Staging Corruption: Chinese Television and Politics*

Christopher G. Rea and Nicolai Volland, eds., *The Business of Culture: Cultural Entrepreneurs in China and Southeast Asia, 1900–65*

Eric Hyer, *The Pragmatic Dragon: China's Grand Strategy and Boundary Settlements*

Kelvin E.Y. Low, *Remembering the Samsui Women: Migration and Social Memory in Singapore and China*

Jennifer Y.J. Hsu, *State of Exchange: Migrant NGOs and the Chinese Government*

Ning Wang, *Banished to the Great Northern Wilderness: Political Exile and Re-education in Mao's China*

Norman Smith, ed., *Empire and Environment in the Making of Manchuria*

Joseph Lawson, *A Frontier Made Lawless: Violence in Upland Southwest China, 1800–1956*

Victor Zatsepine, *Beyond the Amur: Frontier Encounters between China and Russia, 1850–1930*

Patrick Fuliang Shan, *Yuan Shikai: A Reappraisal*

Selina Gao, *Saving the Nation through Culture: The Folklore Movement in Republican China*

Andres Rodriguez, *Frontier Fieldwork: Building a Nation in China's Borderlands, 1919–45*

Yuxing Huang, *China's Asymmetric Statecraft: Alignments, Competitors, and Regional Diplomacy*

For a complete list of the titles in the series, see the UBC Press website, www.ubcpress.ca.

The YWCA in China

The Making of a Chinese Christian Women's Institution, 1899–1957

ELIZABETH A. LITTELL-LAMB

UBCPress · Vancouver

32 31 30 29 28 27 26 25 24 23   5 4 3 2 1

Printed in Canada on FSC-certified ancient-forest-free paper (100% post-consumer recycled) that is processed chlorine- and acid-free.

Library and Archives Canada Cataloguing in Publication

Title: The YWCA in China : the making of a Chinese Christian women's institution, 1899–1957 / Elizabeth A. Littell-Lamb.
Names: Littell-Lamb, Elizabeth A., author.
Series: Contemporary Chinese studies.
Description: Series statement: Contemporary Chinese studies | Includes bibliographical references and index.
Identifiers: Canadiana (print) 20230496814 | Canadiana (ebook) 20230496873 | ISBN 9780774869201 (hardcover) | ISBN 9780774869225 (PDF) | ISBN 9780774869232 (EPUB)
Subjects: LCSH: Zhonghua Jidu jiao nü qing nian hui – History – 20th century. | LCSH: Christian women – China – History – 20th century. | LCSH: Christian leadership – China – History – 20th century. | LCSH: China – Social conditions – 1912-1949.
Classification: LCC BV1360.C6 L58 2023 | DDC 267/.5951 – dc23

UBC Press gratefully acknowledges the financial support for our publishing program of the Government of Canada and the British Columbia Arts Council.

UBC Press
The University of British Columbia
2029 West Mall
Vancouver, BC V6T 1Z2
www.ubcpress.ca

This book is dedicated to

my parents, Harry Bagot Littell and Rebecca Mott Littell.

In addition to unconditional love, they gave me roots and then gave me wings.

And, more important, they let me fly.

Contents

Acknowledgments / ix

Introduction / 3

1   Creating a YWCA Movement in China, 1899–1925 / 17

2   Making a Chinese Leadership, 1925–36 / 53

3   Seeking a Place in a Social Revolution, 1926–36 / 76

4   Claiming National Citizenship, 1937–48 / 110

5   Embracing the Maoist State, 1949–50 / 144

6   Cultivating a Socialist Mindset, 1951–57 / 167

Conclusion / 190

Glossary: YWCA Women, YMCA Secretaries, Christian Leaders, and Related Terms / 196

Notes / 199

Bibliography / 227

Index / 235

Acknowledgments

There is a famous saying attributed to the Daoist philosopher Laozi: "A journey of a thousand miles begins with a single step." Writing a scholarly monograph is indeed a journey of a thousand miles. I would add the observation that one does not make a journey of a thousand miles alone. Many accompanied me on the journey that produced this book. Some joined for a few miles, others for much longer. A few made the entire journey with me.

Xiaoping Cong and I met when we were Spencer Foundation Dissertation Fellows. I met Helen Schneider in the reading room of the Shanghai Municipal Archives. Early in our academic careers, the three of us worked together on panels at innumerable conferences in the United States and Asia. My engagement with them helped me mature as a scholar. There are many others with whom I shared my scholarly work. Three who come readily to mind are Betsy Lublin, Kimberly Manning, and the late Keith Schoppa.

My fellow historians at the University of Tampa have been constant in their support. Al Tillson and Spencer Segalla, however, have been the "go-to" persons for advice on the challenges of historical research and the conventions of historical writing. I credit them with making sure I did not get lost (or plunge over a cliff) on my "journey of a thousand miles."

There are many others in the UT community to whom I am indebted. The librarians at Macdonald-Kelce Library deserve special mention, especially Jeanne Vince, for they facilitated the interlibrary loan of dozens of books that were critical to the development of this volume. Faculty and staff too numerous to mention in the College of Social Sciences, Mathematics and Education were always willing to listen and to celebrate the milestones on my journey.

This book has also been made possible by a University of Tampa Research Innovation and Scholarly Excellence (RISE) Award, David Delo Research Professor Grant, Dana Foundation Grant, and Fred and Jeanette Pollock Research Professor Grant. I also benefited immensely from spending a month as a visiting scholar at the Institute of Modern History at Academia Sinica in Nankang, Taipei. A special thanks to Academia Sinica research fellow Lien Ling-ling, who shares my interest in Chinese women's history, and to my good friend Tseng Chiu-yu, who hosted me during my stay in Taiwan.

There are those outside of the UT community whom I also want to thank. Erik Avasalu translated some of the more difficult post-1949 Chinese textual sources, without which I would have not been able to take the story of the Chinese YWCA into the 1950s. Long-standing friendships with Bruce Leslie, professor emeritus at SUNY-Brockport, and Eli Nathans, with whom I shared an office while we were visiting assistant professors at Ball State University, also sustained me on this journey.

I believe all first-time authors are apprehensive about the publishing process. The personal approach of UBC Press senior editor Randy Schmidt quickly dispelled my fears. He guided me through the always nerve-wracking approval process, providing me with sound advice every step of the way. Production manager Megan Brand was the consummate professional, always responding quickly to my frequent questions. Copy editor Frank Chow fine-tuned my prose. Proofreader Marnie Lamb ensured that the prose was exact. She also provided an index. Cover designer George Kirkpatrick made it clear this book was on the women of the Chinese YWCA. Cartographer Eric Leinberger provided a map so that my readers would not get lost as they navigate the book. I also want to credit the anonymous readers UBC Press selected to review my manuscript. Their insightful comments and critiques made this a better book.

University of Pittsburgh professor emerita Evelyn Rawski suggested I research the YWCA. Carnegie Mellon University professor Donna Harsh made me a better writer. CMU professor emeritus Donald Sutton challenged me to articulate persuasive arguments.

Several important people started this journey with me but are not here with me at its end. The miles we walked together are cherished memories. My parents, Harry and Becky Littell, to whom this book is dedicated.

My husband, Donald Lamb, who selflessly let me pursue my dreams. My UT mentor, colleague, and friend, Connie Rynder. And my best friend outside of academia, Jodie Syford.

Finally, to my brothers Bill, Bob, and Tom and their families; my daughter, Tina; and all my family and friends in and outside of academia, especially my cousin John Harrison, my heartfelt gratitude. Knowing you were always there made all the difference in the world.

The YWCA in China

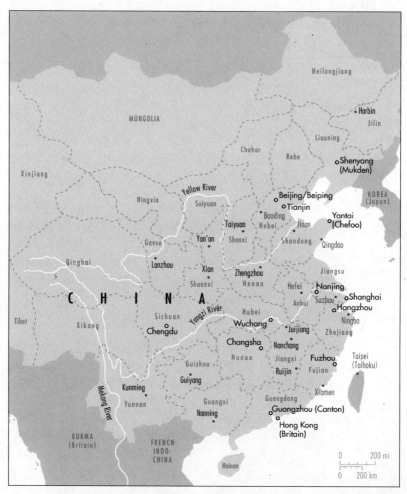

A map of China highlighting the YWCA city associations that had been established by 1928.

Introduction

The YWCA in China examines the Chinese Young Women's Christian Association (YWCA) from its unconventional beginning in 1899 to its embrace of Mao Zedong's state-building project after 1949. It traces the YWCA's history through the lens of the national headquarters office and its leadership in order to answer the critical question of what made it possible for a Christian organization that arrived on Chinese soil as a foreign transplant and cultural interloper to embrace Mao's revolution a half-century later. This book argues that the YWCA gradually evolved to become Chinese in staff, policies, and programs. By 1949, its Chinese leadership believed their Christian-inspired social reform goals aligned with Mao Zedong's revolutionary aims.

The process of Sinification began in 1907 with World YWCA general secretary Clarissa Spencer's directive that the neophyte association be made "Chinese" as quickly as Chinese women could be secured to lead it. Sinification was completed in March 1950, when the women on the all-Chinese YWCA national executive committee declared the association to be "wholly Chinese" for the first time in its history. The process of Sinification, however, was not driven solely by World YWCA policy but by YWCA women on the ground in China who sought to make a Western-inspired Christian organization relevant to Chinese women, Chinese society, and the Chinese state during the turbulent first half of the twentieth century.

There are four parts to this argument. First, the YWCA attracted Chinese Christian women because it provided them with a framework

3

to work out modern identities on their own terms and enabled them to lead public lives that were fulfilling and at the same time served as witness to their Christian faith. Second, the World YWCA's policy of indigenizing local leadership and the commitment of foreign secretaries to carrying out that policy, coupled with the YWCA's high standards, advanced educated and strong-willed Chinese women into positions of leadership in the national office. Third, the Chinese YWCA leadership replaced Western-inspired reform agendas with programs that made sense in a Chinese context and shifted the association's priorities from moral and material uplift to the pursuit of social justice. Fourth, the YWCA women on the ground in China who drove Sinification included both Western and Chinese women. This book focuses on four of them: Grace Coppock, Ding Shujing, Deng Yuzhi, and Cai Kui.

Grace Coppock was critically important during the association's formative years. She was the second Western secretary sent to China. In 1908, she became general secretary of the Shanghai city association, the first YWCA city association organized in China. Five years later, in 1913, she became national general secretary. From the day she was appointed general secretary of the Shanghai association, Coppock prioritized the inclusion and promotion of Chinese women as both partners and leaders of YWCA work in China. She identified Ding Shujing as her successor before Coppock's untimely death in 1921. Ding Shujing became the first Chinese national general secretary in 1926. Her tenure was marked by the association's growing self-awareness as a Chinese institution, its increasing progressivism, and the influence of the second, or May Fourth, generation of YWCA secretaries.[1] Two of the young secretaries Ding nurtured, Deng Yuzhi (Cora Deng) and Cai Kui, belonged to that generation.

Deng Yuzhi and Cai Kui joined the YWCA early in Ding Shujing's tenure after graduating from Jinling College, the Christian union college for women in Nanjing. Cai Kui became executive of the editorial department several months after her arrival in the national office in 1927, a fitting position for someone with a degree in literature. She succeeded Ding Shujing as national general secretary in 1936. Deng Yuzhi, who initially was one of the national student secretaries, became executive of the industrial (labour) department in 1930. A trained sociologist and someone who took Jesus's preaching of social equality very literally, she played a key role in the radicalization of the association's outlook on social reform in the 1930s. She succeeded Cai Kui as national general secretary in 1950 and led the association into the communist era.

The YWCA in China brings together several related discussions. The first involves Sinification. This term is often conflated with "indigenization," and there is some overlap. In this book, "indigenization" means putting something (a process, institution, and so on) under native control. Indigenizing the association leadership in China was a World YWCA policy. The expectation was that the Chinese leadership would indigenize the YWCA movement in China under the guidance of the World and American YWCAs. The Chinese leadership did much more than that: they made the association "the stuff of Chinese life."[2] "Sinification" meant that the association became "Chinese" not just in leadership but in policy, goals, programs, and institutional culture. It took five decades for the Chinese themselves to declare their organization "wholly Chinese." During its formative period between 1899 and 1925, Western YWCA women defined the goals for association work in China and developed programs using Western models recognized as the "association way." Some programs emphasized the goal of individual moral and material uplift typical of mission work, while a few reflected the increasingly progressive-era agenda the American, British, and World YWCAs adopted to meet societal needs on a larger scale. As Chinese women advanced in leadership, they mitigated the foreignness of the association and domesticated the "association way" by prioritizing programs that made sense in a Chinese context and to a Chinese mindset. Regardless of their efforts, Sinification was also a historical process subject to institutional realities and buffeted by historical forces. Although by the mid-1920s a decidedly Chinese identity had emerged, in reality the association's dependence on foreign staff and foreign financial support meant that many continued to consider the association a Sino-Western hybrid until it embraced Mao's state-building project after 1949.

The second discussion, woven throughout this book, concerns the YWCA as a Christian organization that was both a foreign transplant and a cultural interloper in China. Part of the process of Sinification included making Christianity and a Christian organization relatable in a Chinese context. This book examines the multiplicity of Chinese YWCA women as *Christian* women. It cannot be assumed that the Protestant evangelical Christianity of Western YWCA women, with its overriding assumptions of cultural superiority, was the Christianity professed by Chinese YWCA women. Chapter 2 explores the religiosities of Ding Shujing, Deng Yuzhi, and Cai Kui to reveal the lived reality and differences of these women's Christian faith.

The third discussion revolves around the emergence of the Chinese YWCA's *nationalism,* first articulated in 1925, which was grounded in China's rights as a sovereign nation. While it would always be a constituent of the World YWCA, the Chinese YWCA also wanted to become an institutional citizen of China. It would make supporting the nation the theme of its second convention, held in 1928 after the Great Revolution of 1927, and third convention, held in 1933 after the Shanghai War. Japan's invasion of China in 1937 became the catalyst for its nationalism as the association threw itself into war-relief work. It is very likely that the association might not have crossed the 1949 divide had it not gone through the crucible of war and learned to make national survival a priority.

The fourth discussion deals with the YWCA's commitment to the Maoist regime after 1949. The reasons behind the decision to support the communist regime included the abject failure of the Nationalist government during the postwar period, the belief that the association's Christian-inspired social reform goals aligned with Mao Zedong's revolutionary aims, and the association's dedication to the Chinese nation-state. Deng Yuzhi was the guiding force behind the embrace of the Maoist state even before she became national general secretary in January 1950. But if Deng Yuzhi was the "guide," the force behind her was a collective one. The official endorsement came at an enlarged national executive committee meeting in March 1950 that included representatives from YWCAs across China. Their declaration was published in the leading Christian journal. This discussion also highlights Deng Yuzhi's leadership in the liberal Christian community, something that is ignored by most histories of Christianity in China.

Finally, this book provides a lens to examine the processes of cultural transmission, cultural adaptation, and cultural negotiations regarding issues of gender, religion, and ideology. Anthropologist Marshall Sahlins has argued that cultural transmission is a complex event, shaped by historical circumstances, particularly the timing and nature of the intercultural encounter, the effect of which may be wholly or partly unexpected.[3] With staffs from up to seven Western countries and most major provinces in China, the Chinese YWCA served as a "zone of cultural exchange," a place where women were introduced to and subsequently appropriated new ideas and individualities. Their choices were worked out in relationships between YWCA Western and Chinese women from both elite and humbler backgrounds and different generations who embraced different religiosities and were committed to different and often conflicting social and political ideologies. In a time when China had no integrative national ideology,[4] and protected by the gendered boundaries of a women's organization, Chinese YWCA women in particular were able to seize opportunities to lead lives of value as professional women and social activists. These women variously held positions of authority, deferred to those who did, or challenged the status quo. Their relationships created synergies of cohesion and generated dynamics of conflict. It must be emphasized, however, that cultural transmission did not happen in just one direction. Western secretaries were also profoundly changed by their experiences in China and their relationships with Chinese YWCA women.

CHRISTIAN NEW WOMAN

"New women" is a discursive term used to describe women in the late nineteenth and early twentieth centuries who contested or openly rebelled against traditional norms. When the term entered the Chinese lexicon, from where, and who first used it are all matters of conjecture.[5] How and why it was deployed for personal, political, commercial, or ideological reasons in early twentieth-century China is the subject of many essays. It is a historically contingent term, its exact meaning dependent on the context in which it is used. In other words, it must be given analytical boundaries but ones that are flexible because there actually were "new women," and their lived experiences reveal "diverse manifestations" of "new womanhood."[6]

In *The Beijing Young Women's Christian Association, 1927–1937*, Aihua Zhang provides analytical boundaries for her category "Christian New Women." She defines them as a "distinctive version of new womanhood featuring practicality, social service, and broad cooperation across gendered, religious, and national boundaries."[7] Christian New Women's most distinguishing characteristic was their Christian faith: "In practicing their new womanhood ... Christianity functioned as a spiritual inspiration and a mental enlightenment."[8] Zhang's statement is important. Whether born into Christian families or converts to Christianity, Chinese Christian women took their faith seriously. Historians need to as well. In a 2017 introductory article to a special issue of the *Journal of American–East Asian Relations*, Jane Hunter emphasized the importance of taking religion "more seriously" as a historical topic, and that included work on overseas Christian missions and converts to Christianity. She noted that in the writings of British and American historians, mission work had been subsumed by the narrative of nation and empire. It was thus presented as "cultural imperialism." For sure, it bore an element of that, which this current book recognizes. However, as Hunter pointed out, a missionary was not answering a call to serve his or her nation or its imperial goals, but to serve God. Many converts were genuinely attracted to Christianity because of its underlying message of love.[9]

In this book, "Chinese YWCA new women" refers to women who served on governing boards or on professional staffs, had received modern and often Western-style educations, and led public lives, all of which were denied women in traditional Chinese society. The extent to which they contested other aspects of traditional Chinese society varied. For example, many of the women who served on governing boards were married and used feminist maternalism as their rationale for "going public."[10] All Chinese YWCA new women embraced the Christian ideal of service. On this point, I am in total concert with Aihua Zhang. The term "new woman" rarely appears in the primary source documents that underpin this book. Thus, as a category of analysis, it remains largely in the background.

RELATED SCHOLARSHIP

The YWCA in China is the first book-length treatment of the Chinese YWCA. It builds on my published and unpublished works on the Chinese YWCA that began with the completion of my 2002 doctoral dissertation, "Going Public: The YWCA, 'New' Women, and Social Feminism in Republican China."[11] It engages with English-language scholarship only. The author is at present ill-equipped to read academic scholarship in Chinese. Fortunately, many Chinese scholars, even those working outside the United States, publish in English, and thus their work is widely available.

A study of the Chinese YWCA and its women fits into a body of scholarship on the Chinese YWCA that in turn is part of a growing body of scholarship on Chinese Christian women. There are three themes, or threads, that connect the scholarship on the Chinese YWCA movement in China with the larger body of scholarship on Chinese Christian women. The first thread is the legitimacy of the study of religion as a historical topic, especially the study of Christianity in non-Christian lands. This is particularly relevant when studying Chinese Christian women. For Chinese women, Christianity was a religion that, like Buddhism, also a foreign import, provided a spiritual space for women that Confucianism denied them. Even more than the message of Buddha, the message of Jesus valued women. The second thread is the project to "restore" Christian women to the master narrative of the history of Christianity in China, from which they are largely missing. The final thread is the importance of bringing to light the diversity of what it meant to be a Chinese Christian woman. The word "Christian" is often deployed as if "being Christian" was a universal experience. Being a Chinese Christian woman in twentieth-century China was a shared experience in many ways. However, whether a woman was born into a Christian family, converting along with family members when a child, or making the decision to convert as an adult, the lived experience of being Christian was personal and unique. When the opportunity presents itself, the diversity of Chinese women's religiosity must be examined.

Historian Li Ma states emphatically that what is missing from the history of Christianity in China are Chinese Christian women.[12] "As long as the stories and history of women are not integrated into this history, narratives and traditions codified by men will remain oppressive to women."[13] Li Ma's point is well taken. Prominent among the historians of Christianity in China is the late Daniel Bays, whose 2012 monograph *A New History of Christianity in China* made few references to Chinese Christian women or their organizations. Despite its prominence as the largest Christian women's organization and its longevity, Bays made only three references to the Chinese YWCA, although he did include Deng Yuzhi and the YWCA's industrial night schools in one of them. However, once his history crosses the 1949 divide, Deng disappears, although she participated in the political consultative conferences in 1949 and was engaged in the process that produced the Christian Manifesto and was one of its original signatories.[14]

The YWCA in China, along with most other recent studies of Chinese Christian women, is part of an effort to restore Chinese Christian women to the history of Christianity in general, and the history of Christianity in China in particular. Scholarship on Chinese Christian women in English builds on the pioneering work of Pui-lan Kwok's *Chinese Women and Christianity, 1860–1927,* which was foundational in this field.[15] Kwok was also the first to discuss the work of Chinese YWCA women. Up to that time, and even for years afterward, studies of the YWCA movement in China focused on the role of its American secretaries, with little attention given to Chinese women.[16] An exception is Emily Honig's study of Deng Yuzhi, "Christianity, Feminism and Communism: The Life and Times of Deng Yuzhi (Cora Deng)." Honig was among the first generation of American scholars to do research in the People's Republic of China. These scholars' "China-centred" studies broke the stranglehold of the "response to the West" approach that had dominated the China field up to the mid-1980s. Honig interviewed Deng Yuzhi for her book *Sisters and Strangers: Women in the Shanghai Cotton Mills, 1919–1949*. Her article on Deng provided critical, first-hand information about Deng's life, religiosity, and social thinking.

Two later works have also discussed Deng Yuzhi. Karen Garner's *Precious Fire: Maud Russell and the Chinese Revolution* (2003), while primarily about radical American YWCA secretary Maud Russell, discussed her lifelong friendship with Deng.[17] There is a place for similar studies that juxtapose the work of Western and Chinese women. In 2011, Christina Wai-yin Wong published "Expanding Social Networks: A Case Study of Cora Deng and Y.T. Wu on Their Roles and Participation in the National Salvation Movement of 1930s China."[18] As the title suggests, Wong examined Deng's activism in the political sphere as Japanese aggression increased and the Nanjing government failed to respond. Wong's study evidenced Deng's early engagement in extra-institutional and highly political activities that helped bring her to the attention of communist organizers. It also provides the context for Deng's long friendship and activist accord with Wu Yaozong (Y.T. Wu). Also important, although the article was written in English, it was published in a Chinese edited volume, and Wong's sources are almost entirely in Chinese.

Before I discuss recent scholarship on the Chinese YWCA, Jin Feng's *A Family Saga: Ginling College* (2009) deserves mention because it is the one other study, at least in English, that focuses on a Christian women's institution. Jinling (Ginling) College was the Christian union college for women in Nanjing, the last of the three such colleges for women to open. Jinling operated from 1915 to 1952, when it was merged with the communist regime's new higher education system. *A Family Saga* shares several themes with this book. Both examine cultural exchanges between Western and Chinese women, explore the advancement of Chinese women to positions of authority, and, most important, show how those women shaped the vision of their institutions. Among Christian women's educational institutions in China, Jinling was arguably the most successful. Among its prominent graduates were two of the women this book focuses on: Deng Yuzhi and Cai Kui. Its first and only Chinese president, Wu Yifang, chaired the YWCA national committee after the association moved its headquarters to Chengdu, the city where Jinling had its campus-in-exile during the Sino-Japanese War. Like many progressive, reform-minded women, Wu Yifang remained in China to serve her nation after 1949.

Scholars have found the YWCA to be a source for topics on reform-minded Chinese Christian women. The association was the leading Christian organization for women before and after 1949. It had geographical breadth, pioneered work with the urban poor and working classes, and provided a framework for women to consider new gender identities and actively engage in society. While this book is concerned with the association's national work, other recent studies focus on local work. Xia Shi's *At Home in the World: Women and Charity in Late Qing and Early Republican China* (2018) and Margaret Mih Tillman's "Mediating Modern Motherhood: The Shanghai YWCA's 'Women's Work for Women,' 1908–1949" (2021) provide a counterpoint to this book.[19] One-third of Shi's book deals with married, nonprofessional women who lacked modern education but who were members of the YWCA and served lower-status women by participating in "charity" service work. This raises the question of how we define those women. Does their volunteer work in YWCA charitable programs make them Christian New Women as it did for the modern educated, married, civic-minded women who served on YWCA governing boards? Is this an example of the "diverse manifestations" of new womanhood?

Tillman examines the Shanghai city association's work with women, one of the foundational fields assigned to the Chinese YWCA by World YWCA general secretary Clarissa Spencer. Significantly, her study covers the entire history of this city association, from its formal organization in 1908 until the dawn of the communist era in 1949, an ambitious project for a book chapter. Studies of this scope, however, are very important given the historical forces that buffeted YWCA work. Tillman's study demonstrates the importance of examining YWCA work at the local level, something that Aihua Zhang's work, discussed next, also does. It is also revealing that of the ten chapters in the edited volume *Spreading Protestant Modernity: Global Perspectives on the Social Work of the YMCA and YWCA, 1889–1970*, Tillman's chapter is the only one on the YWCA. Considering the global reach of the World YWCA movement, it is puzzling why there is only one chapter on the social work of the YWCA. Obviously, the need to write women back into the history of Christianity is a project that extends beyond China.

Aihua Zhang's *The Beijing Young Women's Christian Association 1927–1937: Materializing a Gendered Modernity* (2021) examines the work of

YWCA women in the Beijing city association during the Nanjing decade, when Beijing was no longer the political capital of China. She analyzes the efforts of YWCA women to "localize" their programs to make them responsive to the needs of Beijing women, particularly those of lesser economic means. Their efforts were, in essence, a reassessment of the practicality of the association way, or the modelling of YWCA work in China on Western ideas and methods. Zhang's analysis aligns with that of this book, which also connects the domestication of the association way to the advancement of Chinese women to positions of leadership in the national office.

In *Christian Women and Modern China: Recovering a Women's History of Chinese Protestantism* (2021), Li Ma weaves the stories of a number of influential Christian women like weft threads through the warp threads of the master narrative of the history of Christianity in China, which is dominated by Christian men. Among those women are Zeng Baosun, great-granddaughter of the Qing general Zeng Guofan, whom Ma describes as a "Confucian Christian woman"; Ding Shujing, one of the three YWCA women this book focuses on; and the aforementioned Wu Yifang. Restoring individual narratives of Christian women is important, and Li Ma does it exceptionally well. However, to truly gender the history of Christianity in China, scholars need to move beyond "her-stories" and claim a part of the master narrative.

SOURCES

This book is based as much as possible directly on primary sources. It also engages with a wide range of scholarship from a number of disciplines and continues to value much of the scholarship published in the late twentieth century.

Primary sources on the Chinese YWCA that survived China's tumultuous twentieth century are scattered in archives across the globe. Outside the United States, the most important archives for this book were the Shanghai Municipal Archives in Shanghai and the World YWCA Archives in Geneva, Switzerland. There was some overlap of archival material as many were official reports and correspondence between the national office in China, the World YWCA, and the Foreign Division of the YWCA of the USA. Despite the duplication of material, each document had to be scrutinized. It was not unusual for correspondence sent to the World YWCA's general secretary and the head of the Foreign Division to "look" identical but end in personal and sometimes confidential comments directed specifically to the addressee.

In the United States, the China Records Project at the Yale Divinity School Library and the Sophia Smith Collection of Women's History at Smith College were primary research sites. Rather than having me travel to New York City to do research at the YWCA of the USA headquarters, their librarian offered to arrange for me an interlibrary loan of the China microfilms from Record Group 5, which covered international work. The offer was readily accepted. Unfortunately, the returned microfilms failed to arrive back at the YWCA of the USA office and thus have been lost. The YWCA of the USA archives have since been relocated to the Sophia Smith Collection at Smith College. The microfilms that are "missing" are so noted in the finding aid for Record Group 5 International Work, YWCA of the USA Records, MS324.

Many hours over several summers were spent at the Library of Congress, both in the inspiring Thomas Jefferson Building and in the James Madison Building where, at the time the research was conducted, the periodical reading room was located. It was there that I scrutinized twenty years of the *North China Herald*. Exhaustive online research added to the source base as well. It was online research that revealed that British YWCA secretary Margaret Garvie did not leave China in spring 1950 with all other foreign secretaries but remained another year, leaving in spring 1951, most likely because of the Christian denunciation campaign.

The majority of YWCA sources, including those from the Shanghai Municipal Archives, were in English, as most were copies of official correspondence and reports sent overseas. There was a cache of documents in Chinese that, although proportionally smaller, were invaluable. Critical among them were the 1951 and 1957 issues of the *YWCA Magazine* and Deng Yuzhi's commemorative volume (Deng Yuzhi xiansheng jinian wenji) published by the national committee of the YWCA of China after her death and sent to me by the World YWCA staff. The latter included Deng Yuzhi's own history of YWCA industrial work, her remembrances of leading Shanghai intellectuals, her description of her service on the political consultative conference that produced the interim constitution for the People's Republic of China, and other select writings. The memorial volume also included touching tributes from colleagues and relatives written after her death in 1996 that provided insights into her personal life and personality.

The lack of personal papers of the three women who are the focus of this book is understandable given the turbulent history of twentieth-century

China and the fact that after 1949, and especially during the Cultural Revolution, the existence of such papers put Christian women, their families, and friends at risk. I have done my best to capture their voices from the sources I do have.

As already mentioned, the YWCA of the USA microfilms from Record Group 5 have been lost. For the sake of brevity in this monograph, I have cited only the microfilm reel number for each document. My dissertation, however, includes fuller citations based on the original YWCA of the USA finding aid. Those citations may prove useful if the missing microfilms are ever located. Regarding the World YWCA Archives, several years after I did research at the World YWCA headquarters, they reorganized their China files to conform to the way their other country files were organized. Thus, my citations most likely no longer match those in the reorganized China files. Citations give the box numbers, and the bibliography provides the names of the specific files and document folders I used from those boxes. They may serve as a "breadcrumb" trail for future researchers.

NOTE ON CHINESE CHARACTERS, ROMANIZATION, AND NAMES

I use traditional characters for names and terms as they appear in my primary sources. I use pinyin romanization in keeping with current scholarly conventions except for commonly known names of historical figures, such as Chiang Kai-shek and Sun Yat-sen. In a few instances, I was unable to identify the Chinese characters for the name of a Chinese YWCA woman and simply used her name as it appeared in a document.

CHAPTER DESCRIPTIONS

The YWCA in China combines thematic, biographical, and chronological approaches. Chapter 1 combines thematic and chronological discussions. The main portion of Chapter 2 is composed of biographical accounts of the lives of Ding Shujing, Deng Yuzhi, and Cai Kui that are arranged thematically. Chapters 3 to 6 are arranged chronologically for the most part.

Chapter 1, "Creating a YWCA Movement in China, 1899–1925," examines the first quarter-century of the YWCA movement in China, when power and authority were mostly vested in Western women. These women worked methodically to expand the association to cities beyond Shanghai, to establish the association way as the model for program work, and to implement the World YWCA policy of developing local leadership.[20]

Chapter 2, "Making a Chinese Leadership, 1925–36," examines the lives of Ding Shujing, Cai Kui, and Deng Yuzhi (Cora Deng), the three most influential YWCA women, each of whom served as national general secretary. Their lives and careers reveal the cultural politics of devolution and how power relations were negotiated. It is important to understand how their early lives and educations shaped their religiosity and social thinking, and how they envisioned the YWCA movement in China. Being a "YWCA Christian woman" is not a generic category of analysis. It is imperative to know these women as individuals and to connect their visions for the YWCA movement in China to their lives.[21]

Chapter 3, "Seeking a Place in a Social Revolution, 1926–36," covers the decade of Ding Shujing's tenure as national general secretary and the period when Cai Kui and Deng Yuzhi assumed leadership of their respective national departments. The chapter is organized around key events and turning points in the history of the Chinese YWCA, which highlight the gradual "domestication" of the YWCA's association way and the growing focus on China-centred policies and programs. These key events also highlight the shift to Christian-inspired social activism, especially in educational work with factory women.[22]

Chapter 4, "Claiming National Citizenship, 1937–48," examines the YWCA during the Sino-Japanese War and the civil war that followed. Wartime contingencies forced the association to "democratize," or decentralize its decision-making process. The war also made national survival and nation-building association priorities. For YWCA women, the war gave new meaning to living one's faith.

Chapter 5, "Embracing the Maoist State, 1949–50," examines events from January 1949 through the end of 1950. It retains as much as possible the voices of the YWCA women who led or just lived through that intense period. Deng Yuzhi became national general secretary in January 1950. The association's all-Chinese leadership declared their unequivocal support for Mao Zedong in March. Deng emerged as a leader among liberal Christians seeking a place in "new China."

Chapter 6, "Cultivating a Socialist Mindset, 1951–57," examines how YWCA women made painful decisions and pragmatic choices as they integrated a socialist mindset into their Christian world view. It describes how YWCA women found themselves continually proving their loyalty. In 1951, they participated in the Christian denunciation campaign, spurning their relationships with the "imperialist" World and American YWCAs. In the following years, Chinese YWCA women participated in various campaigns, including the 1957 Anti-Rightist Campaign. This chapter also traces the efforts of the World YWCA to reconnect with their Chinese constituent.[23]

I

Creating a YWCA Movement in China, 1899–1925

The whole stress will be upon securing Chinese secretaries and turning them loose to evolve a program for an Association that is made out of the stuff of Chinese life.

– Helen Thoburn, 1925

The YWCA entered China as a foreign transplant and cultural interloper, carried by the currents of the missionary enterprise and the expansion of the World YWCA overseas. Editorial department executive secretary Helen Thoburn acknowledged in her 1925 annual report that the Chinese YWCA had grown out of "the mission impulse," admitting it would have been better "if the association here could have been started in the first place out of the genuine desire of Chinese women." By 1925, the situation had changed. A Chinese woman had finally been appointed national general secretary, to take office the following January. While the actual transfer of leadership would be accompanied by challenges, Thoburn insisted that was better than "maintaining an artificial piece of work here just because we have the Western machinery and the impetus to do it." For the next few years, "the whole stress will be upon securing Chinese secretaries and turning them loose to evolve a program for an Association that is made out of the stuff of Chinese life."[1] That had been the intention from the beginning. It had simply taken a quarter of a century to achieve it.

This chapter examines the history of the Chinese YWCA from its precipitate beginning when its fraternal counterpart, the Young Men's Christian Association (YMCA), organized the first YWCA national committee in 1899, to the critical year of 1925. It argues that while there were many important developments between 1899 and 1925, the latter was the transition year of the YWCA in China into becoming a Sino-Western hybrid, ending the formative period that Helen Thoburn described as "our life as an organization trying to be Chinese."[2] The first indication of that transition was Ding Shujing's appointment as incoming national secretary. Another key marker of that transition was a forceful statement of support for Chinese aspirations of national sovereignty in the face of foreign imperialism made by the Chinese leadership of the national committee after police in Shanghai's International Settlement fired on Chinese protesters on May 30. The May Thirtieth Incident sparked protests across China that were violently suppressed. These events led Western secretaries to take a political stance and oppose imperialist policies, such as extraterritoriality, that disadvantaged Chinese in their own country.

The early history of the Chinese YWCA was mostly about Western women's vision for the YWCA movement in China and what they believed Chinese women needed because they dominated the ranks of YWCA secretaries. Many Western secretaries were wedded to the evangelical and missionizing goals of individual moral and material uplift that were the focus of the World YWCA's early expansion overseas. However, as the World YWCA matured, so did its focus, and by the mid-1910s it pursued a more progressive reform agenda focused on larger societal needs, although it approached reform from a Western perspective. That same shift in focus occurred in the YWCA movement in China.

The force behind that shift was Grace Coppock, the second foreign secretary sent to China, who initially served as general secretary of the Shanghai city association and later as national general secretary. Her biographer maintains that her religious faith was a "product of her era," an observation that would have been true for most of the first American secretaries sent to China. Born on the Nebraskan prairie in 1882, the youngest child of five, Coppock believed in the inner strength of women, perhaps a legacy of her strong-willed, tenacious mother, who managed the family farm after her husband's death three days before Grace was born.[3]

One of Coppock's primary goals was the inclusion of Chinese women in the work of establishing the YWCA movement in China. Prairie-bred practicality resulted in her yielding to the need to bring trained secretaries and women with specific expertise from abroad. Before her untimely death in October 1921, she did two things that impacted the future of the Chinese YWCA in significant ways. The first was hiring British industrial welfare expert Agatha Harrison in 1920 to open a national industrial department and commence work in the field of industrial reform. Second, also in 1920, she shared with a colleague her intent of finding a Chinese woman to replace her, and she believed she had found that woman in the new general secretary of the Beijing city association, Ding Shujing.

THE HISTORICAL CONTEXT OF THE YWCA MOVEMENT IN CHINA TO 1925

The first two and a half decades of the YWCA movement in China were marked by iconic dates in Chinese history: 1900, 1911, 1919, 1923, and 1925. In 1900, the Boxer uprising became a global event with the seizure of the British legation in Beijing. The name "Boxers" refers to a peasant religious cult called "Boxers United in Righteousness." Social dislocation in west Shandong Province caused by floods, drought, the absence of local elites, and the intrusion of Christian missionaries accounts for the rise of the movement. For Shandong's peasants, however, the cause was missionaries and their foreign religion. Violent attacks on missionaries in west Shandong and adjoining provinces began in 1898 but remained small in scale. They were reported in the most incendiary terms in foreign papers, however. The Qing court was initially ambivalent toward the Boxers. When Western nations responded militarily, the vacillating court sided with the Boxers in the hope of driving foreign imperialists from their shores. The escalation of hostilities with the siege of the British legation in Beijing, the arrival of an eight-nation expeditionary army, and the defeat of the Boxers became iconic events in the Western imagination.[4] It should be noted that, although the Boxers were defeated, their cause was not. The association of foreign imperialism and Christianity would not only take root but prove to have staying power.

After the humiliating 1901 Boxer Protocol that ended hostilities was forced on China, Chinese reformers renewed calls for a modern centralized state, and revolutionaries demanded the overthrow of the Qing, or Manchu, dynasty. In this tense climate, the Qing instituted reforms. They created a Western-style school system, abolished the centuries-old civil service examination system, and took incremental steps toward constitutional monarchy. A decade of conservative reform did not quell revolutionaries determined to overthrow the Qing dynasty, which they did in 1911 with the Xinhai Revolution. The attempt to establish a republican government failed under the inept rule of its first president, Yuan Shikai. After his death, and despite the continued existence of republican forms of governance, regional warlords seized control of most of China.

In this climate, radical intellectuals like Chen Duxiu, Li Dazhao, and Cao Yuanpei looked for an alternative ideological framework to save China. These leading writers, journalists, and educators set in motion the New Culture Movement, an iconoclastic rejection of traditional Chinese culture and embrace of Western democracy and science dating from 1915, when Chen Duxiu launched his *New Youth* magazine. Another current of the New Culture Movement was its being anti-superstition, and in that vein it rejected both Confucianism and Christianity.[5] When the New Culture Movement merged with the nationalistic, anti-imperialist tide generated by the May Fourth Movement, the various currents created a tidal wave. The May Fourth Movement began on that date in 1919, when Beijing University students protested the decision taken at the Paris Peace Conference to give Germany's concessions in China to Japan and the acceptance of those terms by China's weak Republican government. Student protests spread across China, politicizing an entire generation of young Chinese, among them future YWCA secretary Deng Yuzhi.

According to the late Daniel Bays, a leading historian of Christianity in China, by 1921 Chinese intellectuals had adopted anti-Christian rhetoric for two reasons. The first was what Bays called the "reification of Science," which targeted Christian beliefs as largely being superstition. The second was the association of foreign imperialism, with its roots in the capitalist system and expressed through empire building, with the idea that the purpose of Christian missionaries was to make the Chinese compliant to, if not complicit in, their status as a colonized people.[6] As a movement, however, the first phase of the anti-Christian movement lacked coordination, and although there were vocal protests, as during the international meeting of the World Student Christian Federation held at Qinghua University in Beijing in 1922, it had little impact on Christian missionaries or the Christian community as a whole. It was not noted with interest in national YWCA records.

In 1923 the Russian Communist International (Comintern) brokered an alliance between Sun Yat-sen's Nationalist Party (Guomindang, or GMD) and the fledgling Chinese Communist Party (CCP). The Comintern forced the CCP to become a "party within a party," a subgroup within the GMD. Its radicalism was unabated, however. The United Front sought to wrest military control of China from the warlords and end its economic control by imperialist nations. While its goals were clear, it was not united in its ideological goals, and when its armies marched north in the summer of 1926, they travelled different routes under different leaders. In the meantime, the United Front's opposition to Western imperialism again made targets of Christian missionaries and Christian institutions. As mentioned above, on May 30, 1925, a clash between Chinese labour activists and gendarmes in the Shanghai International Settlement resulted in the death of several Chinese protesters and sparked protest all over China. It also reignited anti-Christian attitudes. The renewed anti-Christian movement was aggressive and violent and would last until 1927. When United Front armies marched north from Guangzhou in the summer of 1926, Christian churches, organizations, and schools were targeted, including the YWCA.

Not only was the Chinese YWCA buffeted by these events, but it had corresponding major events of its own. The first national committee was formed in 1899.[7] The first secretarial conference was held in 1911. In 1919, a Chinese woman became the chair of the national committee, assisted by Chinese officers. The year 1923 saw the first Chinese YWCA national convention, and in 1925 the national committee appointed Ding Shujing national general secretary.

THE MANY WORLDS OF THE CHINESE YWCA

From its inception, the Chinese YWCA had a relationship with the World YWCA, an organization that itself was fairly new. The World YWCA was a product of the separate developments of YWCA movements in England and the United States in the mid-nineteenth century. According to the first official history of the World YWCA, the British association took the lead in extending the movement overseas through its Colonial Division. As the association spread to non-Christian countries, YWCA women began to confront their identity as cultural interlopers. Another issue that influenced the formation of the world organization was the spectre of competition between the British and American YWCAs as the Americans also became interested in seeding their movement abroad. The British YWCA invited the American and seven other national YWCAs to an international conference in London in 1892 to discuss closer relations and coordination between the organizations. These efforts led to the formation of the World YWCA, with its own constitution, in 1894.[8] The energies of its founding women were focused on establishing a place for a multi-denominational women's institution among the many existing male-dominated Christian organizations. At its first world conference in 1898, the World YWCA accepted responsibility for the development of the association movement in non-Christian lands, but only when invited by missionary communities. Following the trends set in the British and American associations, the World YWCA also defined its mission as serving both the individual and society. Because of this, it came to see itself as a social movement and not simply a women's organization.[9]

The World YWCA eventually divided the responsibility for YWCA expansion to non-Christian countries between the United States and Britain in an unofficial but workable arrangement that came to be known as the "scheme of relationships." The United States was made responsible for China, Japan, the Philippines, the West Indies, and Central and South America. Britain was responsible for its colonies. The two associations shared responsibility for the Indian subcontinent.[10] This constituted an organizational "world system," which, although considered pragmatic and necessary, carried colonial overtones as both Great Britain and the United States were imperial powers. Despite the policy of the World YWCA to promote local leadership, it was believed that Western secretaries, with their professional expertise and understanding of the YWCA's ideals and methods, were necessary to set up an association in a foreign land.

THE CHINESE YWCA

Despite the scheme of relationships, the Chinese YWCA never developed exclusive ties to the United States. National general secretaries, starting with Estelle Paddock (1905–13) and continuing with Grace Coppock (1913–21) and then Ding Shujing (1926–36), invited secretaries from many countries to serve in China. This was partially due to the presence of many different imperial powers in China and thus missionary organizations from many different Western nations. It was believed particularly necessary for the Chinese associations to have British secretaries to deal with the more parochial British expatriate communities and mission organizations. Most of the Western secretaries who served in China were

Americans. Several long-serving American women played key roles in mentoring Chinese women. For the most part, however, foreign secretaries served only two five-year terms.

The YWCA of the USA provided the salaries and living expenses for the American secretaries in line with its agreement with the World YWCA office. The YWCA of the USA sought sponsorship from local YWCAs, private donors, and other groups to support a single secretary. For example, Grace Coppock was initially supported by a well-to-do private donor and later by the University of Nebraska.[11] Those funds were sufficient to enable the secretaries to maintain a Western lifestyle, something that was believed necessary for their health and safety. Until at least the mid-1920s, foreign secretaries resided in association compounds, but they paid for their accommodations. The YWCA of the USA also provided funding or helped arrange loans for special projects, such as building a campus for the Normal School for Hygiene and Physical Education in Shanghai and constructing a YWCA headquarters building in the downtown area of the International Settlement. It also provided scholarships for Chinese secretaries to attend the YWCA National Training School in New York City. Otherwise, both the national office and local Chinese associations were expected to be self-supporting. For that reason, finance campaigns were an endemic feature of association life and served as one of the most elemental ways YWCA secretaries and members engaged in civic life. Also, despite the emphasis on "making the work Chinese," neither national nor local secretaries and volunteers hesitated to fundraise in foreign communities or among foreign businesses. Both Western and Chinese secretaries also went to the United States on fundraising tours to ensure that the Foreign Division of the YWCA of the USA had the funds it needed to support China.

THE YWCA AND THE YMCA

Despite the protocols for expansion set at the first World YWCA conference, it was actually YMCA secretaries Robert Lewis and D. Willard Lyon who organized the first YWCA national committee in Shanghai in 1899, appointing the wives and sisters of YMCA secretaries to serve on it. Their action followed a pattern begun in mission countries such as India, where YMCA secretaries would organize a women's association at the same time they organized their own local association. The Chinese YMCA was only four years older than the YWCA, and both associations developed slowly during their first decade. In 1905, ten years after its founding, there were only two YMCA city associations in China, one in Shanghai and one in Tianjin. Ten years after its founding, the YWCA had one city association in Shanghai. At that point, however, the YMCA began a period of rapid expansion, whereas the YWCA did not. In 1914, the YMCA had 25 city associations and 105 student associations, while the YWCA had only 3 city associations and 30 student associations. During the remainder of the decade, the YWCA actually exhibited proportionately greater institutional growth: by 1920, it had 12 city associations and 89 student associations, while the YMCA had added only 5 new city associations and 69 new student associations.

Membership numbers illustrate more dramatically the relative difference between the male and female associations, although such numbers are not terribly reliable for either of them. In 1912, the YMCA had 4,631 city association members and upward of 4,459 student association members. Total YWCA membership in 1914 was 1,300. At the end of the 1910s, the YMCA had 41,699 city association members and 29,639 student association members, compared with only 1,862 members in city associations and 4,552 in student associations for the YWCA.[12] Throughout the 1910s, the YMCA's total membership was seven times greater than that of the YWCA.

The YMCA was more aggressively evangelistic and determined to attract Chinese elites to their organization. The 1907 China Centenary Missionary Conference devoted much discussion time to the propagation of the faith. After the conference, the YMCA held periodic revival-style meetings throughout major Chinese cities aimed at attracting students, officials, and other "influential Chinese." YMCA evangelists John R. Mott and George Sherwood Eddy spoke in China in 1907, 1911, 1913, 1914, and 1915. These meetings may have largely accounted for the rapid spread of the YMCA during these years.[13] There is some indication that Eddy's preaching also attracted women. At least one American secretary held evangelical meetings in nine cities attended by government school students. However, the demand for such meetings was so great, and the resulting interest in Bible study classes so overwhelming, that the YWCA evidently did not pursue that approach further.[14]

One of the problems in promoting the YWCA movement in China was a lack of understanding about the association and its goals. This was not surprising. Delegates at the China Centenary Missionary Conference had been equally mystified – and possibly threatened – by the presence of a nondenominational women's association, affiliated with a network of similar associations with a world headquarters in London. Many women simply regarded it as another missionary society, and not one they should necessarily prioritize. Grace Coppock pointed this out in her first annual report. Although she believed she could build up a membership quickly by offering women interesting and engaging programs, she sought an initial membership that would commit wholeheartedly to the YWCA.[15]

As a result of moving slowly, cautiously, and extremely methodically, by 1919 there were only five organized city associations: Shanghai, Canton, Fuzhou, Tianjin, and Beijing. Pre-organization work had begun in Shenyang (Mukden), Hangzhou, Changsha, Nanjing, and Hong Kong, and six other cities waited for qualified secretaries to begin pre-organization work. The pace of expansion was slowed by the World YWCA policy requiring missionary communities to invite the YWCA to establish an association in their city.[16] Pre-organization work then began with assessing the needs of a city, finding women willing to serve on the governing committee, and, most important, getting a pledged membership large enough to support the new association. This was necessary because, except for foreign staff sponsored by their home countries, the national committee expected city associations to be self-supporting and to contribute to the budget of the national office. Further slowing progress, city associations were usually not organized until a trained woman was in place to serve as general secretary. This required appeals to the United States to find a suitable person who, even after she arrived, spent up to two years in language school before being considered ready to assume her duties.[17]

Gender was an important variable in understanding the growth patterns of the two associations. Men outnumbered women in school enrolment and social service organizations because education and public service remained social and cultural markers for the upper-class man. For new women, education and public service conveyed additional status, but their identity largely remained in their roles as virtuous wives and good mothers, even if those roles were being reinterpreted in modern ways. As a men's organization, the YMCA drew from a larger public constituency from the beginning, and with the abolition of the civil service examination system, it also offered an alternative form of service and intellectual community to elite men deprived of the traditional academy.

Although their organizations and methods were similar, a critical difference between the two was their relationship to parent organizations outside China. The Chinese YMCA maintained almost exclusive ties to the American YMCA. While the YMCA and YWCA would work together at the local level in the future, their relationship at the national level was a bit fraught. The World YWCA eventually curtailed YMCA initiatives to forge some sort of alliance and ensured the future autonomy of the worldwide YWCA movement. Its women on the ground in China ensured the same for their association. When a World YWCA memorandum was circulated to member associations in 1919 suggesting that the YMCA and the YWCA cooperate in countries where both were weak, Grace Coppock replied that she assumed that did not apply to China. She noted that while the national committee saw some advantages in limited cooperation, they also believed that "by all means" the YWCA needed to keep its identity and independence in matters of management and policy.[18]

THE CHINESE YWCA's FORMATIVE YEARS

The YWCA of the USA sent two women to serve as the first YWCA secretaries in China: Estelle Paddock, who served as the first national general secretary in 1904, and Grace Coppock, who became the general secretary of the Shanghai city association after completing her language training. Most of the other early secretaries were also American, so it is not surprising that the organizational structure, as it evolved over the first years, modelled that of the American association and became what Helen Thoburn, quoted at the beginning of this chapter, would describe as a "hothouse plant." Coppock became the second national general secretary in 1913. She had the greatest impact on the formative years of the YWCA. Like the national general secretaries who followed her, she interjected her vision for the association mission in China. The principles she considered essential to advance the YWCA movement included the inclusion of Chinese lay volunteers and professional staff, emphasis on quality programs even if this required programs be smaller in size, and attracting a core of dedicated members rather than seeking a large membership whose numbers impressed but who were mostly interested in what the association could do for them and not in what they might be able to do for it.

Coppock's ideas on the spiritual purpose of the YWCA matured over time as her prairie-bred Christian beliefs confronted an ancient civilization whose intrinsic values she found meaningful. She believed that Christianity in China could use "some Confucian ideals in the foundation." By 1920, she was insisting on an ecumenical spirit as YWCA women sought to instill "the biggest possible idea of God, and His plan for all people" in their work. "The social gospel appeals [to the Chinese]." For this reason, she emphasized social service, and the YWCA mission to women became tantamount to introducing them to social service. The same message went out to YWCA women. "The missionary is a demonstrator both in life and as to work."[19]

In 1907, World YWCA general secretary Clarissa Spencer toured China. She, Paddock, and Coppock attended the Centenary Missionary Conference in Shanghai from April 25 to May 8, along with over a thousand China missionaries and guests from abroad. Spencer suggested that the fledgling association pursue work with urban women, whom she deprecatingly referred to as "women of leisure," and work with female students in government schools, the latter a field the Missionary Conference readily ceded to it. Critically important, Spencer realized the urgent need for more YWCA women on the ground in China. She appealed to the British and American YWCAs to send out young women who were "spiritual, refined, cultured, college-educated linguists with leadership ability." After discussions with the two American secretaries, she also insisted that the work in China be made "Chinese" as quickly as "suitable" Chinese women could be found to lead governing committees and work as professional staff. Harriet Taylor, an American YWCA executive who travelled to China just weeks later, concurred with Spencer's directives but also believed that establishing strong city associations was vital.[20]

The national office followed those directives, especially the one regarding city associations. It spent the next dozen years expanding to cities across China. Many city associations were located in treaty ports – ports forcibly opened to foreign trade by unequal treaties signed in the nineteenth century – because they were locations with a large enough Christian population to support a local association. Nontreaty port cities like Beijing and Nanjing had sizeable missionary communities or major Christian universities.

The national and city associations also developed programs for urban women and students, worked out in broader and more imaginative ways than Spencer may have anticipated. This was due to the influence of the YWCA women on the ground in China, especially Grace Coppock. Coppock's tenure as a secretary was immediately marked by her refusal to accept the position of general secretary of the Shanghai city association until it hired a Chinese associate general secretary. Ding Mingyu (Mary Ding) was finally, if reluctantly, hired by the Shanghai governing committee. Ding Mingyu was Christian-educated but had minimal experience.

When the Shanghai governing committee questioned the wisdom of hiring her because of her inexperience, Coppock declared, "But a Chinese
secretary who knows her own people will make fewer mistakes than I
would without her."[21] Ding Mingyu remained part of the YWCA family
for the rest of her life, serving as a secretary, board member, and friend.
The Shanghai city association celebrated her eightieth birthday in 1956.[22]

Work with Urban Women

The YWCA's real if modest success in expanding to a dozen Chinese cities by the end of its first two decades was largely due to the fact that its
city associations addressed the needs of a wide range of urban women.
However determined the general secretaries of the various city associations were to emulate Coppock's efforts to create a core of dedicated
members, the reality was that to get an association up and running, they
needed a pledged membership sufficient to support it. Thus, attractive
as well as meaningful programs were an imperative. Work with urban
women had been the catalyst for the development of both the American
and British YWCAs in the mid-nineteenth century.[23] Clarissa Spencer
thought that this earlier work should serve as a model, albeit with modifications.[24] Such work also directed the efforts of the independent-minded
YWCA women toward respectable, maternalistic lines of work. Thus,
Christian leaders might have been alarmed had they read the report
of the first secretarial conference held in 1911, where eight secretaries
stressed the need to teach women "how to lead or how best to direct
the powers that in them lie" so they could avail of the opportunities the
"new" China offered.[25] As an underpinning ideology, "maternalism" for
YWCA women was not deployed as a rationale for their social reform
work but rather as an empowering innate female quality that provided
them with unique insight into social problems, their origins, and their
solutions. Spencer's descriptive phrase "women of leisure" played off the
missionary stereotype of upper- and middle-class Chinese women as idle
and lacking real purpose in life. The fact that some women had little with
which to occupy their minds was not ascribed to an essential female flaw
but to extenuating circumstances, especially the lack of places to meet
and opportunities to learn. One of the association's earliest emphases was
in providing places for community and fellowship "where women may
meet and make friends with one another, drink tea together, play games,
listen to music and touch other women's lives."[26] Bringing these women
together provided YWCA secretaries with the opportunity to introduce

new ideas into the lives of their members and visitors. A primary goal for work with "women of leisure" was to involve them in social service as a way to introduce them to the fundamental precept of Christianity, since to association women, "social service" and "Christian service" were one and the same. City association members created free schools for poor children and organized relief projects.[27] While there was an amount of token participation, the association sought to train those with more serious interest in the intricacies of social problems. In 1919, the Shanghai city association held a ten-day Social Service Institute that included a class on aspects of social service, lectures on social problems such as opium addiction and women in industry, and visits of inspection to three social service projects.[28]

The broadest area of the YWCA's early work was with "old-style" and "new-style" wives and mothers. If a distinction can be made between these two groups of women, it would be that the latter had attended new-style schools. The YWCA secretaries sought to fill a void in these women's lives once they left school. An early brochure stated:

> At best, a Chinese woman is in school but a few years, and then she must be reached by some agency other than school. The Young Women's Christian Association, by opening seven days a week for such women, seeks to provide them with true fellowship, classes, group meetings, and those things which shall make them better home makers and more intelligent mothers, as well as to fit them for unselfish service beyond the home.[29]

Among this group, the association had a special interest in those young women who converted to Christianity while attending mission schools but then married into non-Christian families or in other ways lost touch with the church. One strategy for averting this was to hold parties for graduating classes to introduce them to local association work.[30]

One of the ways in which the YWCA arguably contributed to women's education was by creating courses for young married girls and older women who did not qualify for government schools.[31] YWCA reports and brochures published from the 1910s through the early 1920s reveal a great variety of course offerings – English, Chinese, Chinese classics, psychology, modern inventions, famous women, typing, sewing on machines, "fancy sewing" or embroidery, lace making, singing, folk dancing, organ, piano, drawing, painting, games, gymnastics, foreign and Chinese cooking, home decoration, hygiene, first aid, and home nursing.[32] Lectures on a wide variety of topics supplemented formal course offerings. Topics included social problems, current events, etiquette (Western and Chinese), physical education and health, travel, art, and music.[33] Critics viewed these activities as "luxury for the few not unlike a girls' finishing school" and lacking in intellectual discipline. The YWCA viewed them as being an "easy first step to a life of bigger interests."[34] A 1917 article in the *Chinese Recorder* mentioned that both the YMCA and YWCA worked "for the educated," namely, the elite classes, but added that "their final aim is not confined to this class."[35] As will be seen from the discussion of industrial work below, it was not.

Early Work with Students

The 1907 Centenary Missionary Conference charged the YWCA with working with students in the newly opened government schools, and even the YWCA noted the opportunities this field opened for it. Work with students had been among the first initiatives of Estelle Paddock when she became national general secretary in 1904. Her work had been exclusively with mission schools as the Qing court, which had just opened Western-style government schools for boys in 1904, did not open them for girls until 1907. Opening schools for girls did not so much constitute a reform as it was a means of controlling reform that was taking place outside of the court's purview. In the previous decade, there had been a proliferation of both mission schools and private gentry schools for girls. Such efforts accelerated when Qing educational reforms in 1904 excluded girls. Confronted with this activity, Qing officials came to fear that unless the government introduced public education for girls and controlled the content of female education, they risked losing control of their national reform agenda. In 1906, they placed elite schools under the control of the ministry of education, and in 1907, established regulations for girls' primary schools and women's normal schools.[36]

In 1917, the YWCA had only four student YWCAs in government schools. Why did it describe this progress as "perceptible growth"?[37] The main reason for this was the conservative nature of government-run girls' schools. When Qing officials expanded the educational system to include girls, their purpose was to inculcate in young women Confucian morals. This policy continued into the early years of the Chinese republic. Although the provisional constitution granted religious freedom, when the new parliament met for the first time in early 1913, staunch Confucianists petitioned it to make Confucianism the state religion. After months of debates between Confucianists and Chinese Christians lobbying against such a move, the parliament added an article to the provisional constitution that recognized Confucianism as "the great root of moral cultivation."[38]

The lack of trained student secretaries also greatly impeded student work. Throughout its first decades in China, the YWCA depended on the expertise of Western secretaries. Each new program area waited until trained secretaries arrived from abroad. This was true in student work and later in industrial and rural work. Estelle Paddock, the first national general secretary, worked tirelessly establishing student associations herself. The national office finally acquired a student secretary in 1916. The addition of five additional student secretaries resulted in the increase in total student associations in mission and government schools from fifty to seventy-two by 1919.[39]

Recognizing the importance of student work in government schools, YWCA student secretaries organized conferences for students from non-mission schools during the winter vacation, and in this way put them in touch with local city association work.[40] They also tried to reach students in gentry and government schools through mission school students. Students could be very innovative. In Beijing, eight student associations formed a union committee and published a newspaper suitable for distribution in government schools.[41]

One of the association's boldest moves in its effort to reach students in government schools was training physical education teachers, who would then be hired to teach in those schools. However, what ended up as a decision to create a Normal School for Hygiene and Physical Education in Shanghai began as something else entirely. Observing the great success of the YMCA in attracting members because of its sports and physical education classes, Grace Coppock asked the YWCA of the USA to send a physical education expert to China when she was still general secretary of the Shanghai city association.[42] The only reason she gave at the time was her belief that physical education programs would attract women "like no other YWCA endeavor."[43] Serendipity brought Coppock and forty-eight-year-old physical education pioneer Abby Mayhew together at the YWCA's National Training School in New York City in 1911. Mayhew was eminently qualified and, despite her age, was willing to come to China to assess the field and advise the Chinese YWCA. She accepted a two-year assignment in 1912, but, like a number of YWCA secretaries, ended up making China her home for several decades. Mayhew's first task was to study the field. By the time she finished, Coppock was national general secretary, and Mayhew joined her on the national staff.[44]

The Normal School for Hygiene and Physical Education

The interest in physical culture was part of the reform discourse on how to strengthen the weak Chinese body. For this reason, calisthenics were introduced into the newly opened government schools. The gendering of calisthenics accompanied the expansion of government-sponsored education for girls. Educators insisted that calisthenics needed to address the gender-specific physiological and psychological needs of boys and girls, which in turn led to the recognition that trained women physical education teachers were needed to replace the Japanese instructors initially hired.[45] The YWCA national leadership saw a role for itself in training Christian-educated physical education teachers to fulfill that need. In 1913, the national committee decided to establish the Normal School of Hygiene and Physical Education in Shanghai's International Settlement. Years later, Abby Mayhew said that it was because the school provided the association with the means to spread the "gospel of the body" to the greatest number of women and girls, and to train future leaders in the field of health and physical education.[46] Nonetheless, the YWCA's investment in creating the Normal School for Hygiene and Physical Education and later building a separate campus for it was unusual and would never be repeated.

The Normal School fit the mission of the YWCA because the health of the body was linked to the well-being of the soul. Abby Mayhew noted that "the National Committee of the Young Women's Christian Association early saw that ... in order to produce sane and vigorous Christians who could 'put on the armour of God' and fight to the end, we must help them first, as Christ did, to build up strong and health [sic] physical lives as the foundation for the spiritual superstructure."[47] Such statements make clear that although the goals of the Normal School naturally aligned with those of nationalistic reformers and educators in China, the YWCA had a clear agenda of its own in establishing the school. The school would contribute to the creation of a strong Chinese body, and thus to a strong Chinese nation. At the same time, however, the school's graduates would seek to Christianize society through example and to further the association movement.

It was a bold undertaking given the limited financial resources of the association, its staffing shortages, and its focus on geographical expansion. However, the endeavour had Coppock's full support and, at that stage in the YWCA movement in China, the national general secretary had more control over setting priorities than future general secretaries would have. The Normal School would also meet another important goal: provide young Chinese women with opportunities for professional growth.

The Normal School opened in 1915, in a small space where Mayhew had taught fitness classes. Soon after, it joined the national office and the Shanghai city association in a large shared compound. Even after the national office relocated and the school expanded into the vacated space, the school was cramped, so much so that in 1919 the national committee purchased three acres of land and built its own campus – institution building in its most literal sense. Coppock was exuberant at the school's success despite the small number of graduates and the ongoing staffing problems. In 1919, she wrote: "I believe that nothing we are doing has counted more toward Christianity than the Normal Training School. It is looked upon generally as by far the best school of its kind in China."[48] Yet, four years later, the association began discussing affiliating the school with a four-year college. In 1925, the school joined with Jinling College in Nanjing. In 1930, the YWCA ended its relationship with Jinling and its involvement in the training of physical education teachers. Why?

The official reason was the re-evaluation of the Normal School's training program and the decision that four years of schooling were needed to prepare physical education teachers.[49] Four other important reasons, however, sprang from both external circumstances and internal dynamics. China's socio-political landscape had changed. Early reformers had referred to China as the "sick man of the orient." The Normal School had reflected the need to strengthen the Chinese nation by strengthening the Chinese body. After 1919, radical intellectuals blamed China's problems on Western imperialism rather than on inherent cultural weaknesses. Therefore, the school's goal of strengthening the Chinese body for China no longer resonated. In 1920, the national committee endorsed the pursuit of industrial reform work and agreed to campaign for child labour legislation. Coppock's death in 1921 was the fourth reason: in many ways, it left the association rudderless. The national committee struggled for six months to name a new national general secretary. Their eventual choice was Rosalee Venable. She faced major tasks in that role, including supporting the child labour campaign, planning for the first national convention, and grooming Ding Shujing to become the next national general secretary. Agreeing to accept the affiliation of the Normal School with Jinling was simple in comparison.

Industrial Work

Industrial work was actually the Chinese YWCA's first endeavour. In 1904, the national committee hired American Martha Berninger, who worked locally at Shanghai's Margaret Williamson Hospital, as its first secretary. She held small classes for factory women in a rented house in a mill district until 1907, when she resigned because she felt more like a missionary than a social worker. Her resignation may or may not have coincided with the visit of the World YWCA's general secretary, Clarissa Spencer; in any case, Spencer turned the fledgling association away from its industrial focus because it lacked the resources to create the type of programs needed by women workers.

By 1907, however, the World YWCA was waking up to the need for industrial work. The 1906 Paris world conference called for national committees to study how they could adapt YWCA work to the pressing needs of factory women. This call was renewed at the Berlin conference in 1910, where resolutions were passed asking member nations to address social and industrial conditions. Both conferences fell short of directly charging member associations to take direct action, however.[50]

Grace Coppock had been interested in industrial reform before she came to China, and she brought that interest with her to the national office when she became national general secretary in 1913.[51] The growth of Chinese industry after the outbreak of the First World War made it impossible for the association to ignore the problems of industrialization. In Shanghai alone, the growth of the cotton industry was dramatic. Between 1913 and 1918, the number of cotton spindles increased by 35 percent. By 1920, the increase since 1913 stood at 70 percent. The increase in number of looms was even greater. Between 1912 and 1918, the number of looms operating in Shanghai cotton mills grew by 57 percent. By 1920, the number of looms had more than doubled over the previous seven years.[52]

As early as 1917, Coppock had asked the YWCA of the USA to send an industrial expert to China. In 1919, after three Shanghai factory owners petitioned the YWCA to conduct welfare work among their female workers, Coppock made a similar request to the British association.[53] Sometime after that, she again pressed her case with the United States, noting that with association work in three industrial cities, the YWCA needed at least two foreign experts.[54]

The following year, she travelled to the United States with YWCA secretaries Fan Yu Jung and Ella MacNeill, the latter one of the first secretaries sent from Australia.[55] They attended the national convention of the American YWCA held in Cleveland in April. According to most histories, it was the World YWCA Committee meeting held later that year that provided Coppock with the persuasive power to get an industrial program started in the Chinese YWCA. What happened at the American YWCA national convention most likely had a dramatic impact on Coppock, but also influenced the actions taken by the World YWCA Committee several months later. At the convention in Cleveland, the large contingent of working-class members joined forces with industrial secretaries and convinced enough of the conservative nucleus at the convention to "formally support workers' rights, to educate its own members about workers' problems, and to embrace an overtly political role."[56] Coppock may have influenced the eventual outcome when she addressed the convention and spoke of the desolate conditions under which female mill workers laboured in China. Among other actions, the convention endorsed the "Social Ideals of the Churches," which included recommendations for principles of industrial justice, and requested that the American association's national board consider a set of labour standards for factory women, such as "an eight-hour workday, prohibition of night work, [and] the right of labor to organize."[57]

Coppock also spoke of the plight of Chinese factory workers when she addressed the World YWCA's first postwar meeting, held in Chambéry, France. At the end of the meeting, the leadership joined with other international women's organizations in claiming peace and social justice as women's issues. Among the social justice issues it embraced was industrial justice. The World YWCA recommended that member associations engage industrial secretaries to study, research, and teach industrial issues, and to work with other societies from "the standpoint of disinterested service" to pressure governments to enact and enforce legislation where needed. The conference further urged:

> Whereas in the present imperfect social order it is necessary in the interest of justice that groups of industrial workers should have the opportunity of combining to improve their status and voice their needs, we *recommend* that the Young Women's Christian Association encourage organisations among women workers, and give opportunity for its members, through lectures, discussion circles, and other methods, to become acquainted with the principles underlying such organisations.[58]

The policy statements issued at Chambéry are critically important, for they provide context for what appeared to be brazen statements by later industrial secretaries in China who called for organizing a labour movement among factory women. In fact, they *were* brazen when made in Shanghai's International Settlement, which was suffused with Western imperialism. The 1920 policy statements did not mark a turn to the left by the World YWCA, but signalled that perhaps more radical action was on the horizon in order to empower working women. At least, that is the message YWCA secretaries heard.

Coppock brought the World YWCA's directive to develop industrial departments back to China. An acquaintance recommended that she consider Agatha Harrison, director of a welfare workers' program at the London School of Economics, as an expert to study ways for the Chinese association to engage in industrial reform work.[59] When World YWCA representatives interviewed Harrison, they hesitated because she subscribed to no particular church denomination and readily admitted that while she had a "very definite faith," she had been "put off" by organized religion in her youth; she also reserved the right to decide for herself regarding the need for taking Christianity to non-Christian lands. Being a committed, churchgoing Christian was a prerequisite for becoming a YWCA secretary at that time. This policy would not be eliminated until the third Chinese national convention in 1933.[60] Coppock, however, overcame the reluctance of the World YWCA, understandable given her long search for an industrial expert.

The question of Harrison's religiosity is important. Scholars only tend to problematize Chinese women's relation to Christianity and ignore the diversity of religious beliefs among Western women. Harrison, however, experienced an epiphany after meeting Coppock: "Her overwhelming faith literally pulled me up short. She showed me the unfairness of bringing my western conception of the Church's failure on this industrial question of China, and made me see that I'd got the chance of proving I was wrong."[61]

Harrison eventually came to believe that the church was the only force with the potential to bring about true reform because China was at the beginning of its industrial development.[62] By the time she left China in January 1924, she believed that the most important attribute of an industrial secretary was "a great belief in Christianity." She also believed that future industrial secretaries should be chosen from among the YWCA women already in China.[63] Her brief sojourn in China had convinced her of the need to be on the ground in order to understand China's social needs.

Barely a month after her arrival, Harrison recommended that the association begin "making opinion."[64] Her first visits to Chinese factories convinced her that illiterate factory women lacked the ability to organize. Emily Honig points out in her study of women in Shanghai textile mills that factories commonly hired women workers from a single locality, and thus native place identity, rather than class consciousness or worker solidarity, defined textile worker identity.[65] Helping these women organize "to improve their status and voice their needs" would have seemed to be a near-impossible task. Harrison also believed that factory owners did not want "genuine" programs but only superficial "'see-what-we-do-for-our-workers' kind of work." She saw ameliorating working conditions through legislation as fundamental to any genuine reform.[66] "Making opinion" was emblematic of the Christian social campaigns that endeavoured to "awaken the individual conscience on a massive scale."[67] "Making opinion" also described much of the climate of urban China during the May Fourth era. Respecting Harrison's expertise, as they had the expertise of Abby Mayhew, the national committee adopted "making opinion" as the association's approach.

The national committee appointed Smith College graduate Cheng Wanzhen to assist Harrison. Cheng had begun working for the YWCA editorial department and the *China Daily News (Shenbao)* soon after her return to China in 1919. A YWCA colleague described her as poised and articulate, with "a remarkable understanding of Anglo-Saxon thought and expression."[68] Cheng assisted Harrison and used her journalistic skills to educate the YWCA's constituency and the larger Chinese community about labour issues. She moved easily between English- and Chinese-speaking communities, and between moderate and more radical circles. Even the Chinese Communist Party acknowledged her as an industrial expert and workers' advocate.[69]

Cheng Wanzhen was exactly the type of Chinese secretary the national office sought. She was educated, fluent in English, a skilled writer in both English and her native language, able to cross cultural boundaries, and a skilled interlocutor. Her contributions to the first years of the national industrial program were many, but she decided to work only part-time after her marriage in 1925. The YWCA lost her permanently when she resigned due to ill health the following year, leading to the closure of the national industrial office for several years.

The Chambéry resolutions suggested cooperation with other organizations. Both Coppock and Harrison set out to find other groups to work with, although initially Harrison expressed concern that by joining with others the association might receive little recognition for its contributions. Coppock responded that "in this industrial question the association may have to lose its life but in losing it, it will find it."[70] Although Harrison remained concerned, the national committee agreed with Coppock.[71]

The YWCA found two groups to work with. The first would become the National Christian Council (NCC), which was in a pre-organization phase when Coppock approached it. Coppock had been appointed to chair a subcommittee to study the church's relation to economic and industrial problems and submit a report at the NCC's first meeting the following May.[72] When she died suddenly in October, Cheng Wanzhen replaced her as chair of that subcommittee.[73] When the NCC convened in May, it endorsed the standards set by the International Labour Organization: no employment of children under twelve, one day's rest in seven, and limitations on work hours.[74] It also created a standing Committee on the Church's Relation to Economic and Industrial Problems.

The second group was the Joint Committee of Shanghai Women's Clubs, an organization the YWCA essentially created. Sometime just before or after Coppock's death on October 15, Harrison invited the American, British, and Shanghai (Chinese) clubs to meet and discuss their shared interest in child labour, an invitation all three clubs accepted.[75] She called it an "epoch-making event" because the clubs were so clearly divided along national lines.[76] These women would soon confront the staunch patriarchal and misogynist milieu that thrived in the colonial world of the International Settlement. In discussing the complications faced by a Christian women's organization in Shanghai, it must be borne in mind that for the YWCA there was the additional factor that whether their social community was the traditional Chinese world dominated by Confucian norms or the imperialistic world of Chinese treaty ports, those social communities were all dominated by men.

The YWCA dominated the Joint Committee. Each club appointed three representatives. The British Women's Club chose YWCA national committee member Mrs. D. MacGillivray as one of its three. Cheng Wanzhen represented the Shanghai Women's Club. The YWCA had its three seats, and Harrison was a de facto member. Thus, there were six YWCA women on the Joint Committee.[77] Harrison wrote World YWCA industrial secretary Mary Dingman that "each day I come more and more to the realization that though there is plenty of good will on this industrial question it has no backbone. I think the Association will have to be that backbone."[78] It was a role the association did not shrink from. Harrison, and later Dingman, who replaced her, became closely and often solely identified as the committee's leaders by the foreign residents of the International Settlement.

Cheng Wanzhen published three articles on industrial topics in 1922. In March, she published on the Second International Congress of Working Women in the widely circulated *Ladies' Journal*.[79] The other two articles appeared in *YWCA Magazine,* one on the creation of the YWCA industrial department and the other on the campaign for labour legislation.[80] In the latter article, Cheng emphasized the need for a national labour policy. She discussed the creation of the Joint Committee and its intent to get every woman in the settlement interested in the labour question and to involve them in working to improve the lives of working women. She concluded that article with the YWCA's role in that work:

> The YWCA originally sought to elevate the spiritual, intellectual, physical and social lives of Chinese women so that they could reach their highest potential and come together as a group to fulfill their obligation to God and the world … These goals for Chinese women include all Chinese women. As working women have not had the opportunity to develop their potential, the YWCA must provide them with opportunities by promoting a labor movement. The Association cannot do this alone; it must join with other groups to help working women seek happiness and well-being.[81]

Cheng's mention of the YWCA's providing working women with "opportunities to develop their potential" aligned with association rhetoric and would not have raised eyebrows. The idea that the YWCA should promote a labour movement in order to provide them with more opportunities aligned with the World YWCA's policy statements at Chambéry, but few of Cheng's readers would have known that. Thus, her words may have been considered those of a liberal-minded labour advocate.

The Joint Committee began by studying conditions in Shanghai factories. It addressed its concerns and recommendation to the Shanghai Municipal Council in a letter dated February 9, 1923, urging the council to do three things: abolish night work for children under twelve, provide part-time schools in factory districts under the council's authority, and extend the health department's jurisdiction to include the supervision of factories.[82] In June, the council created the Child Labor Commission. Some YWCA histories state that this action was a result of "pressure" from the Joint Committee, which suggests that in just three months a small group of reform-minded women became a genuine moral force in a very patriarchal community.[83] This interpretation ignores the larger world of politics in the International Settlement, which included months-long debates over educating the settlement's Chinese children, and another over the exclusion of women ratepayers (taxpayers) from the list of those eligible to stand for elected office. One woman ratepayer, Dr. Margaret Polk, had publicly challenged the council in a letter to the *North China Herald* in which she accused them of deliberately leaving off the names of women ratepayers. She called for the American and British Women's Clubs, the YWCA, the Women's Christian Temperance Union, and all other women's organizations to "unite in seeing that women's interests are guarded."[84]

The Shanghai Municipal Council commissioned a study on employment of children in mills and factories and invited the Joint Committee to submit names to serve on it.[85] Creating the Child Labor Commission and inviting the Joint Committee's participation solved several dilemmas for the council. First, it obviated the need to take any action regarding schools for Chinese children; at the same time, it made the council appear responsive to the issue of child labour. Second, it provided women with an avenue of service. The Joint Committee stood as an example of women's ability to take coordinated action. Polk's call for women to raise the issue of political rights undoubtedly disturbed the council. By creating the Child Labor Commission, the council allowed women to choose how they would serve the community and, obligingly, women chose the route of maternalistic service. The council appointed three women to the commission: Agatha Harrison, Song Meiling (former YWCA secretary and future wife of Chiang Kai-shek), and prominent Chinese physician Shi Meiyu (Mary Stone).[86]

When Harrison left China in January 1924, secretary Mary Dingman arrived to serve in an interim capacity. Dingman had spent several months in Shanghai the previous year, assisting Harrison. This was insufficient to prepare her for the challenges she would face when Western imperialism clashed with the Chinese desire for sovereignty. Several months after her arrival, Cheng Wanzhen published another article in the *YWCA Magazine* that, while promoting the child labour campaign, also severely criticized Western views of China's working poor:

> Most people ... say "Industrialization in China is still so young, what is the use of passing labor legislation? China has so many poor people, what more do they want besides a job?" People who speak like this ... fear that labor laws will put limits on capitalism and cause great difficulty in world markets ... [T]hey feel that the poor should work from dawn to dusk ...

they should simply work all the time. Rest and relaxation, sanitation, education, recreation, entertainment, all of these luxuries belong to the rich. As for the poor, as long as they do not starve to death, they should be content.[87]

Cheng's impassioned comments reminded her YWCA colleagues that, although she had a "remarkable understanding of Anglo-Saxon thought," she was Chinese and took certain aspects of the ongoing debates over Chinese child labour very personally. As debates in the *Herald* and Cheng's writings reveal, there were clear undertones of race and class in the debates over the welfare of the settlement's Chinese children.

Against this backdrop, the Child Labor Commission carried out its work. When it published its report in July, the *North China Herald* called the report "one of the most significant documents published in this country," and described the recommendations as "humane, moderate and conservative."[88] Those recommendations included a minimum age of ten for child employment, to be raised to twelve in four years, a maximum twelve-hour workday for children under fourteen, and no night work for children. The newspaper believed that the commission's report could not be rejected "even by the most avaricious and hard-hearted."[89] But it was.

The Shanghai Municipal Council decided it needed the settlement's ratepayers to provide it with statutory powers to remediate industrial conditions. The next ratepayers' meeting was not until the following April, however.[90] In the intervening months, there was no aspect of the issue that was not raked across the pages of the *North China Herald*.[91] This debate masked another controversial topic – the printed matter, or press, bylaw. Control of Chinese printing companies located in the International Settlement had been an issue since 1916. The Municipal Council wanted to restrict "scurrilous and seditious" literature through a seemingly benign requirement that printing companies register with the council. Chinese printing guilds opposed this restrictive legislation as the International Settlement was a haven from Chinese government and warlord control. The bylaw had been reintroduced at every ratepayers' meeting since 1917 but always failed, not because of Chinese opposition but because there was never the necessary quorum to pass a bylaw.[92]

The April 15, 1925, meeting was no exception – it failed to attract a quorum and adjourned without even discussing the child labour bylaw.[93] Between the debate over the meeting's failure and a petition for a second meeting signed by seventy-six ratepayers, the council took the unprecedented step of scheduling a second meeting for June.[94] This action did

not forestall debate or prevent allegedly communist propaganda attacking the conservative nature of the proposed child labour bylaw.[95] There
was equal agitation against the press bylaw from the settlement's Chinese
businessmen. In this climate, Chinese members of the Joint Committee
feared repercussions from their community if they continued to campaign for a child labour bylaw linked to the press bylaw.

Cheng Wanzhen decided that the harm the press bylaw would do to the
Chinese press outweighed whatever might be accomplished through the
child labour legislation. She hoped that the second meeting would also
fail to reach a quorum. Mary Dingman could not accept that opposition
to the press bylaw was the reason for all the agitation, and had difficulty
accepting Cheng's position. Even though thirty leading Chinese organizations and firms signed petitions supporting the child labour bylaw
but opposing the press bylaw, she failed to make the connection between
opposition to the press bylaw and the rising feelings against any form of
foreign control over Chinese life in the settlement. A history of industrial
work published after Dingman's departure noted that the "obscurity in
which the Chinese and foreign groups are cut off from understanding
each other's real motives in a community such as this blocked her way."[96]

Two other groups "cut off" from understanding each other were conservative men and civic-minded women. Some conservative men objected in very uncivil tones. W. Bruce Lockhart wrote a letter to the *North
China Herald* directly attacking the YWCA for an ill-conceived and costly reform plan:

> If Shanghai signs a blank chit at the next Special Meeting of Ratepayers
> on June 2 at the behest of the hard-luck story of one of these young things
> from the Young Women's Christian Association, that blank chit ... has to
> be paid ... Miss Agatha Harrison and Miss M.A. Dingman who are the
> origin and energy of this YWCA agitation show a most laudable interest
> in other's people's children ... When Miss Harrison and Miss Dingman
> know as much as I do, and have good working experience of the subject it
> will not be necessary for me to draw public attention to the parable in the
> Bible – the one about the young ladies with the lamps – (possibly members
> of the YWCA of those days!) – the young ladies *who forgot the oil for their
> lamps!* Do you remember it?[97]

But it was labour unrest rather than inflamed rhetoric in the *North China
Herald* that ended the campaign. Tensions erupted into violence when a
Japanese factory guard killed a striking mill worker on May 15. Students

protested and some were arrested. On May 30, a large, angry crowd of more than fifteen hundred converged on a police station in the heart of the settlement where they believed those students were being held. Afraid that they would be overrun, police opened fire, killing or wounding over a dozen people. The May Thirtieth Incident spawned nationwide protests that caused more violence and deaths. The situation in the International Settlement was so grave that on June 1 the Shanghai Municipal Council declared martial law.

In the middle of this crisis, the Municipal Council held the ratepayers' meeting. It adjourned after fifteen minutes, once again short of a quorum. One reason was that many men were serving with the defence force as the city struggled to restore order.[98] Sometime after that, a letter to the editor of a Shanghai newspaper attacked the Joint Committee as "a group of women reformers" who "obviously had no realization of the economic factors involved."[99] With their actions criticized and their cause defeated, the Joint Committee temporarily disbanded. It organized again the following May as the Joint Committee of Shanghai Women's Organizations, and expanded its membership to include other foreign women's clubs and such organizations as the Chinese Women's Suffrage Association and the Chinese Women's Christian Temperance Union. It remained active until the war with Japan. One of its first tasks was to write a history of its first social campaign. The YWCA remained an active member.[100]

Ironically, the women of the YWCA who had worked hardest to get the child labour bylaw passed felt only relief when the meeting was declared "never to have been held."[101] Even Mary Dingman commented that "it is now a real question in the minds of some as to whether there ought ever to be another attempt to get this By-Law adopted ... A complicated international situation exists ... so we must wait." As she left China, she found some comfort in the fact that Chinese who opposed the extension of foreign control over their lives and country did believe in the principle of limiting child labour.[102]

The Chinese leadership on the national committee distanced themselves from the indignation of the foreign community and refuted foreign press accounts that explained away the nationwide protests as communist influenced. They stated emphatically that the protests came from "forces deep in the inner spirit and history of the Chinese people." The protesters opposed the imposition of foreign laws on Chinese residents. The committee pledged "to aid in all possible ways in the securing of such justice and in all processes, which may help to bring about a better

understanding and a right relationship between our own people and the
foreign nations concerned." Both Chinese and foreign staff endorsed that
statement. However, the fact that they considered it separately suggests
that the political realities of the International Settlement, where foreign
and Chinese belonged to separate communities, momentarily intruded
into the YWCA.[103] It is possible that when the foreign staff met separately, they began to recognize their complicity in Western imperialism, living as they did in a settlement that was considered to be foreign soil, and
whose residents were by treaty immune from prosecution under Chinese
law, a principle called "extraterritoriality." Some American secretaries had
the courage to petition the US State Department to revoke this principle, but to no avail.[104] Extraterritoriality ended only in 1943 when the
United States signed the Sino-American Treaty for the Relinquishment
of Extraterritorial Rights in China, which ended a century of extraterritorial rights and allowed limited immigration of Chinese into the United
States.[105]

The national committee's response to the May Thirtieth Incident
was a key marker in the history of the YWCA in China. While future
events would receive more attention, it was a rare moment when the
national committee came out of the shadows and spoke publicly, assert-
ing the right of the Chinese people to their national sovereignty, and
sent a clear signal to the International Settlement's municipal government and foreign residents that the foreign-inspired association had a
Chinese soul because the voices that spoke about "our own people" were
clearly Chinese. The national committee's Chinese leadership could not
be easily dismissed either, for they themselves did not live in the shadows.
The *North China Herald* recognized committee chair Gong Hezhen as a
leader among serious-minded Chinese women.[106]

The story of YWCA industrial work in 1925 was not entirely about
the child labour campaign. In March, the national committee agreed to
lend Lily Haass to the National Christian Council to serve as its industrial executive. Haass, originally a Beijing city association secretary, was
studying at the London School of Economics and planning to return as
a national industrial secretary. In a letter to national general secretary
Rosalee Venable, she questioned the wisdom of reassigning her, without knowing that the decision had actually been made the day before
she wrote her letter. Among her many concerns, most of which turned
out to be valid, was that working through the NCC would be slow and
cumbersome, and that it would not prioritize local work as the YWCAs
would. She also worried that the embryonic industrial "department,"

which had not yet been formally organized, would fail for lack of staff and resources. She was bold enough to ask if she could do both jobs – serve as NCC industrial executive while still having a special responsibility for YWCA industrial work. Her request was denied.[107] When she returned to China to assume her new job, Haass worked closely with Shanghai city association secretary Edith Johnston to plan how that city association would continue its local industrial work, but on September 15, Johnston died.[108]

The national office had already been trying to secure a British secretary for national industrial work. Left on the staff were Dan Dexing, who was listed as industrial executive, and Cheng Wanzhen, who was working only half-time after her marriage. Both were temporarily reassigned as local Shanghai city association secretaries. Dan resisted this designation, but it became a moot point as health concerns forced her to leave by the end of the year. Cheng resigned midway through the following year for the same reason.[109]

Unable to find a suitable British woman to replace Johnston, who was Irish, the association settled on Australian Eleanor Hinder, who agreed to come for two years to finish Johnston's contract.

MAKING THE WORK CHINESE

"Making the work Chinese" had been the goal from the time of Clarissa Spencer's visit in 1907. Spencer essentially meant making its leadership Chinese. It had also been Grace Coppock's goal, although she first had to build up the YWCA movement in China by hiring foreign secretaries to establish city associations. It took two decades for indigenization to begin bearing fruit. "Indigenization" and "devolution" are the terms this book uses to describe the transfer of leadership to Chinese YWCA women, whether lay volunteers serving on governing boards or professional staff who performed executive functions and led program work.

The transfer of leadership to the Chinese women who served on governing boards occurred earlier, was more widespread, and was a less formal process as there were no specific qualifications other than being Christian, being educated, and being willing to serve a diverse community. The situation was different for professional staff. In 1918, the national committee decided that for a young Chinese woman to be accepted for the training program for association secretaries, she must have a middle school education and some experience with her local association, and the recommending association had to agree to hire her when the training was completed.[110] College-educated Chinese women were actively recruited by the national office. Appointing a Chinese woman to a professional position was one thing; enabling her to exercise the authority of her position was quite another. Western women, many of whom came to China to fulfill their own professional ambitions, did not always step back willingly and let their Chinese colleagues lead.

Devolution proceeded slowly for several reasons. The first was the nature of the organization itself. Speaking in the United States in 1925, future national general secretary Ding Shujing pointed out that in the beginning Chinese women neither grasped the purpose of the YWCA nor understood the needs of China's women. Subsequently, they understood the association a little better but thought it was just another mission organization, so they came to "help" the foreign women with their mission work. To Ding, it was at the first national convention, held in 1923, that Chinese women finally had a "self-awakening," and stepped forward with questions, criticisms, and considerations.[111] Ding Shujing's observations represent a Chinese voice attempting to interpret the Chinese experience to a foreign audience. Devolution was also slowed because of the lack of educated, professionally minded Chinese women. In 1920, there were only 117 women enrolled in Christian colleges and universities throughout China.[112] A third reason was the nature of the work itself. At the 1919 secretarial conference, Grace Coppock stated in her address to conference participants: "We should now turn very seriously to the enlarging of the Chinese staff. It will be hard for as a vocation, the secretaryship of the YWCA is still new. It carries a heavier responsibility that most women carry as teachers."[113]

The life of a YWCA secretary was intense. Even a local secretary travelled frequently. They organized and attended conferences and training institutes in China, and were often sent overseas for advanced training. Such opportunities for professional training attracted Chinese women to the YWCA, but they also became a pretext for leaving for easier jobs.

Finally, family pressure to marry and ill health cost the association many promising Chinese secretaries. After marrying, some former secretaries continued as members of governing boards, so the YWCA did not lose their knowledge and talent entirely. Ill health was a constant factor. Even if the association did not lose a secretary, it often lost her services for a time. For example, both Cai Kui and Deng Yuzhi had to take leaves of absence because of ill health.

Leadership on Governing Committees

Chinese leadership developed first among the women who volunteered on association governing committees. When the Shanghai city association organized in 1908, its governing committee consisted of both Western and Chinese women. Four years later, all of its members were Chinese. Shanghai city association general secretary Grace Coppock noted that when Western and Chinese women sat on the committee, meetings were held in English, and Chinese women were not always able to follow the discussions. Western women also tended to make quick decisions, causing Chinese members to hesitate, being unwilling to commit themselves to matters they were not sure they fully understood. In Coppock's opinion, the all-Chinese committee was a more effective governing body.[114]

> No one who has ever attended one of those meetings of the Directors would ever say that the Chinese will not speak out their opinions. And they are full of ideas for the extension of the work. They talk so fast (and not *always* strictly according to parliamentary rule) that it is hard for me sometimes to get a word in.[115]

Unlike in Shanghai, Chinese lay leadership dominated city associations in Beijing, Fuzhou, and Changsha from the time each was established. Those cities had a number of educated Chinese Christian women willing to serve, and in Guangzhou, Chinese women had the fortitude to start their association without the help of the national office.[116]

The national committee included representatives from all city associations and additional members who lived in Shanghai and made up the executive committee of the national committee. The constitution passed at the first national convention in 1923 made the executive committee the policy-making body for the association, somewhat diminishing the ability of the national general secretary to act independently.

In its first three decades, both Chinese and Western women served on the national committee. Starting in 1915, all officers except the chair were Chinese. In mid-1919, Hu Binxia became chair. Future chairs included Gong Hezhen and Sheng Zuxin. These three were among Shanghai's most educated women. Hu graduated from Wellesley, Gong from Barnard, and Sheng from Columbia. Their years in the Unites States should not suggest that they did not consider the YWCA from a Chinese perspective, but theirs would have been a comparatively cosmopolitan view. Hu Binxia served as national committee vice chair from 1915 or 1916 to midway through 1919, when she became chair. The year 1919 was the first year Sheng and Gong appeared on committee lists, although, as few committee lists were complete, they might have begun serving a year or two earlier. Gong took over from Hu in 1922 and chaired the national committee until at least 1928, when there is a gap in the records. Sheng served as vice chair. When the records pick up again in 1932, Sheng was listed as chair, but the following year, Gong was again listed as chair. She served in that capacity until 1937, and continued to be listed as a member of the national committee until the end of the war with Japan. These three women were not alone in the length of their service. Wang Guoxiu, who led the national committee after 1949, first appears on the national committee list in 1934 as the committee vice chair.[117]

The important role of the national committee has not been emphasized in other histories of the Chinese YWCA. In addition to making policy, the executive committee approved programs and hiring decisions. Committee members also oversaw the work of each department, as each department had an advisory committee chaired by a committee member. Thus, the lay volunteers were more fundamentally involved than the terse minutes of their monthly meetings indicate. Further, decisions taken at those meetings were based on first-hand knowledge as well as the reports of the national general secretary and her professional staff. The national committee approved each stage of Ding Shujing's advancement. It stalled the decision to transfer Deng Yuzhi from the student department to the national industrial department for months (internal politics played a role in the delay). After Ding Shujing's unexpected death in July 1936, the national committee delayed appointing Cai Kui the permanent national general secretary for two and a half years, for reasons that documents only hint at. After the May Thirtieth Incident in 1925, the national committee defended the Chinese residents of the International Settlement whose protests over the erosion of China's sovereignty had resulted in the shooting death of students at the hands of the settlement police. The national committee would speak out against Japanese imperialism in even stronger terms after the Shanghai War in 1932. Finally, it would be the national committee that declared the association's support for Mao Zedong and his state-building project in March 1950.

Leadership among Professional Staff

Finding qualified Chinese women became the quintessential dilemma of the Chinese YWCA. For foreign staff, the YWCA's professional ideal was high, requiring secretaries to hold college degrees, to be trained in YWCA organizational methods, and, if possible, to be experienced in their fields of expertise. As noted earlier, the standard for Chinese staff at the local level was more modest, requiring only a middle school education and time spent in YWCA training programs. Understandably, Chinese women with college degrees were highly sought after, but they also had other options besides association work, and those options increased as the years passed. As already seen, retaining secretaries was also a serious problem.

Exacerbating the problem from the perspective of local city associations was the fact that when a Chinese secretary began to show real promise, the national committee tapped her for service on its staff, thus depriving local associations of the very women they needed to make local work Chinese. This was exactly what happened in the case of Ding Shujing. Ding joined the staff of the Beijing city association in 1916 and became its first Chinese general secretary in 1920. In 1923, the national committee brought her to Shanghai to work as secretary for the first national convention as the first step toward grooming her to become the national general secretary, which she did on January 1, 1926.

Numbers reveal progress. The first Chinese secretary was Ding Mingyu, hired as associate general secretary of the Shanghai city association in 1908. She was still the only Chinese secretary, along with one British and six American secretaries, at the first secretarial conference, held at the seaside resort of Beidahe in June and July 1911. At the second secretarial conference in 1915, there were five Chinese secretaries and seventeen Western secretaries. The following year, there were seven Chinese secretaries and twenty-one Western secretaries. At the fourth secretarial conference in 1919, the number of Chinese secretaries had increased to eighteen and the number of Western secretaries to fifty-two. Numbers do not tell the complete story, however. Of the fifty-two Western secretaries, forty-two were Americans and ten were Europeans. Of the forty-two Americans, twenty-one had been in China for less than two years, and only eight had five years of experience. Also, a number of the Western secretaries listed were on furlough and thus not in China. The Chinese secretaries thus likely played a greater role at the conference than the numbers suggest.[118]

From a statistical standpoint, the 1919 figures represent an eighteenfold increase in Chinese secretaries, a tenfold increase in European secretaries, and only a sevenfold increase in American secretaries. It was at the 1919 secretarial conference that Grace Coppock clearly stated, with the foundational groundwork laid by foreign secretaries, that it was time to develop the Chinese secretaryship. The growth in the number of Chinese professional staff over the next five years reflected the focus on that effort. In 1920–21, there were 42 Chinese secretaries and 84 foreign secretaries. In 1922, the ratio was 61/83; in 1923, it was 65/85; and in 1924, the margin had shrunk to 51/64.[119] Anti-imperialist and anti-Christian unrest caused the dramatic reduction in the number of foreign secretaries after 1923. It would also be temporary, as more trained foreign secretaries were needed during the interim as the inexperienced new Chinese secretaries were trained or as new programs required particular expertise. Foreign staff would increase, then decrease again because of the worldwide Depression and Japanese aggression. In 1934, there would be only 11 Western secretaries on the national staff, and 3 in local associations, one each in Hong Kong, Changsha, and Mukden.

The End of 1925: The Year of Transition

It is often not until the end of a year that hindsight brings that year into clear focus. For the Chinese association, the processing of annual reports sent to both the YWCA of the USA and the World YWCA provided the opportunity to explain and interpret events and developments of the previous twelve months. The 1925 report complied by editorial executive Helen Thoburn, some of which was quoted at the beginning of this chapter, and the 1925 report by outgoing national general secretary Rosalee Venable, who had replaced Grace Coppock and promoted the advancement of Ding Shujing, stand as critical measures of just where the YWCA stood as a *Chinese* association. Thoburn reported on the results of a conference of city associations in north China attended by mostly Chinese board and staff members. Those women described Western-inspired associations as being characterized by "departments" and "cooperation," neither of which they understood. Their comment about "cooperation" reflected a policy initiated by Coppock in keeping with World YWCA directives made at Chambéry to cooperate with other groups to achieve certain reform goals. The YWCA had become deeply involved with the NCC, the child labour campaign had been a joint effort with other women's organizations, and the Normal School for Hygiene and Physical Education had just been amalgamated with Jinling College. In Thoburn's opinion, "we have 'cooperated' until no one knows what the YWCA proper, is." As for the remark about "departments," the Chinese participants grasped their organizational role, but the departmentalization of work obscured the main purpose of the association. The participants stated that local associations could not "think out" future programs; Chinese national secretaries needed to lead the way. And the time for them to do it was "now."[120]

Rosalee Venable's report was much in the same vein, except in a broader context. She admitted that although the 1923 national convention had done much, there had not been much original thinking and the regular lines of departmental work, modelled after the American idea of association work, had simply been reported on and the same pattern of work continued down to the present time. A disrupting factor had been the renewal of the anti-Christian campaign and the "new nationalism," both of which threatened Christian churches and the Christian organization because of their foreign origins and foreign leadership. Chinese leadership in local associations became concerned over the possible withdrawal of foreign staff. The previous year, Venable had participated in a meeting of the Beijing city association board as it discussed the possible loss of all the foreign-lead programs such as girls' work, religious education, and social service. The loss of those programs did not seem to matter. What the board members were interested in was a hostel for students coming to study in Beijing and programs aimed at "home life." Unfortunately, Venable did not elaborate on what program changes were made, reporting only that "a year later, their association is far more simplified, and beginning to get closer to what those women understand."

As for her report on work at the national level, in answer to the question: "What are the major departments or committees of your national committee?," she stated that there was no way to reply that year except that they maintained their departmental structure but were "not promoting work along departmental lines." She did not elaborate further, however. She implied that any adjustments must wait until "Chinese women have come through this transition period and taken full possession of their organization." Venable admitted that the shift from being "guardians" would be difficult for some Western secretaries. She did not go as far as Thoburn, who referred to the period to come as "chaos."[121] What her report revealed was that she was at least willing to listen to and entertain ideas that seemed counter to the "association way." But then, she was leaving.

Whatever adjustments might have been made, the bureaucratic division of association work into departments did not end. New departments were added at the national level as programs expanded. In the next few years, this would include the creation of an industrial department and a

rural department. The second of two association histories authored before 1950 also included an organizational chart outlining lines of authority and division of work. That same history, however, emphasized the
democratic values practised in everyday association life.

The first quarter-century of the YWCA movement in China – what
has been described as the "formative years" – occurred against a backdrop
of national struggle for political and cultural standing in an imperialist
world that was attempting to deny China the independence to define
either of those for itself. The failure of the child labour campaign is a dramatic example of how the association was buffeted by historical events.
It also demonstrates how Western-inspired reform models identified the
association as a cultural interloper and foreign transplant. Those foreign
models, or what was called the "association way," would be domesticated
under Chinese leadership (see Chapter 3).

2

Making a Chinese Leadership, 1925–36

I have no right to keep on refusing to take these positions of responsibility when you asked these same things of the foreign secretaries in China, and I as a Chinese woman must do it.

— Ding Shujing, 1923

When Clarissa Spencer wrote, "We must make our work as Chinese as possible ... calling Chinese secretaries as we can find the suitable women," she identified the professional women most identified with the YWCA movement in China. This chapter steps away from the chronological history of the Chinese YWCA to explore the lives, early careers, and religiosities of the three women whose leadership defined the Chinese YWCA after 1925: Ding Shujing, Deng Yuzhi, and Cai Kui. Their leadership anchored the association's gradual transformation from a Sino-Western institution to one shaped by Chinese visions of what the association movement should be in China. Presenting these women's stories in a separate chapter highlights their unique characteristics and qualities, underscoring the different ways of being Christian and a leader among the ranks of YWCA women.

Clarissa Spencer could not have anticipated the cultural politics that complicated devolution or how historical contingency buffeted the process. There were Western secretaries who had difficulty stepping back and letting Chinese women lead. Among Chinese women, there were power struggles between volunteer leadership on the national committee and paid professional staff, clashes between first- and second-generation Chinese YWCA women and between conservative and progressive women. Untimely deaths accelerated devolution; illnesses delayed it. In the end, regime change required it.

The topic of religiosity is critical for a study of a Christian organization and the Chinese Christian women who dedicated their lives to it. Ding Shujing, Deng Yuzhi, and Cai Kui all were converts to Christianity. Ding and Deng converted along with other family members when they were around ten years old. Cai joined the Society of Friends (Quakers) when she was in her early twenties and studying at Jinling College. None of them ever wrote about her conversion experience or the circumstances that led to it. Each spoke or wrote about her deep and abiding faith, but they lived their faith in different ways.

Ding Shujing, Deng Yuzhi, and Cai Kui are examined from three perspectives. The first perspective considers how their early lives and educations shaped their religiosity and social views. The second discusses why each was identified for leadership, what their pathway to leadership entailed, and who supported or impeded their advancement. The third discusses the visions each articulated for the YWCA movement in China before the War of Resistance against Japan. As this chapter covers Ding Shujing's entire tenure as national general secretary, her vision for the association is discussed in depth. Deng Yuzhi's and Cai Kui's visions for the association will be more briefly touched on in this chapter then developed more thoroughly in Chapters 4 and 5, which cover their years as national general secretaries.

Early Life and Education: The Shaping of Christian Womanhood

To understand Ding Shujing, Deng Yuzhi, and Cai Kui as leaders, it is important to know about their early lives and education even though those discussions predate this chapter's time frame. Where were they born, and into what type of family? How were they educated? How did each conceive of herself as Chinese, Christian, and woman? What ideologies centred their lives in the shifting socio-political landscape of China?

Born in 1890, Ding Shujing matured in a China of traditionalists, gradualist reformers, and anti-Manchu revolutionaries. Key political markers in her early years were the Boxer Rebellion in 1900, which resulted in the oppressive Boxer Protocol, and the Xinhai Revolution in

1911, which ended two millennia of imperial rule but did not result in a democratic republic. Deng Yuzhi, born in 1900, and Cai Kui, born in 1902, came of age during the political chaos of the Warlord Era, which began even before President Yuan Shikai's death in 1916. The key political marker in their lives was the May Fourth Movement in 1919, which ushered in an era of nationalistic, iconoclastic, and anti-imperialist fervour. The different Chinas these three women grew up in essentially placed them in two different generations.

Ding was born in Linqing, a city of some consequence at the confluence of the Wei River and the Grand Canal in west Shandong Province, near the Shandong-Hebei border, on February 17, 1890.[1] Her family reportedly greeted her arrival with joy because she was the first girl in several generations. Already with a son, they could give way to joy at having a daughter. Little is known about Ding's parents except that they educated their daughter and converted to Christianity when she was ten or twelve. That both parents welcomed a daughter and educated her suggests some acceptance of progressive ideas. The fact that Ding was accepted at mission schools indicates that her feet had not been bound, another sign that her parents were forward-thinking. Still, their conversion raises questions because, according to Ding's own recollection, her mother was a devout Buddhist. The fact that Ding attended mission schools, first in Dezhou and then in Tongzhou, and later attended the North China Union College for women speaks to her parents' commitment to educating their daughter, and Ding's own desire to pursue her education. It also explains their exposure to Christianity. Who converted first, and why, is a moot point. Ding Shujing's Christian faith became a defining feature of her life and her womanhood. From her writings, it was an ecumenical faith, one that respected the spiritual lives of non-Christian women.

Deng Yuzhi was born on September 11, 1900, in Shashi, Hubei Province.[2] Her father's family had large land holdings. He was a Qing official who, while Confucian in outlook, was socially progressive, as indicated by the fact that he joined the anti-footbinding society. Deng had a younger sister and a brother. When she was eight, her father accepted a position in Changsha, the capital of Hunan Province and an educational and cultural city that was a centre of radical thinking. Her parents enrolled her in the liberal Zhounan Girls' Middle School, along with her sister and sister-in-law. Its famous alumni included communist organizer Xiang Jingyu; Xiang's future sister-in-law Cai Chang; Mao Zedong's first wife, Yang Kaihui; and socialist writer Ding Ling.[3] Xiang was five years older than Deng, and Ding Ling was four years younger,

so it is doubtful that Deng knew either. But Cai Chang was her age and
Yang Kaihui only a year younger, so she may have known them.

Deng's parents died in the early 1910s (some accounts say they died
when she was ten), after which she lived with her grandmother. Like
Ding Shujing's mother, Deng's grandmother was a Buddhist who converted to Christianity, apparently influenced by the missionaries at the
Yale-in-China Hospital who cared for Deng's dying father, and the Bible
women who comforted the family after his death. Deng and her sister
converted as well, presumably for the same reason and at the same time.
As with Ding Shujing, Christianity became a defining feature of her life
and underpinned her social views, including her radicalism. Her life story
confirms the deep and abiding meaning she found in Jesus's message.

Deng's grandmother enrolled her in a mission school, Fuxiang Middle
School for Girls. Deng claimed some credit for this, explaining that she
wanted to learn English. At Fuxiang, Deng joined the student YWCA.
Of the three women who became future general secretaries, she was the
only one whose connection with the YWCA reached back to her youth.
She joined the YWCA specifically because of its service orientation. Thus,
from the beginning, "YWCA" and "service" were linked in her mind,
much like Jesus's life and social justice would be linked. Her entry into
the political arena also began at Fuxiang, where she served as president
of the student self-government association and in 1919 organized and
participated in student protests. Her early "radical" inclinations thus had
many wellsprings: her progressive family, the milieu of Changsha, and
the May Fourth Movement. All shaped her womanhood.

Fuxiang was critical to Deng in another way as well. The feminization
and professionalization of the mission field in China had brought a new
style of female Christian educator to China, one who provided an example of how to live independently even as she taught the gospel of gentility.[4] The teachers at Fuxiang inspired Deng, for, by her own account, it
was during those years that she rejected the idea of marriage and became
intent on getting a college education.

Little is known of Cai Kui's early life and education, but they differed
in important ways from those of either Ding or Deng.[5] Cai was born into
a non-Christian family in Hangzhou, Zhejiang Province, on May 28,
1902. Unlike Ding and Deng, she converted to Christianity as a young
adult, while attending Jinling College. Hangzhou was one of China's
culturally elite cities, having been governed during the Tang dynasty by
the famous government official and poet Bai Juyi and during the Song
dynasty by statesman and poet Su Shi (Su Dongpo). Zhejiang Province

belonged to the region south of the Yangtze River known as Jiangnan. Trade transformed this region into one of the wealthiest and most urbanized areas in China during the Ming and early Qing dynasties. The region gained a reputation of being progressive, particularly regarding education. Cai's family appears to have followed in that tradition. Her father studied in Japan to become a medical doctor, a choice of what was modern and needed for China. When Cai entered middle school in the 1910s, the conservatively inclined educational system offered only two tracks for girls, vocational training or normal school. Cai chose vocational training. Little else is known about her middle school years, but it would be hard to imagine they were not touched by the May Fourth Movement.

All three women attended Christian colleges for women. Ding attended North China Union Women's College, which became the first institution of higher education for women in China when it opened in 1907. Its opening corresponded with the Qing dynasty's struggle to retain its imperial mandate by initiating reforms such as the introduction of Western-style public education (in 1904 for boys and 1906 for girls), abolishing the centuries-old civil service examinations (1905), and making tentative steps toward constitutional monarchy. North China Union College was a logical choice for Ding because of its location in the north and the fact that Chinese was its language of instruction.[6] It was also the only choice other than going abroad. She graduated first in a class of three in 1911. The small graduating class was typical of the early stage of women's higher education in China. The country underwent a cataclysmic change when the Xinhai Revolution overthrew the Qing dynasty a few months later, ending two millennia of imperial rule. For women, however, it was a world largely unchanged: the constitutional assembly denied women suffrage in 1912, the government school system continued to promote Confucian ideals of womanhood, and marriage, rather than career, remained women's primary life goal.

Deng Yuzhi's plans for a college education were complicated by her grandmother's insistence that she go through with an arranged marriage after she graduated from Fuxiang. This remains the most puzzling aspect of Deng's life story. Given what is known about her tenacity, it is difficult to understand why she agreed, but agree she did on the condition that she be allowed to practise Christianity and attend college. After the wedding, her husband's family refused to honour their agreements, so Deng ran away, sheltering at Fuxiang, where she continued to study English so she could pass the entrance exam of Jinling College, whose language of instruction was English. Her husband's family failed to lure her back, and in fall 1920, she entered Jinling. During her sophomore year, her husband and his family tried legal means to compel her to return. Jinling president Matilda Thurston intervened, getting Deng a job with the YWCA in Shanghai. From Shanghai, Deng was sent to work for the Changsha YWCA.[7] It was there that she met YWCA secretary Maud Russell, who became her mentor and lifelong friend. A Christian socialist (and later a committed Marxist), Russell provided Deng with her first opportunity to work as a social activist by involving her in the Changsha YWCA's small industrial program. In 1923, Deng returned to Jinling, where, despite a mediocre academic record, she graduated with a degree in sociology in 1926. Russell convinced her to give up her dream of becoming a teacher and accept a position in the YWCA national office.[8]

Although not yet a Christian, Cai Kui also chose to enroll in Jinling. What led to her decision is not known. Perhaps it was the location, or perhaps the breadth of a curriculum that offered something other than teaching or nursing, the professional tracks most readily open to women. Cai had a literary bent. She entered Jinling in September 1922 and graduated five years later with a degree in literature.[9]

Cai converted to Christianity during her Jinling years, joining the Society of Friends Fellowship in Nanjing.[10] Quakers were among the smallest denominations in China. They made few converts even though they were the least dogmatic Protestant denomination. Renowned Chinese philosopher and cultural commentator Lin Yutang stated in *My Country and My People*:

> The Chinese, therefore, make rather poor Christian converts, and if they are to be converted they should all become Quakers, for that is the only sort of Christianity that the Chinese can understand. Christianity as a way of life can impress the Chinese, but Christian creeds and dogmas will be crushed, not by a superior Confucian logic but by ordinary Confucian common sense.[11]

What Lin Yutang meant, and what may have attracted Cai Kui, was that Quakers eschewed creeds and dogmas, believing every individual could discover the divine spark within them through contemplation. Quakers further insisted that Christianity was best expressed through personal example and service.

When Cai entered Jinling in 1922, China's youth had undergone a political awakening. Even Jinling students had participated in May Fourth student protests and sought to form a student union branch at the college. Cai made only one brief reference to being politically engaged during her youth. In 1938, she explained that although she had been exposed to radicalism, "the knife is sharp, and I did not have the courage to play with it."[12] Despite such a declaration, she married a man who had been intimately involved with the first years of the Chinese communist movement, which suggested that her views and sympathies may have been far from moderate. She steered away from politics on a professional level until she became YWCA national general secretary during the war with Japan.

The personal and professional lives of Ding, Deng, and Cai followed quite different trajectories. The one thing they had in common was that, once they went to work for the YWCA, they remained a YWCA secretary for the rest of their careers. Ding never married. Whether or not her parents arranged a marriage for her is unknown. Given that they had already demonstrated a certain liberal-mindedness, they likely deferred to Ding on the matter of marriage. Most college-educated women married college-educated men, so when she graduated from college, her options would have narrowed. Once she went to work for the Beijing YWCA in 1916, she would have met single YMCA secretaries interested in marrying an educated Christian woman, but perhaps she never met a man she considered suitable, or the attractions of a career outweighed the social advantages of marriage. Both in China and the West, many women chose not to marry simply because, for the first time, they had that choice. She had four nephews, so her extended family life might have been quite fulfilling. Also, not having had a sister, Ding might have found the sisterhood within the YWCA personally satisfying.

After graduation, Ding taught at a mission school in Shandong. She returned to Beijing in 1914 to teach at the Bridgman Academy, the middle school associated with North China Union Women's College. In or around May 1916, she became embroiled in a controversy when the academy board appointed her to replace a more experienced Western teacher and a few board members claimed that she lacked the necessary qualifications.[13] About five months later, Ding joined the staff of the newly organized Beijing YWCA city association.[14] The change in careers may have resulted from a deliberate choice to leave an uncomfortable environment, or Ding may have simply taken advantage of a new opportunity. Whatever motivated her, the Beijing YWCA quickly recognized the potential of its newest secretary.

Deng Yuzhi's rejection of her marriage was a defining event in her life because she gained the freedom to fulfill her ambitions. However, according to a memorial address written by her nephew Deng Zhenying, Deng Yuzhi remained close to her family and was affectionately referred to as "Big Daddy" by her nephews and nieces. When her sister-in-law died in 1922, both she and her younger sister cared for them. When her brother remarried and his second wife lacked mothering instincts, Deng continued her involvement. According to her nephew, she was so fond of him that she brought him to live with her when she was sent from Jinling College to Mt. Lu to recover from a bout of tuberculosis. She also took him to live with her in Shanghai after her graduation in spring 1926, and sent him back to live with his father only when she left Shanghai to attend the London School of Economics.[15] It is difficult to challenge this account even though no YWCA documents corroborate it. There are very few official documents that comment on either Western or Chinese women's personal lives. Nonetheless, Deng Zhenying's recollection adds a very human dimension to Deng Yuzhi's life, softening the image of a woman known for her wholehearted dedication to serving the Chinese working classes and the Chinese nation-state.

After graduating from Jinling, Deng Yuzhi accepted a position as a student secretary on the national staff in Shanghai, an ideal fit as she had belonged to a student YWCA at Fuxiang. Deng would not remain a national student secretary for long, however. By fall 1927, she had become the choice of senior national staff to reopen the national industrial department, which had closed when Cheng Wanzhen resigned the previous year. Because of her unconventional life, getting the more socially conservative national committee to agree to her transfer took time. She would not be named a national industrial secretary until 1928.

Cai Kui also went to work for the national YWCA after graduating from Jinling in 1927. It is quite possible Deng recommended her to the YWCA. Over time, the association hired a number of Jinling graduates.[16] Cai joined the staff of the national editorial department. Unlike Ding, who never married, and Deng, who left her marriage, Cai married Chen Wangdao in September 1930.[17] He was a noted scholar of rhetoric and a professor at Fudan University in Shanghai. Historically, Chen is remembered as the first person to translate the *Communist Manifesto* into Chinese and as one of the founding members of the Chinese Communist Party in 1921. Although apparently very ardent, he left the party around 1922, apparently over disagreements with Chen Duxiu, one of the party's co-founders. He would not formally rejoin the party until after 1949.[18]

A biographical sketch in the Jinling College archives noted that Cai had the "good fortune" to have a husband who believed that "women should find full and free expression of their talents and personalities through professional life."[19] Chen's early writing certainly demonstrated his strong advocacy for women's economic independence.[20] The couple had one son.

These three women had very different personalities. Ding's colleagues described her as very dignified, with a good sense of humour, and as being *re xin* (enthusiastic or zealous). She was also strong-willed and, while she listened to the advice of others, she followed her own dictates. Lily Haass, the longest-serving and most influential of the American secretaries, described Deng Yuzhi as "a rare thing" because she was interested in economic questions, and as being "keen mentally." Even more, she considered Deng her intellectual equal: "I find her unusually stimulating, mentally able to meet my mind at any point that I touch."[21] A Chinese colleague reminisced about Deng's boldness:

> At that time the buses in Shanghai were graded as first-class and third-class. Once, as a Chinese man dressed in old clothes tried to board a first-class bus, a Western foreigner attempted to pull him off the vehicle. When Deng Yuzhi stopped the foreigner from doing this, the man said, "This is an English bus!" Deng Yuzhi said, "Go home and take a look at a map – what country is Shanghai in? It's in China, not England." Thus, the Westerner was forced to stay his hand.[22]

Lily Haass is the source of much of what is known about Cai Kui's personality. She described Cai as having a nervous temperament and not always able to deal well with criticism or adverse situations. Haass also lauded her tact and finesse with people during their travels outside of Shanghai during the first months of the war with Japan.[23]

More is known about Ding's advocacy of peace and her internationalism and religious inclusiveness, and Deng's Christian socialism, than about Cai's Christian humanism. Ding Shujing's mother had been a devout Buddhist before her conversion to Christianity, and her devotion left an indelible mark on Ding. One night when she was young, Ding awakened to see her mother kneeling in prayer before a little altar with lighted candles and incense. Years later, a friend recounted her description of that moment, how "something in the expression of her mother's face and attitude entered deeply into her [Ding's] consciousness and she experienced a feeling of awe and worship, and a sense of inner life within herself that she never lost."[24] This "sense of inner life" may have been one source of Ding's religious inclusiveness, for while she believed Western secretaries sent to China should have a deep-rooted Christian faith, she also insisted that they understand the truth in other religions.[25]

From the time of Deng Yuzhi's involvement with the student YWCA at Fuxiang, her Christianity was rooted in Christ's message of addressing social inequities, and especially serving the downtrodden. Other currents converged with her Christian outlook. She and friend Maud Russell studied Marx together.[26] In the 1930s, her friend YMCA secretary Wu Yaozong promoted the social gospel movement.[27] All these influences merged into Deng's insistence that Christians change the present economic system, which was "absolutely contrary to Christ's way of life." She was not the only YWCA secretary to find the capitalist system a contradiction to Christ's message, nor the only Christian voice to suggest that Christianity learn from communism. All indicators point to the fact that by the mid-1930s, Christian socialism had become the wellspring of her faith.

Cai's involvement in the Christian Literature Commission in the 1930s, while a natural offshoot of her professional training and work as editorial department executive, reveals her belief that Christian values contributed to Chinese life.[28] Few of her writings before the outbreak of the war with Japan survive in the archives, so discussing her religiosity is problematic. However, looking at the sum total of her writings that do exist, it is evident that from the time of her conversion to the Society of Friends, Quaker principles, referred to in this book as "Christian humanism," defined her religiosity. Stated in a 1938 letter to Sarah Lyon of the YWCA of the USA, those principles included justice, love, brotherhood, and peace.[29] Although such principles were shared by all YWCA women, they clearly expressed the core of Cai's Quakerism.

The age difference between Ding and the younger Deng and Cai meant that they experienced very different Chinas and, in that sense, belonged to different generations of Chinese women. The China that Ding experienced in her youth, although in the thrust of change, clung to traditional values and ways of viewing women. Ding exemplified a modern woman in many ways – she was college-educated and single, and pursued a career. But the source of her professional authority was maternalistic rather than revolutionary. Ding had witnessed the Boxer Rebellion as a child, then the Xinhai Revolution as a young adult. Given her work for the YWCA and dealings with American and European women during her early years in the Beijing city association and later the national office, it is not surprising that Ding embraced the internationalist agenda that transnational women's organizations adopted after the First World War, and that among the causes that most animated her was the pursuit of peace and social harmony.

Deng and Cai, on the other hand, belonged to the May Fourth generation, although they represented different tendencies within the torrent of cultural iconoclasm and cultural regeneration. Deng was unconventional, outspoken, and politically inclined. Cai was unconventional in her own right, continuing to pursue a career full-time after her marriage and the birth of her son, leaving both to study abroad and travel for the association. She was not as politically inclined as Deng, however. Neither woman fit easily into the middle-class mould that defined most national committee members through the 1920s and into the 1930s. Both women confronted obstacles in attaining the positions of leadership that would eventually enable them to influence the trajectory of the association movement in China.

Pathways to Leadership

The YWCA singled Ding out for leadership early in her career. In 1919, three years after she joined the Beijing city association, she was sent to the United States for six months to acquaint her with association work and to present the "best" of Chinese womanhood to American women as a means of raising funds for China. They chose her despite her not yet being conversant in English, something that apparently was not remedied during that first trip. Ding visited more than fifty associations. The fact that the Beijing YWCA welcomed her back in 1920 as its first Chinese general secretary suggests that she had been identified for advancement before her departure.[30] The report noting her appointment came just a short time before the May Fourth demonstrations, which eliminates the possibility her appointment was a reaction to student nationalism. That outgoing general secretary Theresa Severin stayed on as "advisory secretary" also suggests that Ding required an additional period of tutelage as, to paraphrase Helen Thoburn, "she found her way."[31]

Ding's rapid promotion may have reflected an effort by the Beijing city association to secure her talents for their own work. It was a prudent move as national general secretary Grace Coppock was looking for a Chinese woman to succeed her and confided to at least one fellow secretary that she believed Ding to be that woman.[32] Coppock, however, died unexpectedly in October 1921. Although the national committee deliberated for six months, it is unlikely that it considered Ding. In the end, the committee chose Rosalee Venable as the new national general secretary.[33]

For the history of the YWCA movement in China, the fact that Venable knew of Coppock's interest in Ding Shujing is important.[34] Even more so is the fact that she acted on this knowledge. She assumed office in September 1922 intending for Ding to succeed her, and within months the national committee brought Ding to Shanghai to serve as executive secretary for the first national convention, planned for October 1923.[35] The national convention and the drafting of a constitution would make the Chinese YWCA a full constituent of the World YWCA.

In February 1923, the national committee invited Ding to become associate general secretary. Ding initially declined the appointment, even after the committee asked her to reconsider.[36] After much persuasion on Venable's part, she accepted the position, stating that "I have no right to keep on refusing to take these positions of responsibility when you have asked these same things of the foreign secretaries in China, and I as a Chinese woman must do it."[37] She also agreed to serve as acting general secretary when Venable went on furlough after the convention.[38] The national committee, however, decided to send Ding to the YWCA National Training School in New York on a scholarship provided by the YWCA of the USA.[39] This decision identified Ding as the choice for future national general secretary, and her acceptance of the scholarship indicates that she understood that.

In February 1925, while Ding was completing her training in the United States, Venable peremptorily resigned, and the national committee invited Ding to replace her beginning on January 1, 1926.[40] Ding accepted the appointment, albeit reluctantly.[41] Six months after assuming her new office, she wrote Venable: "You remember that night when I told you how I should hate this job and how you said I had accepted it and I must therefore wait a little while before I made up my mind what to do about it? Well, I am not unhappy in it, I tell you privately I simply adore it!"[42] Given the circumstances in China when she assumed leadership, Ding's admission indicated that she was not daunted by the challenges she faced.

Ding's promotion to national general secretary should have been the archetype of devolution for the YWCA, but it would not be repeated. Both Deng Yuzhi's promotion to national industrial secretary and Cai Kui's to national general secretary revealed the behind-the-scenes tensions of devolution when the national committee disagreed with the recommendations from ranking professional staff. It is important to note that it was Chinese women, not Western staff, who attempted to block the advancement of both Deng and Cai, and in both cases, it was Western staff and their Chinese allies in the association who pushed for the promotion. On the other hand, Deng Yuzhi's promotion to national general secretary in January 1950 illustrates how seamless the process could be when there was only one logical candidate, everyone on the ground recognized that fact, and delay was not an option.

Deng Yuzhi's history with the YWCA is the most unusual of the three for several reasons. First, she was the only one of these three women who had belonged to a student YWCA or worked for a city association before completing her college education. It was during that period that she met her lifelong friend Maud Russell. She also became close to Lily Haass, as Haass's effusive praise for her indicates. Deng seemed to attract advocates: Matilda Thurston, who protected her at Jinling; Russell, who recommended her to the national office; and Ding Shujing and Lily Haass, who promoted her transfer from student secretary to industrial secretary. A final, significant difference was that Deng worked for the association for the entirety of Ding Shujing's and Cai Kui's tenures as national general secretary before she herself was appointed national general secretary in 1950. She thus followed women who had proven the potential of Chinese women to lead the YWCA movement in China.

Other than serving as national general secretary and leading the YWCA into the communist era after 1950, Deng Yuzhi is best known for her leadership of the national industrial department, her passionate advocacy for social justice for China's working classes, and her connections to Shanghai radicals. Deng began her career with the YWCA as a student secretary. Within a year, Ding Shujing and Lily Haass wanted her to be made an industrial secretary and to reopen the national industrial office, which had closed in 1926 after Haass was lent to the NCC and the one remaining national industrial secretary had resigned for health reasons. Haass genuinely saw the future of industrial work in China with Deng:

> Miss Teng [Deng], to my mind, combines in a rare way an ability to see in the large and abstract with a natural firsthand approach to workers including those that she meets in everyday life. I think she has the mind and personality that will make her a real leader in industrial lines, and undoubtedly she has a very deep and real interest in the subject.[43]

Despite the recommendations of Ding and Haass, the national committee delayed approving Deng's appointment for six months.[44] Exactly who
objected and what their objections were cannot be ascertained from official documents. Her life had been unconventional. She was bold and outspoken. There was a lot for conventional women to be concerned about.

Few in the YWCA regarded Deng with the suspicion that the un-
named members of the national committee did. National student secretary Gertrude Steel-Brooke thought so highly of Deng that she devoted
an entire letter to writing about her in February 1928 while they jour-
neyed together. "She ... is a person of keenest mind whose education has
taught her to really think and draw conclusions ... She is filled with an
idealism and a desire for the fullest expression of life that will brook no
temporizing when once the call comes clearly enough."[45] One can only
imagine Steel-Brooke's reaction when, a few months later, she found out
that Deng had already received that call.

In early 1928, Haass was released by the NCC and became the executive in the newly created national industrial department. The national
committee finally approved Deng's appointment as a "trainee" in that
department in April.[46] In early 1929, the national committee agreed to
send Deng to the London School of Economics, a signal that she had
passed some litmus test and would be accepted as a full-fledged industrial
secretary.[47]

Haass's enthusiasm over Deng's advancement was again shared in a letter to Mary Dingman and Agatha Harrison: "She is a very rare thing in
China, the college woman who has an interest herself in economic questions. She is unusually keen mentally ... Her enthusiastic response to new
ideas and her penetrating criticism of them indicates that she is unusually
well fitted to get the most possible out of her foreign study."[48]

In June 1929, the national committee announced Deng's appointment as national industrial secretary effective the following summer.
While this appointment was necessitated by Haass's furlough, the furlough conveniently coincided with Deng's return, a move reminiscent
of Rosalee Venable's resignation in 1925 to make way for Ding Shujing's
promotion.[49] Upon her return, Haass took up the responsibilities of national personnel secretary, and she held that position until she left China
in 1945.

Deng used her position as national industrial secretary to inject more
liberal Christian ideas and radical approaches into the YWCA industrial
program. Her social and reform philosophy was a sharp rebuke of the
missionizing and maternalistic approach of the past. A number of YWCA

women, Chinese and Western, volunteers and staff, shared her view and did not hesitate to articulate their critique of the capitalist economic system in China or the Christian imperialists who supported it. Deng's work as national industrial secretary and her promotion of a Christian economic order will be discussed in Chapter 3.

Cai Kui's entire career was also spent in the YWCA national office. She joined the national editorial department after finishing college in 1927, and became its first Chinese head shortly afterward. Her promotion to head a department was thus quick and, unlike Deng's, readily accepted. In 1930, Cai co-authored an association history with Lily Haass that became a mainstay for YWCA historians.[50]

In July 1934, the national committee named Cai acting national general secretary while Ding Shujing went on a "working" furlough.[51] Cai's appointment was not necessarily an indication that she was being singled out as a possible successor, as no one would have been expecting the forty-four-year-old Ding to retire anytime soon. The role of acting general secretary was probably mostly "acting," as nine Western secretaries dominated the national staff, led by the experienced Lily Haass, who was both the personnel and the city secretary at that time.[52] A year later, Ding announced that she planned to retire,[53] but before she could do so, she died of sepsis caused by a severe tooth infection, on July 27, 1936. Cai had been appointed acting general secretary two weeks earlier.

Ding Shujing was thirty-five when she was named general secretary, and had worked for the YWCA for nine years, first in Beijing then in Shanghai. She had been identified for leadership early and groomed for the top executive position. Cai was thirty-four when she was named acting general secretary after Ding's death. She had worked for the YWCA for nine years, all in the editorial department, except for a year as acting national general secretary in 1934, during which she continued her work as editorial department head. Why was Cai named only "acting" national general secretary after Ding's death? When Ding Shujing died, Cai was returning from a year of study at Columbia University Teachers College in New York City, so her familiarity with the YWCA Foreign Division staff should have been seen as an advantage.[54] Her return through Europe and India had also given her recent international experience. The question remains: Why was Cai named only acting general secretary? Was the national committee waiting for her return? They had not waited for Ding Shujing's return from the United States to name her national general secretary. For whatever reason, the national committee hesitated to make Cai's appointment permanent, and it continued to hesitate for two and a

half more years. She was not confirmed as national general secretary until
January 19, 1939.[55]

LEADERSHIP AND ATTITUDES TOWARD WESTERN
SECRETARIES: DING SHUJING

The documentary record provides only Ding Shujing's discourse on
Western secretaries. When Cai Kui became national general secretary,
there were few Western secretaries, but she would comment on her attitude toward them in her postwar plan. Shortly after Deng Yuzhi became
national general secretary in 1950, the few remaining Western secretaries
were sent home, so there was no need to form an opinion.

While in the United States, Ding also spoke several times with members of the Foreign Division of the YWCA of the USA. During these
meetings, she outlined key elements of her leadership and management
philosophy: an emphasis on programs that met real needs, and an insistence on the importance of Western secretaries to provide expertise and
to mentor Chinese secretaries. She spoke decisively about what support
the Foreign Division needed to provide to ensure the continued growth
of the Chinese YWCA. Ding considered the quality of Western secretaries to be of paramount importance, and held strong views on how they
should be chosen and trained. She implicitly criticized how young women
had previously been selected, by noting how Chinese women perceived
the shortcomings of those who either failed to adjust to their new life or
did not make the contributions expected of them. Among other things,
Ding emphasized that a candidate should have a clear understanding of
the purpose of her coming to China, that she understand she "is not a
traveler or a leisurely visitor; she has a real responsibility and business waiting for her there." Ding believed that anyone sent to China should have a
deep-rooted Christian faith and also a clear understanding of the truth in
other religions. A Western secretary must, above all, remain open-minded
toward the new things she would experience in China.

On the matter of training and preparation, Ding was equally specific,
and her comments again reflected her ecumenism, her internationalism,
and her interest in the power of the group. First, a new secretary should
become thoroughly acquainted with every kind of Christian movement
because the Christian movement in China worked closely with those in
the West. Next, she should study all kinds of women's movements in
America and internationally because "Chinese women today, especially

thinking women to whom we would trust our leadership, are very interested in international women's movements." Her third point was that all candidates for China should study comparative religions and the history and philosophy of China. Finally, Ding considered it very advantageous if, before travelling to China, candidates met with Chinese women studying in the United States, because "it is a loss both to us in China and to the association here not to have close contact with such outstanding Chinese women." She concluded her address with these words:

> In recruiting secretaries I think we should use the scientific way, and not merely propaganda or the emotional way. It should be made clear that in going they enter upon a world task to which they should give themselves wholly both in a study of the needs and in the service. They should go in the spirit of those who feel "The world is my country." I know that these things are already in your minds, but they are so strongly in my heart that I must say them to you in this last meeting with you.[56]

In speaking out so definitively on issues of leadership, Ding Shujing claimed these ideas as her own. They were, however, the product of nearly ten years of involvement in YWCA work, tutelage under both Theresa Severin and Rosalee Venable, and two trips to the United States.

Envisioning the YWCA Movement in China

Each of the women had her own vision of what the YWCA movement should be in China. Those visions were shaped by their religiosities, their service as the senior executive, and the events happening around them that buffeted their lives. This section explores Ding Shujing's vision when she was national general secretary, Deng Yuzhi's evolving vision of a just social order both within the association and in society at large, and Cai Kui's thoughts when she first became acting national general secretary. The fuller visions that Cai Kui and Deng Yuzhi articulated when they became national general secretary will be discussed in the chapters that cover their tenures in that office.

Ding Shujing: The Internationalist

Ding began her tenure as national general secretary already with a vision of what she wanted the YWCA movement in China to be. She articulated

that vision in speeches she made while attending the YWCA National
Training School in the United States in 1925. The vision centred on her
belief in internationalism and in the collective power of women to bring
about world peace.

One can only speculate on the exact origins of Ding's commitment
to the cause of international peace and cooperation espoused by many
world women and their organizations during the interwar years. What
type of woman was committed to this cause? Carrie Foster describes
them as "community internationalists": "In a world where militarists
and nationalists were becoming even more bellicose, these social workers
and educators, these wives, mothers, sisters, and daughters were thinking in terms of family, community, and the brotherhood of mankind.
It was not that they loved their country less, but rather that they loved
humanity more."[57]

At its first post–First World War meeting at Chambéry, France, the
World YWCA had embraced women's internationalism. Grace Coppock
brought the spirit of Chambéry back to the Chinese YWCA. Ding may
have met Women's International League for Peace and Freedom president
Jane Addams when she visited China in 1923.[58] Whatever the source of
her views, Ding articulated them clearly when she attended the World
YWCA Service Council meeting at the World's quinquennial convention
in Washington, DC, in May 1925. It was also clear that, while others
may have influenced her, Ding's view also sprang from China's internal
strife. She spoke of the negative and divisive influence of nationalism in
China, and of how the Chinese YWCA promoted international cooperation and friendship to fight that spirit. She pointed to the five nationalities represented on the Chinese YWCA staff and the decision taken at
its first national convention not to limit membership to Chinese nationals. "Is this not significant in its emphasis on internationalism? I do believe true international solidarity, which is our goal, can come only when
the whole world can act together in a degree of cooperation closer and
more effective than we have as yet." In her opinion, the foundation of
internationalism was the spirit of unity and cooperation that came when
"women have come to see the power of the group over the individual in
accomplishing their desires." The YWCA, she argued, demonstrated the
power of the group by bringing women of different social standings, different educational status, different religious denominations, and different
nationalities together to develop international understanding.[59]

Early in her tenure as national general secretary, Ding expressed
her beliefs "publicly" in YWCA brochures and pamphlets. She saw

"internationalism" as part of China's heritage, not simply as a modern or Western concept, often quoting the Confucian classics. For example, in a 1926 brochure, she quoted a famous passage from the *Book of Rites*: "When the Great Way prevails, the world belongs to all. Men of great virtue and talent are elected who will cultivate mutual trust and promote universal understanding. Thus, men do not regard only their parents as parents, nor treat as their children only their children."[60] Ding imbued the passage with a Christian message: "The Confucian saying above means that when 'the Great Will,' that is, the will of God, is carried out the world will belong to all of us with no dividing lines between us, and we will all enjoy a 'world state' of peace."[61]

Ding Shujing also held up the YWCA as a model international community. In her first years as national general secretary, the number of foreign staff allowed her to continue to present the association in that light. There had been secretaries from five foreign countries in 1925. Most Western secretaries had always been American, with a few Britons and others from the anglophone world or Europe, but the most important thing to Ding was that their numbers remained large enough for her to claim that the association was "international" in composition and outlook. In 1932, she clearly stated that goal to a friend at the YWCA headquarters in New York:

> In earlier days it was customary to think of the relationship of the American and China Associations in terms of the building up of a national movement in China which would eventually become independent both in staff and finance. Now our growing conception of internationalism leads us to believe that we shall draw no hard and fast lines which shall constitute artificial barriers to mutual sharing, and we look forward to a continued relation of cooperation and sharing for mutual benefit between our two countries. We hope that you share this conception.[62]

Ding's vision countered the policy of devolution. It can only be imagined how she felt as the number of Western secretaries decreased dramatically in the early 1930s, from around a hundred at the beginning of the 1930s to thirteen in late 1934. Some left because their term of service ended. Home associations no longer could finance others because of the Depression. Still others left because a qualified Chinese woman had been found to take over their positions. Still, as Ding proposed to her friend in New York, she planned to "draw no hard and fast lines" when it came to retaining American women who wanted to stay, even if there were

Chinese women who could do the same job. She made an entreaty to that effect at the third national convention in 1933. Few at the convention shared her view, however. Even if Western staff were being withdrawn for financial reasons, most saw it as "wholly in line with the original policy of turning over to Chinese leadership as rapidly as secretaries could be recruited and trained."[63]

Ding did not lose hope in her internationalist vision, especially in the cause of peace, even after Japan invaded Manchuria in 1931 and attacked Shanghai in January 1932. In November 1935, she attended the national convention of the Japanese YWCA as a representative of the World YWCA Council. According to Chinese YWCA national secretary Talitha Gerlach, Ding went because she wanted to foster the international fellowship of the YWCA movement. She came away impressed with the spirit of fellowship that permeated the meeting and with renewed hope because the Japanese women she met had been eager to know the truth of the situation in China.

Deng Yuzhi: A Christian Socialist

What we know about YWCA women comes from their own words or writings, the writings of others, or what is inferred from the things they did. All three sources provide a wellspring of information on Deng Yuzhi. Her Christian faith was rooted in the social and spiritual messages of Jesus's life. She expressed those beliefs in the politicized tones of a Christian socialist.

Deng's vision for the YWCA movement in China up to 1950 was for it to break down its own class barriers and be instrumental in creating a Christian-inspired economic order. She articulated this vision publicly at the first industrial secretaries' conference held in September 1927, which she attended as a guest. On the first day of the conference, during a prolonged discussion on how to provide "abundant life" for factory women, Deng abruptly interrupted the discussion to insist that the association dare not remain a middle-class organization. Seeing the situation through the lens of a sociologist, she insisted that individual secretaries' formation of personal relationships with labour leaders was not enough, and that the association itself had to officially step forward in support of the working classes.

The recommendations that came out of the conference included Deng's call for creating a self-directed women's labour movement and for creating an understanding of labour issues in order to work toward a

Christian social order.[64] It would be three years before Deng could pursue the vision articulated by those goals. When she finally took over the national industrial department in 1930, the thinking within the association had begun to catch up with hers. At the 1930 industrial secretaries' conference, national general secretary Ding Shujing stated: "Our special job is with industrial girls and women. The most talked about subjects these days in China are industry and agriculture, hence we are in a very important field. Finally, we should maintain the purpose of working *with* industrial workers, not *exclusively* for them."[65]

Shortly after that conference, Deng returned from a year of study at the London School of Economics to assume leadership of the national industrial department. She continued to raise an impassioned voice and demand that China's foreign and native industrialists create a just economic order. She specifically appealed to the conscience of Christians. In a 1934 published article, her words screamed from the page: "It is also time that followers of Christ helped those who are exploited to build the attitude that will eventually do away with this system that kills their souls! We are challenged to do something to release the captives and set the bruised free!"[66]

When Deng became national general secretary in January 1950, she was fifty years old and had worked for the YWCA for half her life. The Chinese YWCA was no longer a "hothouse transplant" and in almost all respects was fully indigenized. Deng's vision had also matured. She was a committed nationalist with a fondness for international ties, and a Christian socialist with a fondness for Maoist principles. She no longer needed to be concerned with creating a new economic and social order. She did need to ensure the continuation of the YWCA in that social order. On a larger scale, she needed to ensure the continuation of Christianity in the new social order. She would achieve both of these goals.

Cai Kui: A Christian Humanist

Cai Kui's early years at the Chinese YWCA were spent in the editorial department, considered part of the "functional division" (Administrative Division), according to a YWCA organizational chart.[67] In that capacity, two of her major accomplishments were co-authoring the association history with Lily Haass and editing the Christian Literature project. What official correspondence she undertook in her first years in the national office, if of any consequence, has not survived. The earliest indication of how her Christian humanism would shape her eventual vision for the association movement came in a speech she made at the Far Eastern regional conference in Colombo, Ceylon (Sri Lanka) in October 1936 on her way back to China after a year of study at Columbia Teachers College. She attended the conference as acting national general secretary along with national committee chair Wang Guoxiu.

Cai spoke about the Chinese women's movement, pointing out that Chinese women's rights were now protected by law and many men supported sexual equality. Still, she admitted, inequities persisted. The weight of tradition continued to be a great obstacle, constitutional guarantees aside. She then turned to the contemporary situation in China. She believed that the Chinese people had a newfound confidence in themselves and their country, a constructive attitude that was compelling service groups to consider concrete and practical programs since "the masses" now insisted on deeds rather than words. "'Unification' is the word that predominates the whole field of our political and social movements. The more encouraging thing is that the liberation movement in China today is not led by a few radical intellectuals as in the past, but the great masses."[68] It is very difficult to decode this part of Cai's speech, especially considering that she had been absent from China for a year. "The masses" is not a term that was commonly used in YWCA documents in the 1930s, but when it was used, it reflected the vocabulary of those with leftist leanings. It is commonly thought that Cai drafted her own letters and speeches, so it is likely that Wang Guoxiu may have had input into her speech on this occasion. Wang's own ideology, like that of most national committee members, is not remarked on in archival records. However, it should be noted that she chaired the YWCA national committee after 1950 and remained its chair at least until 1957.

Cai concluded by stating that the Chinese YWCA did not support "blind and narrow nationalism" but upheld righteousness and justice. "We YWCA workers must not let ourselves be dragged into the whirlpool of extreme irrational nationalism." She admitted that "at home we are sometimes criticized as a denationalized organization, yet we cannot help giving sympathy to the people who are struggling for existence."[69] Here she spoke very broadly, to all the women assembled:

With regard to the international policy of the World YWCA, I feel that the Association has two important duties. First, it must train people to put the love of Christ into practice, thereby teaching them to exercise world public opinion along the lines of justice. Second, it must study the basic causes of political and economic conflicts and encourage intellectual cooperation among nations ... It is in the spirit of Christ's love our Association suggests that one of the themes in the 1938 [World] council meeting should be women's responsibility for concrete training for world peace. Women must be called on to act in the present international situation.[70]

Cai's remarks echoed the philosophy Ding Shujing had advocated for years and were in line with the overall mission of the World YWCA during the interwar years. However, they also reflected the Quaker principles that were at the core of her Christian humanism.

In many discussions of Christianity in China or of Chinese Christians, an individual's Christian identity is lost, as if context mattered more than subtext. Chapter 2 examined the religiosity of Ding Shujing, Deng Yuzhi, and Cai Kui to provide the subtext. All three were converts. The conversions of Ding and Deng were essentially "social conversions," as they converted along with other family members. Cai's conversion to Quakerism as an adult must have been carefully considered, and the unusual choice of the Society of Friends must have spoken to her need for a spiritual home. Ding's religiosity was also unique in that her spiritual awakening appeared to have come from witnessing her mother at prayer before a Buddhist altar, rather than her conversion to Christianity. Watching her mother's sincere devotion, she experienced "awe." As for Deng, it quite possible that without Jesus's gospel of social revolution – for that seems to be Deng's understanding of his life – Christianity might not have become her life-animating principle.

This chapter also examined the social mindsets of the three women. Historical circumstances appeared to shape how each viewed society and the wider world. Ding Shujing grew up in a world of imperialist intrusion, revolutionary foment, the overthrow of the ancient imperium, and then world war, all of which were likely the genesis of her advocacy of internationalism. On the other hand, both Deng Yuzhi and Cai Kui were shaped by the May Fourth Movement, leading to Deng's outright rejection of tradition and Cai's more measured response, with her conversion to Quakerism as part of that response.

Chapter 3 picks up the chronological history of the Chinese YWCA by examining Ding Shujing's tenure as national general secretary and the start of Deng's and Cai's long careers with the association and their early taste of leadership responsibilities.

3

Seeking a Place in a Social Revolution, 1926–36

People often speak of Christianity as being opposed to Communism. This is a dangerous antithesis, as Communism may have some ideals which Christianity might well use.

— Mrs. Jin Longzhang, March 1932

The decade from 1926 to 1936 were years when, to paraphrase Helen Thoburn, the Chinese YWCA began to be made the "stuff of Chinese life." These were the years of Ding Shujing's tenure as national general secretary and the advancement of Cai Kui and Deng Yuzhi to executive leadership in national departments. The period ended with Ding's death and Cai's appointment as acting national general secretary. This chapter is organized around key events and turning points in the history of the Chinese YWCA and highlights how external events continued to shape the association leadership's decisions regarding its policies and programs. The association's industrial programs are used as a lens to trace the evolution of its social thinking from an emphasis on maternalistic and moral reform to an emphasis on building a society based on social and economic justice. YWCA industrial secretaries embraced a liberal interpretation of Christianity, domesticated the foreign-inspired "association way," and sought to break down the association's middle-class identity and make it inclusive. The connection of industrial secretaries in both the national office and the Shanghai city association to Shanghai's radical intellectuals and communist underground would be relevant to the association's future survival.

The ten years from 1926 to 1936 also roughly correspond to the period referred to as the Nanjing Decade (1928–37), when the Nationalist government ruled from its capital in that eastern Chinese city. The bridge between the May Fourth era and the Nanjing Decade was the period known as the First United Front, the Soviet-brokered alliance between Sun Yat-sen's Guomindang and the neophyte CCP. The goal of the First United Front was to unify China, which meant wresting territorial control from competing warlords and driving foreign imperialists from China or, at minimum, ending their economic privileges without inviting reprisal. Despite its name, United Front factions did not share the same revolutionary goals. During its early months, the United Front's leadership fought over a number of political and military issues and split into opposing factions: a coalition of conservative and right-wing groups led by Chiang Kai-shek, who had won the struggle for leadership of the GMD after Sun Yat-sen's death in 1925, and the Comintern-supported leftists. The military campaign to unify China began in July 1926, with separate armies, reflecting ideological divisions, marching north. The communist-led armies marched through central China, eventually making Wuhan their stronghold, while Chiang Kai-shek's army marched up the coast, reaching Shanghai in March 1927. The "Great Revolution" appeared to be succeeding when Chiang turned on his allies in April and destroyed the alliance.[1]

As this chapter will show, however, at the beginning of the Nanjing Decade, YWCA women held out hope that revolutionary China would bring about a "new" China, and committed themselves to that effort.

The Shanghai City Association Takes the Lead in Industrial Work

Australian Eleanor Hinder had never worked as a YWCA secretary before coming to China. At the personal invitation of Mary Dingman, who had previously met Hinder in Australia, Hinder visited Shanghai in 1924 while on an international study tour of industrial welfare work financed by her employer, Farmer and Company Limited, Australia's most prominent department store. From Shanghai, she travelled to Japan, North America, and Europe, where she attended several international conferences and

visited the International Labour Organization in Geneva.[2] Thus, when
the Chinese YWCA sought a replacement for Edith Johnston and failed
to find an English candidate needed to deal with the British expatriate community, Hinder was a logical alternative. More important, she
agreed to come for two years. Hinder arrived in China in February 1926,
when China was still reeling from protests caused by the May Thirtieth
Incident.[3]

At the time, the Shanghai city association did not have a separate
industrial department, and Hinder's task was to create one. The first
thing she needed was a staff. She convinced membership secretary Gong
Peizhen, who was considering a return to school to study social work, to
join the industrial staff by promising to arrange for her work to count
toward the practical requirements of her degree. Hinder described her
as "the most intelligent girl on the local staff, by far." She then engaged
returned student Qian Cuige, whom she called "just ripping," effusively
praising her as "dainty and pretty, and full of the most surprising initia-
tive. She is willing to get into the most radical movements for the sake of
getting [in] real touch with working women."[4] Qian assisted Hinder in
her first project. At first, they tried to contact women labour leaders but
that failed. Few in number, the women had become wary due to police
and military raids against trade unions the previous fall.[5] Hinder then
tried a different approach. With Qian's help, she rented a room near the
Nanyang Tobacco Factory and began giving English classes. Her purpose,
however, was to find a few women who had the potential to be developed
into future trade union secretaries. She believed that labour leadership
must come from the labour class.[6] How long these classes lasted is not
clear, but they led Hinder and Lily Haass, still on loan to the NCC to
propose a settlement-type project in an industrial district, where Western
and Chinese industrial secretaries would live together and conduct health
and educational work.[7]

The proposal was most unusual. Industrial districts were definitely
outside the domain of middle-class women, and definitely not suited
for foreign women. The growing strength and organization of the labour
movement and the increasing number of strikes made the situation in
these districts quite precarious. Though settlement work was identified
with maternalistic ideals of women such as Jane Addams, even she may
not have opened her Hull-House Settlement project in an alien city full
of animosity toward foreigners.[8]

By the fall, Hinder had found a house to rent in Zhabei, one of the
poorest and most congested industrial areas, and began preparations

for herself, Haass, and three Chinese secretaries to move there in late November. Haass commented:

> It will mean a tremendous thing to our Chinese secretaries if they can get
> a first-hand knowledge of industrial women and their problems instead of
> trying to do all of their work from an office. They have clearly in mind that
> we are not doing any slumming in any superior way but opening the way
> for the development of Chinese leadership among the women workers.

After they moved in, Haass wrote: "It is amazing how simply and natural-ly the silk filature people come to us. The direct approach to labor doesn't seem so difficult when you're right in its midst." While Hinder reported encouraging progress in contacting both working women and manage-ment, Haass worried about the Chinese secretaries as labour unrest and strikes, organized and supported by left-wing radicals, invited new police raids and put Chinese secretaries at risk of being caught up in them.[9]

The settlement house experiment was short-lived. Although the clash-es between labour organizations and the municipal government compli-cated their mission, the end actually came when Chiang Kai-shek's troops seized the house for use as barracks after his army arrived in Shanghai at the end of March. Hinder had few regrets, however, because "we found out many things, and we know now what to recommend for such work in more normal times. It is a way to work: it is the nearest thing to a prac-tical programme that this association and its Chinese membership has evolved, and the Board [of the city association] has learned something by the experiment."[10]

In mid-April, Hinder bluntly assessed the overall situation: "Our every move has relation to Chinese internal politics."[11] Several weeks later she published an article, "The YWCA Seeks Its Place in a Social Revolution," in the *"Green Year" Supplement*, the English-language sup-plement to the YWCA's magazine. Broadly speaking, the revolution she was referring to was Chiang Kai-shek's United Front campaign to unify China, the unity of which he had already destroyed. The "social revolu-tion" ironically referred to the support the CCP contingent within that shattered front had garnered from peasants and workers as they marched through central China. Hinder envisioned three roles for the association in carrying this revolution forward. The first was to "make the services of the Association available to groups of women workers in relation to the labour movement ... to the end that the movement may stabilise and become more intelligent." The second was to work through the women's labour movement to get the government to regulate employment practices. The third was for the association to induce employers to voluntarily address workers' grievances.[12] Although on the ground in China for only a little over a year, Hinder clearly saw the role of the Chinese YWCA as one that needed to recognize the importance of that "revolutionary" moment and define its goals in reference to the working class.

At first glance, it would be easy to rate the Shanghai YWCA's industrial work between 1925 and 1927 as no more successful than the child labour campaign. In both cases, failure was due to external events. The child labour campaign likely would have failed even without the May Thirtieth Incident. Given the labour unrest in Shanghai, the settlement project and Hinder's goal of contacting women union leaders was problematic from the outset. Hinder, however, had introduced a new approach to industrial work that differed greatly from the policy that had defined it at the national level before her arrival. She was interested in helping to organize labour and had hired staff who did not hesitate to take initiatives. Her published article was a public call for the association to "seek its place in the social revolution" by assisting the labour movement. When industrial secretaries held their first conference in September, they would frame questions and make recommendations that had been greatly influenced by Hinder.

THE FIRST INDUSTRIAL SECRETARIES' CONFERENCE, SEPTEMBER 1927

The first industrial secretaries' conference was held on September 1 and 2, 1927.[13] Because this meeting followed the NCC's National Conference on Christianizing Economic Relations, where broad social issues had been discussed, the secretaries focused on fundamental YWCA issues such as its middle-class identity, its relation to popular movements, its limited approach to reform, the role of Western secretaries, and the nature of its Christian mission to women, all pivotal questions whose answers would redefine the industrial field and eventually the identity of the association.

This conference brought together three Chinese and three Western industrial secretaries, but numbers do not tell the full story. Also attending were Jinan general secretary Ruth Hoople, national city association secretary Harriet Smith, national general secretary Ding Shujing, Lily Haass, who was lobbying to be released a year early from her assignment to the NCC, and national student secretary Deng Yuzhi. Deng attended because Haass and Ding Shujing had tacitly agreed that Deng would become an industrial secretary.[14]

The conference report, written by Hinder and edited by Haass, read less like a report and more like a transcript of meeting minutes. The terse, unpolished document retained the nuances of the two-day meeting: questions raised but only partially answered, concerns voiced with no solutions offered, and personal opinions interjected whether or not they were on topic. The report was sent to both World YWCA industrial secretary Mary Dingman and Agatha Harrison. The author of any letter, report, or article acts as a filter, communicating what is considered important. In this case, the frank and open relationship among these four Western women, as seen in their frequent correspondence, suggests that the report probably contained a fairly straightforward rendering of the conference.

In evaluating the field, the secretaries believed they needed to support the labour movement and made direct work imperative. Their repeated use of the term "labor movement" raises the question of exactly what groups they were referring to. The GMD had succeeded in suppressing the General Labour Union. Skilled labour and craft unions remained, but since April, they had lost their autonomy to either the underworld or the GMD. Whatever their understanding, the secretaries clearly wanted to establish contact with women workers and help them create a labour movement of their own.

Regarding labour issues, the secretaries noted that in other countries, working-class gains had not come about solely because of "the goodwill among the more leisured groups." Rather, they emphasized, gains had been forced on upper classes *by* the labour movement. The secretaries asked themselves what role the YWCA could play in helping labour groups. At this point, Deng Yuzhi spoke up, insisting that the association dared not remain a middle-class organization. She insisted that individual secretaries' forming of personal relationships with labour leaders was not enough, both acknowledging the efforts of the Shanghai secretaries and pointing out the limitations of their efforts. Rather, Deng insisted that the association had to officially step forward in support of the working classes.

Her boldness at speaking out so critically on the first day of the conference may have surprised some, but her message was not new. It was essentially the point Hinder had made in her May article "The YWCA Seeks Its Place in a Social Revolution" – except that now this message was delivered by a young, bold Chinese secretary.

The secretaries began the second day by emphasizing the changed circumstances of China, noting that "given an emerging labor movement, which, given its own leadership, can be relied upon to achieve for itself, 'direct work' with women workers becomes increasingly important." Everyone agreed on the importance of educational work since a self-directed labour movement needed a literate leadership developed from within its own ranks. Deng Yuzhi again spoke up, saying that industrial women would not find their voice for some time but that the association could make that time come sooner by becoming involved with working women. The conference's final recommendations were that the national industrial department reopen so that it could promote industrial work and expand it to other industrial cities. The role Western secretaries could play was raised, with the conclusion that "no personal approach on the part of a foreign worker is welcome." This did not exclude Western secretaries from the field; it just set the boundaries for the roles they could assume.

The first part of the conference ended with two stated goals for industrial work going forward:

1 To contribute to a fullness of life for working women, through efforts toward improvement of their conditions of work and living, and by seeking to develop a leadership among them, help in creating a self-directed movement toward their own emancipation.
2 To contribute to an understanding of the problems of working women and other women and by society in general, aiming at creating such social thinking as can make toward their fuller life, and toward a Christian social order.

The number of issues covered and the frankness with which they were discussed during the two-day conference suggest the intensity these women brought to their work. Discussions of association policy, class identity, and "tangible" programs revealed their grasp of what needed to be done but not how to do it. Their belief that the association needed to be more inclusive, their honest admission that Western secretaries impeded field work, and the practical problem of finding and supporting trained Chinese secretaries point to the complex organizational relationships within the YWCA that bureaucratic flow charts mask.

The central importance given the labour movement revealed the evolution of thinking on the part of some secretaries. In an article based on the conference report, Lily Haass immediately emphasized the importance of labour: "It was evident that in China, as elsewhere, labour itself will be a most important influence in bringing about changed conditions. It would seem, then, that any contributions we could make to the labour movement might in the end be one of the most telling and valuable services we might render."[15] What Haass could not foresee was that the YWCA work for labour would be a "telling and valuable service" to the YWCA movement in China by making it an ally of Shanghai radical intellectuals.

Despite her involvement in the secretarial conference, Haass was not a YWCA industrial secretary at that time. While she was finishing her studies at the London School of Economics in 1925 and anticipating her return to China to do industrial work for the association, the YWCA national committee agreed to lend her to the National Christian Council to serve as their industrial executive for three years. Although she reluctantly agreed, she found the work troublesome, the YMCA obstructionist, and the operations of the NCC slow and cumbersome. She stewed over the loss of a "national outlook" from within the YWCA. She begged to be released, but the national committee held firm to their commitment to the NCC.[16] Haass, for her part, remained committed to her understanding of the type of industrial work the YWCA should undertake. This gave rise to a conflict with Ding Shujing that has been much noted – and misinterpreted – by historians. In November, after the conference, Haass wrote Mary Dingman an explosive letter after Ding requested that the YWCA undertake a "concrete piece of work" along the lines of the YMCA's model industrial village in Pudong. Haass tried to understand Ding's request: "It is inevitable that to a practical-minded people visible pieces of service should make a great appeal … 'How can you talk education to a people suffering in poverty, poor homes, etc.?' they say." Still, she vehemently disagreed:

> To me the whole thing raises the question whether you can put an association of a type calling for a certain degree of "civilization," material comfort and intellectual advancement, on a people who are still on a low economic plane. Answer please! To some of us who prefer to do a certain kind of advanced "constructive" work it may bring a pretty definite choice as to whether we want to follow Chinese leadership into different, to us non-associational type of work – or go home![17]

Haass must have been genuinely flabbergasted as she and Ding had seen eye to eye on Deng Yuzhi's transfer, and Ding's presence on the first

day of the secretarial conference would have been taken as an endorsement. Ding's request for a "concrete piece of work" may have been her
own, or it may have reflected the national committee's desire as it had not
approved the goals set by the industrial secretaries of training a leadership
for a self-directed women's labour movement. Dingman's response was
cautious:

> I can see clearly that you are being faced with great problems as the
> Chinese take more and more the complete control and develop the work
> along their own lines. I don't think it is a case of foreigners going home
> but it is the more difficult one of standing by as the Association in China
> evolves through a certain phase, which may at the time seem to be not
> according to the ordinary precedence. Really I think of our difficulties
> in the European Associations, I sometimes wonder just what is the true
> Association type.[18]

Dingman's observation that there may not be a "true Association type"
after touring associations across Europe speaks to how defining an influence the British and American associations had been, and how "foreign" those models appeared to be to associations outside the anglophone
world. Dingman did not convince Haass, who continued to see larger
"constructive work," such as education on labour issues and lobbying for
legislation, as fundamental. In a follow-up letter to Dingman in January
1928, Haass stated that she had not "conceded" that the association decided to do "concrete work" because the association membership wanted
it, but because it believed it was a way to reach the labour movement.[19]
     In the end, both Ding Shujing and Lily Haass would find satisfaction
in the industrial program. It is not clear if the national committee ever
endorsed the proposals that came out of the first industrial secretaries'
conference. When it formally organized the national industrial department in 1928, that language was left out of the department's statement
of purpose, leading Haass to remark how much education still needed to
be done among the association's leadership.[20] Haass finished her assignment and returned as the new department's first executive. After months
of hesitation, the national committee made Deng Yuzhi a trainee in the
industrial department. One final decision of the national committee was
to send her for advanced training at the London School of Economics,
clearly identifying her for future leadership.
     Among Deng's first actions when she joined the industrial department
was to tour a silk filature factory in the Zhabei industrial district, where

Hinder's settlement house project had been located. Of Shanghai's eighty Chinese-owned silk filature factories, fifty were in Zhabei. Deng then contributed an article about her visit to a special November 1928 issue of the *"Green Year" Supplement* on the YWCA's industrial work. Her detailed description of the differing experiences of factory workers depending on their specific job (peeling, selecting, reeling, and skeining) and how they fit into a sort of "social hierarchy" based on job, native place identities, and whether or not they had familial connections with management again suggests that when discussing the lives of Chinese women, they cannot be treated as a single category. Deng specifically noted the presence of children in workplaces, both child labourers and the children of women who, because of their eleven-hour workday, had to bring their younger children with them to work. She observed that many of the child labourers looked much younger than ten years, the legal age for employment of children. She also noted their brutal treatment by floor managers, who punished every instance of inattention with a slap or strike from their batons.[21]

At the local level, the Shanghai industrial department introduced literacy classes for industrial women shortly after the first industrial secretaries' conference. Gong Peizhen began with one class near the former Zhabei settlement house.[22] Within twelve months, there were five night schools in five industrial districts, and a sixth that held late afternoon classes for girls who worked the night shift. The night schools were often dependent on facilities belonging to other groups. They used rooms in the YMCA model industrial village in Pudong[23] as well as a community centre run by the Shanghai Baptist College in Yangshupu and another operated by the London Mission Society in the Hongkou district.[24] The YWCA conducted itself very circumspectly, contacting both unions and government bureaus in connection with this work.

Circumspect or not, these night schools came to the attention of communist labour organizers in Shanghai, according to written testimony taken in 1953 from communist organizer Wang Zhijin. Once the Great Revolution of 1927 failed and union organizing was suppressed, the night schools became an alternative means for party members to recruit for their movement. While a few details of Wang's testimony contradict YWCA records, such as her saying that the first Shanghai night school was in Yangshupu rather than Zhabei, by and large it aligns with the latter. Although Wang's account of how successful their efforts were is likely exaggerated (and it leaves out Deng Yuzhi's role, perhaps because she was not personally involved at the most local level), her testimony provides valuable if indirect insight into what students gained from those schools.[25]

YWCA official accounts provide much detail. Each school offered a basic literacy course that ran for six months, meeting for an hour and a half daily, five days a week. They used the four texts in the "Thousand Characters" series developed by former YMCA secretary James Yan for use in mass education projects. After completing the series, students were able to read simple books and newspapers and to write letters. Once a literacy class was organized, one session per week was devoted to club work. "Club work" sounded innocuous, and in many ways it was. However, club discussion groups helped girls understand their place in relation to the entire industrial order, encouraged them to think collectively, and acquainted them with organizational methods, all of which industrial secretaries considered essential to the labour movement. Gong Peizhen pointed out that this nucleus of industrial women, while negligible in the face of the entire problem, was vital in the production of leadership among industrial women.[26] Wang Zhijin echoed Gong's words: "The best method for raising workers' political awareness was, in fact, to expose them to a wide variety of knowledge by raising their level of culture and giving them a firm grasp of reading and writing."[27] She had equally high praise for club work as a useful platform for extending learning and experience outside the classroom, toward the same goals Gong described.[28]

The direct approach through education certainly affected the Chinese secretaries. Although they had not been brought up in the same sheltered environment as their mothers, crossing the Huangpu River by means of a hand-propelled ferry and moving around the streets of industrial districts where even residents were fearful gave real meaning to the phrase "obtain direct touch." As Eleanor Hinder observed, before this time, "not to any great extent have educated girls in China 'taken off the gloves,' in social work, and there are elements of physical danger in this work which call for the use of the term 'bravery' in carrying it out."[29] What these secretaries saw and experienced certainly provided them with a different outlook from that of many of their older colleagues.

The direct approach also altered the relationship between Western and Chinese industrial secretaries. The industrial secretaries' conference had found little role for foreigners in industrial work as it was obvious that they were neither welcome nor safe in industrial districts. Eleanor Hinder had already recognized that her place was in the office, attending to tasks normally performed by junior local secretaries. To her, this was the truest testament of the partnership between Western and Chinese secretaries because it represented "where community of purpose and closeness of sympathy and interest in achievement make the group of secretaries a unit."[30]

THE SECOND NATIONAL CONVENTION, JULY 1928

When YWCA women attended the second national convention in early July 1928, the revolution was not yet over.[31] The new government was not formally established until October 10, and final military victory was not achieved until December. The convention provided YWCA women with the opportunity to consider their place in the "new China." It was a conversation they would repeat thirty-two years later, when they considered their place in Mao Zedong's "new China."

Since assuming office, Ding Shujing had insisted on concrete programs that met the "definite and immediate needs in the community," even if this approach deviated from the accepted association way preferred by Western secretaries.[32] The four general programs convention delegates decided on were education, home betterment, promotion of work for women, and promotion of right international relations.[33]

Delegates also engaged in broader discussions on the type of women the YWCA should serve, the association's relationship to "revolutionary China," and its relationship to the church. Work with women remained at the heart of the YWCA mission. Three of the four programs dealt directly with women. The convention discussion highlighted changes in the association's thinking. The 1911 secretaries' conference defined the association's purpose as teaching women "how to lead or how best to direct the powers that in them lie" so that they could avail themselves of the opportunities the new China offered.[34] The new China of 1911 had been stillborn; that of 1928 promised to be different. In 1911, "women" had meant "women of leisure" and students. Now, as the association grappled with "revolutionary China," it examined its relationship with six categories of women: women in the home, students or young girls (whether or not they were attending school), professional women, industrial women, rural women, and "slave girls, etc.," with concubines coming under the last category.

Gone was the ambiguous phrase "women of leisure," replaced by "women in the home." The category of students had been broadened beyond middle school and college students to include younger girls of school age. Identifying professional women as a distinct group showed a recognition that education and careers, while a means of improving social status and providing economic independence, were not panaceas. The women who served on the YWCA staff knew this first-hand and thus, in a manner of speaking, they included themselves in one of their categories.

The fact that the convention included industrial women as a separate group reflected developments in the industrial field since the first industrial secretaries' conference the previous year. Discussing the needs of rural women indicated the most profound change in YWCA thinking, as up to that time the association had been almost entirely an urban movement. The subject was first raised at the October 1926 national committee meeting. It is unclear why the committee discussed the needs of rural women at that time, but it is likely that accounts of the peasant movement inspired by United Front leftist propaganda had stirred an interest in rural affairs. In April 1927, the national committee accepted a proposed policy statement and work plan for establishing a rural department. The 1928 convention endorsed that policy. After the convention, work began in four centres, focusing on literacy, health, homemaking, and leadership training for rural women.[35]

Under the heading "revolutionary China and the YWCA," delegates discussed their responsibilities to the newly unified nation. Their statement read: "We have arrived at a period of reconstruction. We want to promote a spirit of unity, freedom and equality. The YWCA ought to meet the needs of New China." In 1928, "New China" needed five things: good government, better communities, the right kind of women's movement, good leadership, and good citizens. For whatever reason, the first three were not elaborated on. A good leader was a person who was "a real worker, one who is willing to serve, can work with others, has good influence, character and personality," a description that sounded very much like YWCA women in general, and especially Ding Shujing.

Another part of the discussion addressed how the association could help the labour classes with their problems in revolutionary China. In a lengthy and somewhat ambiguous statement, delegates noted their intention to help labour but said that neither oppression of labour by capital nor strife between the two would be tolerated. The role of the association was to "reconcile capital and labor that they may appreciate the value of cooperation." Considering the support given the child labour campaign in the early 1920s, and the strong anti-imperialist stance the national committee had assumed after the May Thirtieth Incident, such a conservative statement is surprising. It may have reflected a backlash against the more radical statements made in the final report of the first industrial secretaries' conference about helping to create a self-directed women's labour movement. The convention's official statement on labour also confirmed that the association remained a middle-class women's organization in 1928.

Given that the Chinese YWCA was a member of an international women's organization and networked with others such as the Women's International League for Peace and Freedom, international relations remained a subject of vital interest. It was a centrepiece of Ding Shujing's leadership agenda. Recommendations included supporting international organizations such as the League of Nations and World Court, and a study of the causes of international misunderstandings to work toward eliminating them.

The last topic dealt with the YWCA's relationship to the church. The delegates emphasized "living of Christian life" as a way to promote the truth of Christianity. This meant different things to different women. To some, it meant being members of a congregation and being regular churchgoers. To others, it meant emulating Jesus's message of love and his life of service to humanity. Thus, it was an inclusive statement that remained vague. Delegates suggested that the association should promote self-governance in Christian institutions. While this had always been the policy of the YWCA, self-governance for many Christian institutions and mission stations had come about only when missionaries fled before the advancing revolutionary armies in 1926 and 1927. When the Nationalists prevailed, the missionaries returned to their governing positions. The YWCA statement was thus also an objection to that trend. The delegates also came out in support of the indigenous church movement. It had begun in response to anti-imperialist attacks on the Chinese Christian church as a symbol of Western imperialism during the United Front era between 1923 and 1927. Its aim was to create an authentic Christianity.

After the convention, YWCA women in the national office resumed their standard routine. But life had changed. The lack of a strong political centre during the Warlord Era had created a fluid environment that allowed for social and cultural experimentation.[36] Now, the strong hand of government came into play. Although the anti-Christian movement abated as the Nationalists consolidated power, some anti-Christian elements appeared in the Nanjing government. Even the YWCA fell under suspicion as a Christian institution. In the association history they wrote in 1930, Lily Haass and Cai Kui stated that "secretaries, formerly much respected for their zeal in social service, now are condemned as the tools of imperialism, for so they are designated by the propaganda of the Kuomintang [Guomindang]."[37] Such suspicions would be tempered after Chiang Kai-shek's conversion to Christianity in 1930.

Another side effect of the establishment of the Nationalist government was its assumption of civic functions once provided by service organizations. Thus, the YWCA's role as a leader in both social thinking and social service was also threatened: "It [the government] has caused the [YWCA] movement to lose its leadership in social thinking; it has limited the field of service through usurping former fields of Association work; and it has increased the difficulty of obtaining qualified women for the service of the movement."[38]

The YWCA city associations in China did experience difficulty recruiting local women. The national revolution had resulted in the withdrawal of a number of Western secretaries. In 1927, there were fifty-seven Chinese secretaries and only forty-two Western secretaries. In 1929, there were eighty-seven Chinese secretaries and only twenty-six Western secretaries. At first glance, the statistics suggest that recruiting was going well and the pace of devolution was increasing. However, numbers can be deceptive. While twenty-four secretaries were added in 1929, only ten were college graduates. This forced the association leadership to request the World Committee to send twenty-five additional Western secretaries. Devolution was a goal, but YWCA work required experienced women. However, the stock market crash on October 29 prevented the national committee from realizing its hope of significantly increasing the number of new Western secretaries.[39]

THE SECOND INDUSTRIAL SECRETARIES' CONFERENCE, FEBRUARY 1930

The two and a half years between the first and second industrial secretaries' conference saw some advances in the YWCA's industrial programs at the national and local level in Shanghai. The national committee created an industrial department in late 1927 or the very beginning of 1928,[40] although the department's statement of purpose did not include language regarding educating a leadership for a self-directed women's labour movement. The national committee also approved Deng Yuzhi as a trainee in the new department.

The Shanghai city association's industrial program grew. Reports indicate that average attendance at its literacy night schools was 170 in 1929 and 379 in 1930. Over the same twelve-month period, the number of industrial girls' clubs increased from fifty-two to ninety.[41] And, although the national committee had not endorsed educating a leadership for a women's labour movement, secretaries in the literacy school were finding ways to include such training in their classes.

Ding Shujing presided over the second industrial secretaries' conference in February 1930.[42] Once again, it was small meeting, with three Western and five Chinese secretaries attending, including Lily Haass.[43] Deng Yuzhi was still in London. Unlike in 1927, when the two-day conference consisted essentially of round-table discussions, this five-day conference featured twelve presentations and guided discussions by professionals on such topics as economic ethics, international economic relations, and others that dealt not only with methodology but also with the scope and dynamics of industrial problems. Centring many of these discussions was the perceived need to "Christianize" economic relations, which indicated the influence of liberal Christian thinking.

Industrial secretaries recommended that four specific areas be emphasized in the next few years: direct work with working women; education of association members on industrial issues and legislation; research on topics such as living conditions, cost of living, and so on; and stimulation of interest in larger social and economic questions such as capitalism and population problems. Direct work meant "creating an intelligent group of working women who are fitted to help in their own emancipation." The definition of direct work raises the question of whether the national committee had finally approved the goal set at the first industrial secretaries' conference, or whether the industrial secretaries had simply found a nonthreatening way to articulate that goal.

The conference reports, lectures, and discussion outlines indicated a mixture of insight and naïveté, circumspection and open criticism, that make it problematic to ascertain how well these women understood what had transpired in the labour movement over the previous three years. While one section of the conference report noted "the Kuomintang [Guomindang] Movement with its democratic aims" as a factor in recent developments of the labour movement without mentioning the party's continued suppression of any radical elements, another part criticized trade unions for their corruption and misappropriation of money, for forcing skilled workers to join while excluding unskilled labour, for deducting dues directly from salaries, and for being tools of political parties. The report was particularly specific on this last point, noting that outside influences came from communists, the government, and "intellectuals."

It is not clear who those intellectuals were in 1930, but after Deng Yuzhi returned, she may have been able to point them out as she counted many of them as her friends. The disparaging reference to communists would also undergo a change: in just two years, YWCA secretaries and lay volunteers in Shanghai would note that Christianity had a lot to learn from communism. The report's wording does suggest that these women were cautious about their public statements, having attracted the scrutiny of the government.

The conference report identified the needs of the women's labour movement as education on industry, the history of international labour movements, workers' needs and problems, and organizational techniques. The last point referred to learning how to conduct meetings and speak in public. As for the role of industrial secretaries, they were seen as providing some leadership in order to get the movement started. Ding Shujing amplified that point in her address:

> What kind of people ought we to be? First of all, we are a Christian movement. We may differ in methods – some may want to build character by thinking of Jesus as a great personality; others may get people to follow Jesus's way of life themselves. Secondly, since we ourselves have had the opportunity of education we should know how to educate others. We should be in the position of advisors to industrial workers ... we should maintain the purpose of working *with* industrial workers, not *exclusively* for them.[44]

Ding's concluding remark is important because it has been asserted that the YWCA's industrial work remained "paternalistic" until Deng Yuzhi took over the national industrial department in 1930.[45] The fact that Ding so clearly articulated working *with* industrial women as a YWCA goal six months before Deng's return indicates that Deng was not alone in her thinking. The national committee may have remained socially conservative even if they embraced more liberal interpretations of Christianity. Increasingly, however, YWCA secretaries demonstrated a willingness to ignore class boundaries. Ding Shujing, in her capacity as national general secretary, clearly pointed the way forward.

THE FIELD SURVEY OF 1930

In 1929, the Chinese association decided to participate in an international survey sponsored by the American YMCAs and YWCAs. Ding Shujing explained that it was important to study association work because "the extensive changes brought about in Chinese life and social organization by the revolution have necessarily affected our work and give rise to many questions about it."[46]

The field survey for China had been proposed in December 1927 but delayed for many reasons. One was preparations for the second national convention. Another was concern on the part of the Chinese leadership that, as originally planned, the survey would be conducted by "outsiders" and "any study from the outside would not be tolerated in this period of supremacy of nationalistic spirit." The national committee wanted to direct the survey because "it has become a definite desire on the part of our leaders to have a study of the association for our own purposes, to find out where we are, and whether we are on the right track, as well as to make recommendations for the future." The final difficulty, according to Lily Haass, was that the Chinese YMCA had refused the YWCA's suggestion on how to conduct the survey jointly. The YMCA wanted an extensive and costly survey. In the end, the YWCA decided to "proceed on our humble basis."[47]

The field survey was critical as the association found itself in much the same position as in 1907, needing to legitimize its work in China. It lasted six months and used four approaches: interviews, questionnaires, observation, and evaluation conferences. The conferences were held through the early months of 1930 in city associations in Guangzhou, Changsha, Shanghai, Nanjing, and Yantai; by student groups in Beijing, Shanghai, and Guangzhou; and by the national committee and staff. These conferences were credited with creating a way of thinking about the function and work of the association that helped prepare for policy changes. However, as Ding Shujing would later admit to the staff in the Foreign Division in New York, because of the social changes in China, "the purpose of the YWCA changed" but "our recent survey showed a lack of clearness and uniform thinking regarding the situation in China."[48]

The completed reports were given to a survey commission made up of prominent Chinese men and women not associated with the YWCA, including Dr. Hu Shi (Hu Shih). The commission met twice for preliminary discussion and held a third meeting in July to prepare the final report.[49] The final report, titled "A Study of the YWCA of China 1891–1930,"[50] consisted of three parts. The first was an association history co-authored by Cai Kui and Lily Haass. The second contained articles on economics, labour, rural life, political life, women's relation to political life, family, education, vocational education, health, recreation, and religion. The final part contained the field reports. As a result of this study, the YWCA narrowed its work to four fields: industrial work, rural work,

work with girls (whether or not in school), and work in urban centres, i.e., city associations.[51]

The report on the industrial field was written by Gideon Chen, a former YMCA secretary trained in England, who had succeeded Haass as NCC industrial secretary. Chen reported that three factors limited the YWCA's ability to work with labour: its religious nature, its middle-class identity, and the fact that it was a women's association. He noted, however, that the YWCA was among the relatively few women's organizations in China willing to work in this field. He suggested three possible approaches. The first was a revolutionary approach requiring the association to "labourize" its middle-class industrial secretaries and have them live among the workers. He went so far as to propose that the YWCA find secretaries who would act as "field commanders" to facilitate the labour movement. Second, the YWCA could undertake real reform by guiding labourers in the "right direction" – by which he presumably meant organizing – but this approach required secretaries unafraid of being caught up in the political whirlpool, breaking laws, or ending up in prison. His final approach involved advocating for beneficial changes in living and work conditions, conducting educational classes, and providing working women with opportunities for leisure to improve their quality of life.

Chen then offered pragmatic advice. Since the YWCA could not reach out to the entire industrial field, it should adopt the demonstration method with two considerations: a unified policy and concentration. The association should select two issues for serious study and work to make a difference in the lives of women rather than merely seek to make itself "look good" in reports. If the YWCA chose workers' education, it should find the best locale for a model experimental station and select the most qualified secretaries to run it. Chen summarized his advice by saying that sacrificing other equally interesting programs for one that would make a difference was the "law of success in social progress."[52]

The national and Shanghai industrial departments accepted Chen's recommendations and submitted a plan to create a special demonstration project in the heavily industrialized western district of the International Settlement. In September, the national committee appropriated $3,000 to carry out the plan.[53] The Ferry Road Center included four houses on Ferry and Robinson Roads (Xiaoshadu and Laobisheng lu) in the western district. It was an improvement over other facilities because the facilities were rented and not shared, so the association could create and direct programs as it saw fit. The centre became the mainstay of YWCA industrial work in Shanghai, with its industrial centre, a working girls' hostel, and a demonstration project in health care and vocational services. Two YWCA secretaries and two teachers lived in the centre, providing continuous contact with working women.

The hostel was an experimental project in group living and homemaking. Providing hostels for urban women was hardly a new venture for the YWCA – for years, it had supported boarding-style hostels for white-collar working women and students in Shanghai, Beijing, and elsewhere. The Ferry Road Center differed from those in that it sought to teach working girls skills needed to live on their own. Thus, girls could live in the centre for only a few years before being expected to move out and establish their own communal living situations. The Ferry Road Center provided club rooms for recreation, something that trade unions also provided but which women apparently did not use to any great extent, because men frequented them.[54]

Given the prominence of Deng Yuzhi in the history of YWCA industrial work, it is essential to note the importance to the future of the association's industrial program of the years from 1925, when Eleanor Hinder was hired as a Shanghai city association industrial secretary, to 1930, when the Ferry Road Center was established. First, those years constitute one-third of the most viable years of YWCA industrial work.[55] Second, Hinder's "direct approach" and literacy classes became the model for all future work. The actual driving force behind the first five years of the industrial program was arguably Hinder at the local level in Shanghai and Ding Shujing in the national office. While Lily Haass's advocacy cannot be discounted, Ding is the consistent thread that ties all other efforts together. She agreed to Deng Yuzhi's becoming an industrial secretary and, most likely, wore down any resistance to that appointment. She was present at both industrial secretaries' conferences, and although her voice was recorded only at the second conference, what she said there was consistent with the messages that came out of the first conference. This is not to deny the significance of Deng Yuzhi's role as national industrial secretary after 1930; in fact, Deng's "radicalization" of the industrial program ensured that there would be a future for the YWCA movement in China.

The Industrial Program under Deng Yuzhi

Deng Yuzhi returned to China in September 1930 after a fifteen-month absence, having completed studies at the London School of Economics and attended the World YWCA committee meeting at Saint-Cergue,

Switzerland, on her return trip. National committee minutes note her appointment as national industrial executive in March 1931, but it is likely she assumed those responsibilities earlier, as Lily Haass was on furlough. Deng carried out the duties of this office with the help of Eleanor Hinder, who returned in 1930 to assist with various projects for the YWCA national office.[56]

In late spring or early summer 1931, Deng underwent surgery, from which she recuperated very slowly.[57] It is difficult to ascertain how much of a guiding hand she exercised during her convalescence. It is also difficult to know how involved she was with the Ferry Road Center, as there is some ambiguity in the record as to whether the national industrial office or the Shanghai industrial department directed work there. The Shanghai city association continued to operate its night schools for factory women separately from the Ferry Road project, although even in that endeavour, the national office was occasionally involved. The expanded curriculum for all educational work with factory women certainly reflects Deng's vision. New courses included advanced classes in reading, arithmetic, geography, history, letter writing, simple composition, and civics. After Japan invaded Manchuria in September 1931, industrial secretaries added courses on the fundamentals of economics, economic history, the trade union movement, politics, social history, and essay writing, which developed into a two-year worker's education course. Secretaries also instilled an awareness of workers' problems and women's responsibility to do something about their situation.[58]

Industrial work continued in the girls' clubs. There were now two levels of clubs: beginners' clubs for girls sixteen and older who had completed the literacy class and advanced clubs for those who had moved to the next level of course work. These clubs served as a vehicle for raising both the class consciousness and feminist awareness of factory women. YWCA records reveal that in 1932, CCP cultural worker and composer Tian Han helped girls in one club produce plays that served as the basis for group discussions aimed at building confidence and group solidarity. The play *Before Lunch* addressed the evils of night work and questioned whether the interests of employers and workers were the same.[59] The skit *Where to Go?* told the story of peasants who escaped rural poverty only to be abused by factory supervisors. Its underlying message was that workers had to struggle to improve society for the good of all. According to Deng, the message of the play *Where to Go?* was subtle enough not to be clearly identified as socialist commentary by those only interested in watching the working girls' performance.[60]

In her 1953 testimony, Wang Zhijin made no mention of Tian Han or of any YWCA involvement with the work of cultural workers. But accounts from Deng Yuzhi, both shared with historian Emily Honig during interviews starting in 1979 and in essays in her memorial volume published after her death in 1996, clearly indicate that she knew and endorsed the involvement of cultural workers such as Tian Han. Wang Zhijin did mention that club work included activities like singing and stage events. Wang also described larger gatherings held elsewhere because the school buildings were too small for lectures or movie screenings, activities that "made excellent use of YWCA resources to engage and educate more workers."[61] The main thrust of Wang's testimony, however, was how the party cadres "used" the YWCA, took advantage of their resources, and seemingly escaped notice: "We had done everything possible to minimize the American imperialist influence, and even to use the enemy, while performing the work of the party."[62] However, given that Wang gave her testimony in 1953, she could hardly have claimed otherwise.

As industrial girls studied and worked together at the various industrial centres, a few began to stand out as genuinely interested in labour questions. In 1931, there were enough interested girls for the industrial secretaries to organize the first industrial girls' conference with the theme of "Improving the Livelihood of Women Workers." A *daibiao hui* (representative council of factory girls) decided on the conference goals: 1) to broaden girls' outlook by having them meet students from other centres; 2) to identify and study common problems that developed solidarity; and 3) to bring the message of the conference back to individual centres. It was a short weekend conference, reflecting the difficulty working girls had in getting time off, but industrial secretaries considered it a success. As Shanghai city association secretary May Bagwell, one of the secretaries who lived in the industrial centre, wrote:

> Surely if industrial women are to become a part of a woman's movement in China and are to have a share in bringing about social and economic changes for the benefit of all, the hope lies in the type of alive, keen, intelligent girls and young women who are to be found in the YWCA industrial centres in Shanghai.[63]

A second conference, held in April 1932, convinced YWCA industrial secretaries that the leadership they were developing was crucial in order for working women to advance.[64]

Although Wang Zhijin did not mention the first conference, Bagwell's description of it aligned with the specific goals of the cadres working in the night schools. Their primary purpose was recruitment, and Wang specifically mentioned Xu Peiling, who worked for the industrial department and joined the CCP in 1932. YWCA staff lists are snapshots in time, and the fact that Xu Peiling is not listed as a Shanghai association secretary in 1932 does not mean she was not one. Or, as Wang's testimony is not specific, Xu might have been a teacher and thus would not have appeared on a staff list. In total, Wang listed seven women, including Xu, who were either working at the night schools or attending them when they were recruited for the party in the early 1930s.[65]

During her tenure as national industrial secretary in the 1930s, Deng was the only secretary in her department, although she certainly received advice from like-minded secretaries on the national staff. Among them were Lily Haass and the radically inclined Talitha Gerlach. Joining them in 1935 were Gong Peizhen, formerly a Shanghai city association secretary, and Deng's friend and mentor Maud Russell. Haass, Deng, Gerlach, and Russell belonged to a left-leaning foreign study group.[66] Over time, the group came to include radical expatriates such as American journalists Agnes Smedley, Edgar Snow, and Snow's wife, Helen Foster Snow (Nym Wales).[67] Deng counted liberal educator Tao Zhixing and leftist playwright Tian Han among her acquaintances. They provided her with connections to leftist organizations such as the League of Left-Wing Educators and the League of Left-Wing Writers.[68] Deng was also friends with YMCA secretary Wu Yaozong. Both would become involved in the National Salvation Movement, and in 1949, both would be selected by the CCP as Christian delegates to the political consultative conferences that deliberated on the first constitution for the People's Republic of China.

Deng used her contact with the foreign study group to find interesting, knowledgeable, and, more frequently than not, left-wing Westerners to give lectures at YWCA industrial night schools after the Shanghai War. Among them were Americans Edgar Snow, Anna Louise Strong, and Agnes Smedley. Smedley lectured at the night school a second time, after visiting the rural bases of the CCP.[69] Deng's contacts with the Shanghai underground Communist Party also began in 1932. According to her testimony, Tian and others would not necessarily have been identified as "communists" as much as "patriotic workers," which is a possible reason why they escaped the notice of both GMD agents and those on the YWCA national committee who might not have approved.[70]

The Shanghai War, 1932

Increasing Japanese intrusions into Chinese territory after 1928 heightened tensions between China and Japan. They also provided YWCA women with the opportunity to speak out on matters of peace and social justice. Most of those intrusions were far to the north, including Japan's invasion of Manchuria in the fall of 1931 and the extension of its zone of control into China's northern provinces. One of those intrusions was right on the YWCA women's doorstep, however. On January 28, 1932, Japan attacked Shanghai after months of prolonged anti-Japanese activity in the wake of Japan's invasion of Manchuria the previous September and open hostility toward the Japanese expatriate community in the Shanghai International Settlement.[71]

The Shanghai War was brief but destructive. Negotiations to end the hostilities began while fighting continued. The Japanese agreed to a cease-fire on March 5, and a peace agreement was signed one month later.[72] The situations in Manchuria and Shanghai led to a League of Nations Commission of Enquiry headed by British statesman Lord Lytton. Their presence gave YWCA women, led by national committee chair Sheng Zuxin and national general secretary Ding Shujing, several opportunities to demonstrate the collective power of women. The commission received an official statement from the YWCA signed by Sheng Zuxin. The statement opened with quotes from cables sent to the Chinese association from the Women's International League for Peace and Freedom and the International Council of Women, exhorting the YWCA to "stand true" and not swerve from the "path of faith in the possibility of peaceful settlement and in just international action, not to let down in their own efforts in their own country with their own government to the end that the counsels of the League should be the way of settlement."[73]

Sheng told the commission that the YWCA's Chinese constituency had lost faith in the efficacy of international action by peaceful means. "When the enemy was on their soil, ravaging their country, no course was left to them but to support the defenders who were standing for justice." Nonetheless, she continued, YWCA women found the presence of the commission encouraging and waited "with faith and expectancy a successful denouement of League action." The statement concluded with a challenge to the commission to "perform this service for the world."[74] There were more than subtle undertones of nationalism in the official statement, reminiscent of the tone of the national committee statement after the May Thirtieth Incident.

Ding Shujing called a meeting of Chinese women's organizations to address what she considered an oversight by Shanghai's municipal leaders – a failure to include women in their plans for the commission's visit. The Women's Christian Temperance Union, the Women's Suffrage Association, the Women's Rights Association, the National League for Defense, the National Council of Women, and the YWCA formed a coalition called the Chinese Women's League for the Promotion of Women's Rights. They entertained the commission's delegates and other dignitaries at a banquet to provide them with the opportunity to meet Chinese women and hear their opinions on the current international crisis.[75]

The Chinese Women's League spoke out forcefully. It composed a declaration that, although endorsing the commission's mission, maintained that "we shall never waive our sovereign rights which our forefathers have bestowed upon us." It also demanded compensation for losses incurred by the Chinese because of the Japanese invasion of Manchuria and Shanghai. Until these points were satisfied, normal relations "cannot subsist between the peoples of China and Japan."[76]

In an interview with Ruth Woodsmall, a representative of the Laymen's Foreign Missions Inquiry, which was in Shanghai at that time, Ding Shujing and Sheng Zuxin spoke of the importance of that meeting with the League of Nations Commission of Enquiry. Woodsmall noted that Ding and Sheng believed "it is of the greatest importance that this Western Commission should realize that women leaders in China have become articulate. They have thought of them too much in terms of blind faith and ignorance. This meeting they hoped will bring an entirely different picture."[77]

The YWCA's official statement and the declaration of the Chinese Women's League were nationalistic statements. While Ding Shujing did not waver in her commitment to peace, in her writings she clearly linked peace with justice:

> During these months the strength and power of international ties and affiliations have been tested. They have bound us more closely together than ever before, they have influenced attitudes and widened sympathies, and helped us to glimpse the strength which there may be in our unity. We trust that these bonds may grow in strength, and that we who are thereby closely united, may find an effective means to champion the cause of justice and peace, which are so seriously jeopardized today.[78]

During the months before Japan's dramatic withdrawal from the League of Nations in 1934 after the latter condemned its aggression in China, Japanese intrusions increased. A somber note entered Ding's correspondence:

> Recent developments have been an occasion for further heart-searching as to what attitude we, as a Young Women's Christian Association, should take ... The result of these deliberations lead us to reiterate once more our abhorrence toward all kinds of aggression, whether directed toward ourselves or by us, toward others. Yet we cannot but admit as an inherent human right, the principle of self-defense, and the futility of trying to build peace apart from justice.[79]

In her April 1933 letter to YWCA secretaries in China, Ding admitted that there was a lack of consensus on the YWCA position toward ongoing Japanese aggression. The national office decided not to make an official statement that would be interpreted as binding on local associations.[80] Ding's many letters to YWCA secretaries across China highlighted the mental and emotional challenges she faced as national general secretary. This is not to say that Grace Coppock did not face similar challenges, but China was not her country. Ding, and later Cai Kui and Deng Yuzhi, would find these aspects of leadership exhausting. At least Ding and Cai did, and they spoke about them near the end of their tenures as national general secretary.

THE LAYMEN'S FOREIGN MISSIONS INQUIRY

The Laymen's Foreign Missions Inquiry had been organized by seven American Protestant denominations. It sent representatives to study missionary work in Asia from 1930 to 1932, and issued a final report in 1932. The representative sent to Shanghai was Ruth Woodsmall, an active member of the American YWCA who had spoken at the Chinese YWCA's first national convention a decade earlier, and who would shortly be appointed World YWCA general secretary.

The degree to which the social thinking of some secretaries had evolved since the mid-1920s was evident in their interviews with Woodsmall. As a YWCA woman herself, and thus a trusted colleague, she drew out frank, telling comments about the limitations of the church as a framework for reform, and the need for it to broaden its social thinking and approaches

to social issues. Secretaries talked openly of the need for Christians to
disavow imperialism and capitalism and to take a candid look at the appeal of communism and emulate its "for the masses" approach. Such
comments would sound controversial and unrepresentative to those unfamiliar with the history of the Chinese YWCA and its women. From the
time Deng Yuzhi warned the association to broaden its class base in 1927,
to May Bagwell's pointing out of the need for the YWCA to help develop
"class consciousness" among workers, industrial secretaries had invoked
the discourse of Christian socialism and the social gospel. Historian
Robin Porter suggests that Agatha Harrison introduced Christian socialism to YWCA secretaries in the early 1920s; she may well have done so,
but she would not have been the first.[81] Maud Russell, who arrived in
China in 1917, was a Christian socialist. The secretaries who attended the
London School of Economics were certainly exposed to Christian socialism. The social gospel movement also introduced new interpretations of
the nature and purpose of Christian social reform. YMCA secretary Wu
Yaozong was an active proponent of the social gospel movement in the
late 1920s. Whatever the sources – and there were many – these radical
ideas had been circulating for some time.

In their interview with Woodsmall, Lily Haass and veteran secretary
Jane Ward stated:

> A pernicious idea prevalent today is the idea of Christianity saving China
> against Communism. Christianity should study Communism and adopt
> some of its message in its doctrine of good for the masses. Christianity
> versus Communism suggests that Imperialism and Capitalism is justified.
> It is a pernicious doctrine to justify Capitalism and Imperialism on a basis
> of the material progress which they make possible. This is opening up the
> question also as to whether material progress is the end rather than the
> means to an end.[82]

Western secretaries were not the only women to express such views.
Mrs. L.C. King (Mrs. Jin Longzhang), a graduate of Mount Holyoke
College who was vice chairman of the national committee and interim
general secretary of the Shanghai city association, stated similar views.
Woodsmall's notes read:

> The question was raised as to whether Communism is making a strong
> appeal to Chinese young people. Communism, according to Mrs. King,

is likely to attract young people, with its social program, because it seems to offer a definite way out of modern problems. It is positive, whereas Christianity is too passive. Christianity seems to emphasize the other world and have too little contact with life. People often speak of Christianity as being opposed to Communism. This is a dangerous antithesis, as Communism may have some ideals which Christianity might well use. If Christianity is lined up against Communism this may also be interpreted as meaning that Christianity is identified with the other opponents of Communism, namely, capitalism and Imperialism. The Church should endeavor to attract youth by a more positive social program.[83]

These women also explicitly criticized the church for its conservatism, and missionaries for the "backwardness" of their religious thinking. Haass and Ward noted that

the average missionary does not at all represent current American religious thought. Sometimes the YWCA people feel in a peculiarly anomalous position, since, as a part of the Christian movement they are in many people's minds identified with the missionary movement, whereas they are much more closely related in their sympathies to the doubt and uncertainty of the Chinese returned student.[84]

The comments that followed the Shanghai War were more fully articulated at the third industrial secretaries' conference in January 1933. Conference participants explicitly recognized the necessity of class struggle as a means of improving working women's lives, and reiterated the importance of developing a "self-directed" workers' movement. The educational emphasis shifted from working to improve literacy and develop leadership skills, and thus encouraging personal achievement, to training women to organize the working class as a group. To achieve this goal, introductory literacy courses were combined with training in self-expression and group discussion, and advance coursework was upgraded to include a more substantial study of industrial problems such as trade unionism and labour legislation. Many of these ideas had been formulated in March 1932 immediately after the Shanghai War. The conference's final recommendation was that the upcoming third national convention include an "industrial assembly."[85] The inclusion of urban and rural working women at that national convention would be the association's most open rejection of its original middle-class identity.

THE THIRD NATIONAL CONVENTION, 1933

The third national convention had been planned for 1931 but was delayed until 1933 because of Japanese aggression in Manchuria and Shanghai. The convention was driven by the utmost sense of urgency. As one secretary reported:

> So many changes had been taking place in the whole social fabric ... so many new trends were seen emerging with the Association itself, that it became almost impossible to go on further with any clear sense of direction unless opportunity came to examine the present Association program ... and to determine the new emphasis for the period just ahead.[86]

The similarity between this statement and the question raised five years earlier at the second national convention speaks directly to the tumultuous nature of that period.

There were 217 delegates representing thirteen city associations, eighty-nine student associations, four rural centres, and industrial centres in at least three cities. The size of the membership in 1933, with the inclusion of rural and industrial women, was certainly greater than the 1928 membership, estimated at 6,000, and less than the estimated 10,000 reported in 1937. The convention theme, "Building a New Society," reflected the association's determination to participate in the national life of China. The five convention topics did so as well: 1) the nature, purpose, and function of the YWCA; 2) problems of sex, marriage, and family life; 3) what programs the YWCA should provide rural and industrial women; 4) what the YWCA could do to improve political life; and 5) what contribution the YWCA could make toward the solution of "the problem of livelihood." The international interests of the YWCA were reflected in the presence of guests from England, Australia, New Zealand, the United States, and, interestingly, Japan.

Industrial and rural questions received much attention as both industrial and rural women took the stage to give first-hand accounts of how their YWCA programs worked. Claims that the YWCA veterans "accepted naturally" these less educated and less sophisticated women and that these industrial and rural delegates "truly belonged" were probably exaggerated. By official accounts, the newcomers were articulate when describing their worlds, which for the middle-class convention delegates must have been as foreign as the homelands of the international representatives.

On the policy level, the convention made a critical change to the nature, purpose, and function of the association by passing an amendment eliminating the requirement that staff and volunteers be formal members of a church. While affirming their fundamental distinction from other social service organizations because of their interest in the "whole of life" and their belief that religion was a vital factor to have "abundant life," the delegates rejected church membership as "too dogmatic" a test for fitness for leadership.

Another decision, growing out of the field survey and necessitated by diminishing financial and staff resources, was that local associations should concentrate on fewer programs that met local needs and that they could support. Equally important, they were given the power to decide which programs to keep, which to modify or combine, and which to eliminate. How much autonomy this gave local associations is questionable, since not long after the convention Lily Haass, by then the most experienced secretary, became national city association secretary and thus had some leverage in what city associations did.[87]

One final discussion had to do with the withdrawal of much of the Western staff because their home boards could no longer support them as the Depression continued. Another factor in the declining number of Western secretaries would have been voluntary attrition due to China's increasingly precarious situation as Japanese aggression grew. Ding Shujing felt the loss of Western secretaries particularly keenly. Few at the convention shared her view, however. They were concerned over the rapid pace of withdrawal, and it was decided to create a special fund for developing Chinese secretaries. By October 1934, only twelve foreign secretaries remained out of a total of ninety-seven in the late 1920s. Turnovers made maintaining a high level of expertise among Chinese staff difficult. In 1934, forty-six women joined the YWCA staff, which meant that now over half of the eighty-five Chinese secretaries were new.[88] It cannot be known how frustrated Ding became as events and circumstances beyond her control thwarted her ability to maintain an international staff.

1934 AND AFTER: RADICALIZATION

In some respects, YWCA industrial work levelled off after 1934 as a result of the broadening world Depression. Economic conditions caused great unemployment, and those who were employed had their wages cut. In Deng Yuzhi's words, this created a "depression psychology" that stymied a labour movement that had largely lost its momentum due to the failure of an independent union movement.[89] The YWCA remained the only Christian organization that focused on industrial women's problems. Although education and not welfare was the primary purpose of industrial work, the inclusion of some welfare projects ensured the continued support of the more conservative members of the national committee.[90]

In 1934, there were seventy-five secretaries in fifteen city associations working with middle-class urban women. In comparison, there were ten industrial secretaries, four in the national office and six on local staffs, supporting a total of nine industrial centres in four different cities.[91] Mathematically, that was an average of five secretaries directing programs for middle-class women in each city, and two and a half secretaries operating programs in four industrial cities. Considering the higher salaries paid industrial secretaries (because of their training) and the fact that most teachers at industrial centres were not classified as "secretaries," the industrial programs appear to have been adequately supported. In 1934, approximately 864 girls attended classes at YWCA industrial centres in Shanghai, Wuxi, and Tianjin. By 1936, that number had grown to 1,364, an increase of 58 percent.[92] While the overall number seems small, perhaps as a result of the program's association with a Christian organization, in many ways the increase seems dramatic. How to account for it? Perhaps the best explanation, although not the only one, is the radical reorientation of industrial work after the third industrial secretaries' conference, with the recognition of the necessity of class struggle and the need to develop a class consciousness among working women.

Deng Yuzhi set the tone for this early in 1934 with an article in the mainstream English-language missionary magazine the *Chinese Recorder*. She did not attempt to modulate her words:

Has Christianity anything to do with this [industrial] situation? Did Christ not teach us "to preach good tidings to the poor, proclaim release to the captives, and set at liberty them that are bruised"? Thousands of these women and girls are "bruised" by economic pressure and are the "captives" of economic exploitation. So bruised are they, indeed, that their bodies are not decent enough for spiritual growth!

Have we any "good tidings" to preach to these people as to how they can be freed from the exploitation of a profit-making system? Preaching to them as to how to save their souls and get ready to go to heaven in the next life is not enough. The time has come for us to declare that the present system is unreasonable and absolutely contrary to Christ's way of life.

It is also time that followers of Christ helped those who are exploited to build the attitude that will eventually do away with this system that kills their souls! We are challenged to do something to release the captives and set the bruised free![93]

It is not known how missionaries in China or mission boards outside of China reacted to Deng's challenge. Despite the creation of the NCC in 1922, the Christian community in China remained as fragmented in 1934 as it had been when Clarissa Spencer negotiated with its leadership in 1907 to find a niche for a nondenominational women's organization. The article may have brought the YWCA to the attention of the GMD secret police but, for a number of reasons, the YWCA escaped their deeper scrutiny.

One dramatic example of this is the case of Jiang Qing, who would become Mao Zedong's second wife. In 1934, she was assigned by the communist underground to work for the YWCA. She lived in a YWCA industrial centre and taught one morning and one evening class, which left her afternoons free to perform tasks for the party. The YWCA assigned her to visit workers' homes and report on their living conditions, and later sent her to investigate health clinics and small factories. These are all activities Deng Yuzhi described in her brief history of YWCA industrial work written in 1990.[94] As Jiang told her story, she enlisted a number of students to smuggle communist handbills into factories. She was eventually caught carrying handbills, and imprisoned for eight months. She was released because a former student, also imprisoned, contacted the YWCA and arranged for a foreign secretary to come and "guarantee" Jiang's innocence. It is not clear whether she returned to work for the industrial department, but after 1936 she worked for the underground in an area closer to her own interests, the theatre.[95]

Why was the YWCA not suspect? Emily Honig argues that the YWCA industrial programs appeared quite innocuous and the contacts between industrial secretaries and communist cadres were carried out so covertly that they escaped the attention of the Nationalists.[96] Roxanne Witke notes that Jiang Qing believed the GMD relied on the prestige of the YMCA and YWCA to bolster its image, and therefore did not interfere with them.[97] Certainly, the fact Chiang Kai-shek was married to former YWCA secretary Song Meiling, who remained close to the association, provided additional protection.

Despite the YWCA's apparent protection, the GMD secret police were an ever-present threat. The YWCA industrial centres continued to train industrial girls in organizational techniques and, by providing club rooms where women from one mill could discuss their strike efforts, tacitly supported workers agitating for better wages and living conditions. One industrial centre student recalled the following about a strike that started at the Japanese-owned Tong Xing mill in 1936:

> At our school there were women who worked at Tong Xing, so they told us about their strike ... The Japanese finally conceded and raised their wages. When we saw that they got a five-*fen* raise, we all said, "We have to think of a way to demand this too." We at Yong An ended up striking as well.[98]

The YWCA also continued to add to its curriculum. After the National Salvation Movement began in 1936, it added lectures on patriotism, nationalism, and anti-imperialism.[99] Industrial girls also were active in anti-Japanese protests.[100]

DING SHUJING'S DEATH

As Chinese women's advancement into positions of responsibility is part of the history of the YWCA movement in China, so are their decisions to step down from office. Ding Shujing confided her intention to resign to Rosalee Venable when the two friends met in New York at the end of Ding's furlough in August 1935.[101] She said that ten years was long enough to serve, and that other women were capable of carrying on in her place. After her return to China in November, she began to talk openly of resigning. She urged the association to do away with the position of national general secretary entirely and substitute some form of paid volunteer service. Few agreed with her suggestions.[102]

The World YWCA invited Ding to work for them as a permanent representative from Asia to the World Council and initiate "a new era of oriental collaboration." World YWCA general secretary Ruth Woodsmall felt strongly that "Europe should have the benefit of more direct personal contact with Miss Ting." Ding equivocated, not wanting to leave one full-time job for another. Then, she fell ill. She was hospitalized in mid-July with sepsis caused by a severe tooth infection, and died on July 27, 1936. Cai Kui had been appointed acting general secretary two weeks earlier.[103]

Historical events buffeted the formative years of the YWCA movement in China, and continued to buffet the association during Ding Shujing's tenure as national general secretary. The Great Revolution of 1927, Japanese incursions after 1928, and the worldwide Depression in the 1930s were not simply a backdrop; rather, they forced the association's leadership to reconsider its programs and continually redefine its identity as both Christian and Chinese. This chapter has focused on a singular endeavour, industrial work, which is illustrative of the way the association responded to its changing situation and how its thinking evolved. The choice of industrial work was intentional, however, made to highlight the early influence of Deng Yuzhi as historical hindsight recognized her later importance. Her social mindset – the need to Christianize economic relations and prioritize social justice for the working classes – would become the touchstone of the association after 1949.

Chapter 4 examines Cai's tenure as national general secretary. She led the association for thirteen years, during which China was at war either with Japan or with itself. Less known to history than the vibrant Ding Shujing or the outspoken Deng Yuzhi, Cai travelled continually and communicated effectively to keep the association movement functioning under desperate wartime circumstances.

4

Claiming National Citizenship, 1937–48

We are essentially a people's organization, functioning democratically.
— Cai Kui, June 1939

From January to March 1932, the YWCA national office suffered through the brief but destructive Shanghai War. The Chinese YWCA thus was no stranger to conflict. However, nothing could have prepared it for eight years of war with Japan or the three years of civil war that followed. Japan's invasion of China in 1937 tested the strength and resolve of association women. The civil war tested their faith.

This chapter examines how the YWCA national office met the challenge and disruption of war by loosening its bureaucratic structure, democratizing its decision-making, and further localizing its program. These wartime transformations made it possible for the association to cross the 1949 divide. War further provided an opportunity to grow and expand the YWCA movement in the interior. For the YWCA women, it was also a spiritualizing experience, providing them with the opportunity to actualize their Christian beliefs and live the gospel of Jesus. Finally, and critically important, the war provided the YWCA as an institution and its women as citizens the opportunity to contribute to the national survival of their country and, after that, the building of a new China.

On July 7, 1937, troops from the Japanese garrison on the Beijing-Tianjin rail line conducted night maneuvers near the Marco Polo Bridge southwest of Beijing without notifying the local village. Alarmed, the local Chinese militia opened fire, which the Japanese returned. In the confusion, a Japanese soldier went missing. Although he eventually returned quite unharmed to his camp, hostilities escalated and, within days, a simple misunderstanding became the pretext for war. When negotiations failed, Japan attacked. Tianjin fell on July 30 and Beijing on August 8.

As the Japanese high command debated whether to invade China, it reinforced troops already stationed in Shanghai to protect the city's sizeable Japanese population. The battle for Shanghai officially began on August 13. After years of appeasing Japanese aggression in the north, trading land for time as he attempted to exterminate the communists, the previous December Chiang Kai-shek had been forced by one of his own generals into forming an alliance with the CCP to fight the Japanese, creating the Second United Front. Chiang made his stand in Shanghai, throwing all his best troops at the Japanese, partially in the hope of gaining Western support by demonstrating China's will to fight. Fierce fighting continued for three months, thwarting Japanese expectations of a quick victory over a people they despised. It did not result in foreign assistance, however.[1]

The YWCA's location in the International Settlement provided no shelter. On August 14, just one day after the battle commenced, Chinese bombs accidentally fell on its centre. One landed in the Nanjing Road area, one or two in front of the New World Amusement Park, where civilians had sought shelter from the fighting. Others struck near the Bund. By most accounts, several thousand were killed or injured.

Chinese forces erected defence lines along the northern boundary of the International Settlement. Zhabei, the industrial district cradled in the hollow formed by the settlement's northern, central, and western administrative districts, was on the opposite side of those lines and thus witnessed fierce fighting and massive destruction. As the battle raged, the YWCA served as a registration and coordination centre for women volunteers who offered first aid and civil defence classes and ran two of the three dozen or more refugee camps.[2] One camp was for industrial girls dislocated when factories in Zhabei were razed; the other, run jointly with the Chinese Women's Club, was for women and children.[3]

The first months of war disrupted the association's national network and threatened to fracture its organizational unity.[4] Shanghai's defeat meant that both the national office and the Shanghai city association were in occupied territory, along with Beijing, Tianjin, and Yantai. As soon as Shanghai fell, the Japanese army marched to the capital, Nanjing.

Nanjing suffered a hellish nightmare of rape and massacre from December 1937 into January 1938, in which thousands perished at the hands of Japanese soldiers. There are no YWCA accounts of the Nanjing Massacre. In general, official YWCA documents were devoid of any accounts of atrocities committed by either side – and there were atrocities on both sides. Ever conscious of the power of the printed word, association war discourses highlighted how hardships and challenges were overcome, stressing women's ability to endure and, even more, to be strengthened by adversity.

War Travels

After capturing Nanjing, the Japanese pursued the withdrawing Nationalist army up the Yangtze River. Their advance threatened YWCA city associations in Hankou and Wuchang, which, along with Hanyang, made up the tricity area of Wuhan. Wuhan fell in October 1938, ending the first period of the war.

Before the fall of Wuhan, acting national general secretary Cai Kui and national personnel and training secretary Lily Haass travelled to associations in central, southern, and western China. Their first stop was at Hankou, where they met Deng Yuzhi, who was working at the Hankou city association, already "well-entrenched as a social-service provider."[5]

Since the creation of the Second United Front in December 1936, the political life of China had opened up to viewpoints suppressed for years. In early 1938, Wuhan was the de facto national capital as preparations to make Chongqing the wartime capital were proceeding slowly due to transport and other problems. From January to October, Wuhan was open to many influences and, although never reaching the cosmopolitan heights of Shanghai, experienced its own stripped-down version of a cultural renaissance.[6]

Thus, not surprisingly, Haass found Hankou "full of politics": "The 'United Front' means that groups formerly working 'under cover' are out in the open. It seemed incredible that all these people, hunted for years, were coming and going about openly, honored guests at public functions, making speeches, delightful, charming people with kindly eyes, not bitter and sharp." She further observed that "people of every party and group" were eager to talk to representatives of a women's organization. And, more profoundly, Haass found a "new kind of 'cooperation'" both in government circles and in "people's organizations, of which we are one."[7] This was one of the first references in the association's official records to its being described as a "people's organization," a description that would become part of the wartime vocabulary redefining the association's identity.

Among the people Haass specifically mentioned meeting was Deng Yingchao, wife of communist leader Zhou Enlai. The openness of the first years of the Second United Front, and the opportunity to meet with communist leaders such as Deng Yingchao, would prove critical to the YWCA's future. In a 1986 interview, Deng Yuzhi recalled meeting Zhou Enlai, in 1938 the communist secretary for southern China, for the first time when he visited the Hankou YWCA to inspect its relief and anti-occupation work. At that time, he expressed admiration for the association's "charity" work. Extant YWCA documents do not record further contacts between Deng Yuzhi and these important communists. In interviews with China scholar Emily Honig, Deng suggested that Zhou and his wife "recruited" her support for the communist-organized resistance movement.[8]

Cai Kui's narrative of that trip, a composite of notes made while travelling, provided a Chinese view of the changes war was bringing to the YWCA movement in the country. Cai recalled a conversation she had in Hong Kong with Mrs. Shu Houren (Julia Yen), who had served as president of the Hankou YWCA board since 1937. Cai had remarked how difficult it was to keep the YWCA movement going in war, a remark she must have looked back on as naive since at that point the war was only eight months old. Shu disagreed:

> In the past YWCA work was entirely a pioneering adventure. At times it seemed to be super-imposed or forced upon China with a foreign outlook. People took an interest in the YWCA often-times out of courtesy but now a new stage has been reached. Upon the foundations which was laid we are now ready, in fact the time has come when we may build a building of our own.[9]

Shu's observations are important because they come from a member of the governing board of a city association, not from someone at the national office. She emphatically noted that Chinese women were ready to make the association their own.

By 1937, the YWCA had been a conduit for Western ideas for almost four decades. From its origins as a Western transplant and cultural interloper, it had evolved slowly and unevenly, buffeted by political currents

and economic crisis, and occasionally with its own internal power struggles, to become a Sino-Western hybrid. YWCA women knew they must
mould an organization to fit the needs of women in a country torn by a
war that the rest of the world was ignoring. And while Chinese women
worked side by side with the remaining Western secretaries, the stark
reality was that those women could leave and return to countries that
were not – or not yet – at war. During a national crisis, Chinese women
had to take ownership of their situation and their association. The goal
had always been to "make the work Chinese." The war made that goal
a necessity. The February-to-March trip provided Cai with the opportunity to observe both her country and its women with a critical gaze.
Chengdu was a thriving educational centre, home to West China Union
College.[10] It also hosted campuses in exile from occupied areas, including
Yanjing University from Beijing, Nanjing University and Jinling College
from Nanjing, and Dongwu University – later Suzhou University – from
Suzhou. After the association headquarters relocated to Chengdu in 1942,
YWCA women would complain about the city's "sleepy academic environment," which they found a bit stifling.[11] In 1938, however, Chengdu's
atmosphere was suffused with the resilience of students who had made
long and difficult journeys to reach their new campuses. Cai and Haass
then travelled to Kunming, capital of Yunnan Province. The city had
been barely touched by modern influences, let alone Christianity, but
the war brought the southwestern "frontier" province into China's political and social life. Somewhat of a provincial backwater, Kunming was
the most southwestern of the cities Cai and Haass visited. It sprang to
prominence when China's three premier universities, Beijing University,
Qinghua University, and Nankai University, relocated to there in August
1938 and created the National Southwestern Associated University, more
commonly referred to as "Lianda."[12]

The YWCA was there before them. Cai was amazed that in a province
with almost no history of Christian education for women, the YWCA
had exhibited almost unprecedented development. Cai observed that
the association, housed in a building bought for it by the wife of the
governor, had become the centre for women's activities. However, the
Kunming YWCA had not yet met all the organizational requirements
for formal recognition by the national committee. Among other things,
it had not yet found the requisite number of church members to form
an association board.[13] Guiyang, in neighbouring Guizhou Province,
faced a similar dilemma. Its few Christian women and meagre financial
resources hampered preparatory work. Although no one suspected the

war would drag on for seven more years, Cai understood that the association movement would develop along less than regular lines in those frontier regions. She urged the national city department to draft policies and principles for organizing new centres that accounted for wartime circumstances, but recommended that an experienced secretary be assigned to each new centre.[14]

Chongqing contrasted dramatically with its provincial counterparts. It was the economic, industrial, and commercial metropolis of central China. When Cai and Haass visited, it had not yet experienced the massive population influx that it would when Wuhan fell,[15] but it was swollen with refugees. China's wartime refugee crisis was staggering. Estimates range from 4 to 90 million, with GMD estimates of 60 million at the beginning of the war, when refugees arrived in the interior in waves, often having to flee a second time when their initial city of refuge fell.[16]

Cai recounted the abrupt change for those fleeing coastal cities, leaving lives and possessions behind, and for those in the interior who were experiencing their own "invasion." She admired the people caught up in the crisis, and the spirit with which they faced life: "People are definitely spiritually on top of the difficulties ... many people in the interior are homesick and want to come out 'sometime' but their presence in the interior and the adaptation of life as a whole have already brought far reaching changes. This is the stuff from which the New China will be built."[17] She almost prophetically added that "the YWCA has a real share in its task – and in the building we will become a new YWCA."

From her remarks during this and subsequent trips, it appears she sensed that the current struggle had the potential to transform the nation by breaking down barriers that divided people, and through common struggle create a genuine national identity. The YWCA would also have a new identity: its war work would make it an organizational citizen of China.

THE WARTIME FOCUS: RESISTANCE AND RECONSTRUCTION

The national office was accustomed to thinking of the YWCA movement in organizational terms (city associations, industrial centres, rural centres), in developmental terms (pre-organization, organized), or in terms of geographical locations. Now, it classified branches and centres in wartime terms, such as occupied or threatened. Each area presented unique challenges. In the occupied coastal areas, YWCA staffs made the adjustments necessary to remain open and adapted as needed. In any occupied city, Chinese secretaries risked being intimidated or arrested. In treaty ports such as Tianjin and Shanghai, foreign concession areas provided some protection to the city associations located within their boundaries. In Tianjin, the association was in the British concession; in Shanghai, the national office and the main Shanghai city association office were in the International Settlement. However, there were no concession areas in Beijing or Yantai, where a Chinese secretary was arrested. Arrests were also frequent in Beijing. Suspected collaborators were kidnapped and often executed in secret. The Beijing staff "quietly but consistently," and with some success, followed a noncooperation policy, although some questioned how long they could continue to do so. Other precautions included asking Westerners to serve "nominally" on boards and not maintaining lists of staff or volunteers.[18]

As 1938 turned into 1939, the national committee finally confirmed Cai Kui as national general secretary. Henceforth, she would personify the association and her words would convey not only the purpose and goals of the YWCA movement but her own conviction of China's special place in that movement. She would carry those messages with her as she travelled – and she travelled a lot. In April 1939, Cai and Haass attended a regional conference in Chongqing. The conference was unique inasmuch as it was surrounded by war, a situation made clear by Haass: "Did you ever before know of a YWCA conference the location of which was decided on the basis of where there was a good dug-out available to which to flee?"[19] That was reality for the residents of Chongqing, which suffered through 268 bombing raids from the time it became the wartime capital, to 1942, when Japan diverted its air power to the Pacific war.[20]

The conference adopted the theme of "Resistance and Reconstruction." The inclusion of reconstruction highlighted the fact YWCA women had no inkling that true reconstruction was more than half a dozen years away. Representatives from Chengdu, Guiyang, and Chongqing and personnel from the evacuated Nanjing and Wuchang associations attended. Considering the distances and the impediments to travel, the effort to attend speaks of the importance of their work to those women.

Cai's concluding remarks (described by Haass as among the most "masterly" she had ever delivered) emphasized that resistance and reconstruction could be accomplished only through "mass education," which included those present, for YWCA workers were also part of the people: "We are essentially a people's organization, functioning democratically;

from the cooperative efforts of members emerges a joint production." Cai reiterated that their goals could be reached only through cooperation, both through the union of local associations with the national organization and by cooperating with other groups. She concluded that "we are all responsible for the kind of China we have in the future; we have a religious responsibility towards the needy; we built not a new China, but a new world. What kind shall it be?"[21]

Cai's description of the YWCA as a "people's organization, functioning democratically" sounded like words from a script written ten years in the future. She made clear that "people" referred to Chinese of all class backgrounds. Echoing Ding Shujing's address to the second industrial secretaries' conference a decade earlier, both the women who served and the women who were served were united in a common endeavour. The 1938–39 annual report later defined "functioning democratically" as inherent to the YWCA movement, now even more important because of the "regimentation" of wartime.[22] This phrasing was an important marker of evolution – perhaps even a revolution – in thinking since the second national convention in 1928. It suggested the influence of the May Fourth generation secretaries, along with the younger secretaries they now mentored.

In June 1939, Cai and Haass again set off for the interior to attend conferences. Their route is unknown. Japanese-occupied territory was an amoeba-like formation, spreading from Manchuria south along the coast to include half of Zhejiang Province, with bubble-like tentacles reaching into central Hubei and the northern tip of Jiangxi. The Japanese also occupied or had blockaded all major ports south of Shanghai. One of the last of these efforts, the operation to blockade Shantou (Swatow), was underway in June. One way or another, Cai and Haass found a route.

The situation in western China was much the same as the year before. The population was still on the move – probably even more so, given the number of cities that had fallen since their February 1938 trip. Cai rather pointedly stated in a letter to a colleague at the YWCA of the USA headquarters: "To you in the West mention of the migrations of population due to the War may seem an old story, but to us in China it is still a vital factor of national life."[23] Her understated point spoke to a keenly felt reality – what was happening in China in June 1939 remained at the periphery of world attention.

The continuing reality of war, with its hot periods alternating with long periods of virtual stalemate, provided the national staff with time to consider the organic relationship between association branches. Whereas a year earlier, association leadership had viewed the organization as being divided between occupied, threatened, and unoccupied areas, by mid-1939 it was classifying branch associations and centres as actively working or having had work suspended. Some associations remained open and active in occupied cities, such as Beijing, Tianjin, and Shanghai. Others, like Hong Kong and the Guangzhou association in exile in Macao, remained operational even though they were close to areas under military occupation. Most active centres were in free China, although several of them suffered incessant bombing raids.[24]

Already compromised, the situation in occupied cities deteriorated as Japan became emboldened by the lack of an American or European response to its aggression in China. One seldom noted event dramatized just how serious the situation was becoming. On June 14, 1939, the Japanese blockaded the British concession in Tianjin. The "Tianjin Incident" stemmed from the British consul's refusal to turn over four Chinese accused of assassinating a collaborator. Japanese demands escalated, and included the demand to hand over all the Nationalist government's silver reserves in foreign banks. Japanese soldiers strip-searched anyone leaving the concession. When news reached the British press that British citizens, including women, were thus humiliated, the British public became inflamed. Some considered it an act of war, and a few in the government agreed. To engage militarily, however, meant sending the British fleet. French pleas for Britain not to weaken its forces in Europe, and America's refusal to support Britain in an Anglo-Japanese war, forced Britain to negotiate. On August 20, the four assassins were handed over. The silver reserves were not.[25]

IDENTITY, AUTONOMY, AND WAR-RELIEF WORK

The Chinese association had led efforts to organize women's cooperative bodies such as the Joint Committee of Shanghai Women's Clubs, established in 1923, which campaigned to end child labour, and the Chinese Women's League for the Promotion of Women's Rights, which placed women's views before the League of Nations Commission of Enquiry in March 1932. Not only did this strengthen its identity as a leader among women's groups but, as the leader of these groups, the Chinese YWCA was able to protect its autonomy. Maintaining its identity and autonomy remained a goal throughout the war.

During the war, the Women's Advisory Council of the New Life Movement under the leadership of Song Meiling, wife of President

Chiang Kai-shek, became the de facto leader of women's wartime work. While stressing the need for all women to do their utmost, Song tacitly recognized the need for voluntary organizations like the YWCA to work separately rather than directly under the supervision of her organization.[26] For its part, the official YWCA history noted that the YWCA maintained a "cooperative attitude" toward Song's Women's Advisory Council.[27] Song had a long relationship with the Chinese YWCA. She had worked for the association for a year after she graduated from Wellesley College and returned to China in 1917. During the YWCA-led campaign against child labour, Song served on the Joint Committee of Shanghai Women's Organizations and represented the committee on the Municipal Council's Child Labor Commission. She maintained close ties to the association. She was keynote speaker at the annual convention of the YWCA of the USA in 1938, although she had to deliver her speech over the radio.[28] Her long history with the Chinese YWCA may have reassured her that it was an organization that could function usefully without a lot of supervision.

This does not mean that the YWCA did not coordinate with the Women's Advisory Council or cooperate with other organizations. YWCA secretaries lectured in the council's training courses. The YWCA also cooperated with almost a dozen Chinese and international relief agencies in China, and worked especially closely with its fraternal counterpart, the YMCA, on student relief work.[29] The association's leadership, however, also considered war-relief work as part of a larger agenda. In this view, war relief would end but the larger agenda would not. That agenda included expanding and strengthening the association, being increasingly responsive to local needs while not losing sight of the national perspective, and involving more women in more ways in decision-making processes.[30]

It has been argued that the Women's Advisory Council also saw its wartime relief work in a larger context. As with the YWCA, its women were educated and progressive. They sought not only to solve the immediate problem caused by the war and to ensure the survival of the nation but also to establish themselves as capable leaders who should have a role in influencing the future direction of China.[31] In many ways, therefore, the two organizations were of one mindset, with the outstanding difference being the Christian spirit of the YWCA's wartime relief work.

When there were opportunities to benefit from another organization's vision, experience, and expertise, the YWCA did not hesitate. Such was the case with the Chinese Industrial Cooperative (CIC) movement shepherded by New Zealander Rewi Alley. By her own account, it was YWCA secretary Maud Russell who urged the national committee to participate in the first CIC cooperative in Baoji, Shaanxi Province. In April 1939, the national committee endorsed a proposal to send two secretaries to Baoji to train in CIC methods: Zhou Shao Yirong, former Tianjin industrial secretary, now working in the national city department, and Chen Ruifu, who had worked in the rural centre in Songshu, Jiangsu Province, before it closed after the Battle of Shanghai.[32] The association leadership saw the CIC movement as an opportunity to fulfill the promises of the 1933 national convention, which had stressed livelihood and citizenship training. Participation in this movement also gave the association the chance to demonstrate its patriotism by helping increase wartime production, and to demonstrate its commitment to wartime relief, as the CIC movement focused on refugees.[33]

According to his own account, Rewi Alley conceived of the CIC program along with close friends Edgar and Helen Snow. He organized the first cooperative, a knitting factory in Baoji, west of Xian, in Shaanxi Province. While he would have preferred it to remain an independent grassroots movement serving the wartime needs of the people, both government backing (to secure as much non-interference as possible) and government financing were necessary. He enlisted the aid of prominent Westerners, including British ambassador Sir Archibald Clark-Kerr, and eventually secured the support of Song Meiling and, through her, that of the GMD.[34]

One of the two secretaries sent for training in April arrived in Chengdu in June. YWCA secretary Ruth Packard observed the fruits of her labour when she passed through that city on her way to Chongqing and Kunming. For two months, the newly trained secretary undertook the necessary organizational work, investigating potential cooperative members for their skill, their need, and their general fitness to join this new endeavour. Out of an unknown number of applicants, the special YWCA secretary chose sixteen refugee women to organize a sewing cooperative, then taught them both the management and productive aspects of running the cooperative. The women borrowed money for capital from the CIC, contributed what they could afford themselves, rented space in the Chengdu YWCA, and were quickly contracted to produce student uniforms. Their week included an eight-hour workday and six hours of elementary-level study each week. A five-member board of managers met weekly, and once a week the entire membership met in a self-evaluation meeting. For recreation, they participated in YWCA activities. The women who were elected manager and adviser had an even longer work week. They rose early to buy cloth, and were often up late calculating production costs. By November, the cooperative was able to pay back its seed money.[35]

THE YWCA MOVEMENT AT WAR WITH ITSELF

The Chinese YWCA faced another wartime "front": the position of the World and American YWCAs on the war in China. The dilemma for the Americans was that, in accordance with the "scheme of relationships," they supported both the Chinese and Japanese YWCAs. American secretaries in Japan, while not defending Japanese aggression, saw opportunities opening in Japan for the advancement of women, in similar yet dissimilar ways to what was happening in China. Initially, the World YWCA would not call what was happening in China's "war," preferring to refer to it as "China's troubles."[36] In a pedantic statement in 1938, the World YWCA executive committee noted:

> During the conflict the World's YWCA, confronted with questions as to the role of a world Christian movement in relation to international crises, has realized with painful clarity the fact that the World's YWCA cannot indulge in peace pronouncements, since its life as a world movement is bound up with the great national movements in the zone of conflict.[37]

Despite the obvious fact of Japanese aggression, "fellowship" initially allowed some relatively cordial contact between Chinese and Japanese YWCA leaders. In May 1939, two Japanese women returning from the World conference in Madras, India, disembarked for a day in Shanghai and met with their Chinese counterparts to discuss "questions of mutual concern."[38] Subsequently, Western secretaries from the Japanese YWCA paid a visit to the Beijing YWCA. The visitors explained that they wanted to see the situation in Beijing "through the eyes of Chinese people" as well as "through the eyes of realistic internationalists." However, a visit from Japanese national general secretary Taka Kato in the spring of 1940, apparently without advance notice, caught the Beijing YWCA off guard. Kato's visit was interpreted as well-meaning, but it was still perceived as a threat to the unity of the YWCA movement in China.[39]

Concerns over that visit lingered, and in August, Cai Kui wrote World YWCA general secretary Ruth Woodsmall a letter explaining the thinking of the Chinese YWCA. The women from the Japanese national office claimed their visits were "personal." Cai acknowledged that they were "innocent" and intended to "create understanding." However, she believed the visits carried added meaning because of the conflict between the two countries. She was alarmed because she understood Japanese women planned more visits, ostensibly to attend church conferences but actually to develop closer relationships with the YWCAs in occupied areas.

Cai was troubled that her Japanese sisters did not grasp the significance of China's struggle to resist Japanese imperialism. She suggested that Christian civilians in Japan were being used as tools to build Japan's "New Order in East Asia," which, in fact, was a campaign to make China a colonial nation and a subject people: "Is it to be wondered at that we fear the YWCA of Japan is opening itself up to the criticism and suspicion of being a part of the civilian column invading China at this stage in support of the military conquest of territory?" Cai recognized that China was, in turn, being accused of being too "nationalistic," but the YWCA movement in China could not be seen as "accepting" Japanese occupation.[40]

BUREAUCRATIC PRAGMATISM: MOVING THE NATIONAL OFFICE

As the war ground on with no significant support from abroad, the national office realized it needed a relocation plan. On November 1, 1940, the national staff met to discuss what work would remain in Shanghai, what would operate out of a new headquarters, who would remain in Shanghai, who would relocate, and when to move. With a nod to the "democratic" nature of the YWCA national office, the staff suggested that their colleagues already located in the interior be asked for their input.[41]

Ten days later, the national executive committee met to make decisions. Most pressing and perplexing for both procedural and political reasons was how the executive committee would restructure itself. The national committee had always included "resident" members – those residing in Shanghai – and nonresident members, representing local YWCAs throughout the country. The Shanghai residents had made up the executive committee. Now, the national executive committee decided that because of the new work in the interior, a body fully vested with authority needed to be set up as an independent body not subordinate to the current executive committee. A special committee was appointed to study this critical question. The executive committee was more decisive on other questions. All departments except the business department would relocate to Chengdu in February. Chengdu was selected over the wartime capital of Chongqing to avoid "regimentation" as well as oversight of the Nationalist government. On the matter of American secretaries, the executive committee deemed that relocating the national headquarters to the interior constituted a "satisfactory way" of complying with the US State Department's advice that Americans leave China, believing that individual secretaries should make their own decisions.[42]

By December, decisions were finalized for the move. Cai Kui sent an announcement to national associations overseas. She described Shanghai as an "isolated island" with increasing limitations on freedom that, when coupled with the vast migration to the interior, made the interior a more appropriate location for the national headquarters. As with much of Cai's previous correspondence, she presented the move as an opportunity to expand work into the interior rather than simply a necessity of war. Leadership would be transferred to an acting executive committee, with those members remaining in Shanghai being renamed the "Shanghai committee of the national committee."[43] Jinling College president Wu Yifang, who had relocated with her college from Nanjing to Chengdu, agreed to chair the acting executive committee.[44]

1940: A YEAR IN RETROSPECT

In reading official histories and articles written for publication, such as Lily Haass's "New Trends in the Young Women's Christian Association," published in the *Chinese Recorder* in January 1941, it is important to remember that the Chinese association fully understood the power of print and had used publications to shape its public persona for years. Haass would have been acutely aware of her audience, both in China and overseas. More than many, she was wedded to the broader goals of the YWCA movement and the methods needed to achieve them. This, coupled with her twenty-seven years of service to the Chinese YWCA and her seniority over any other woman, Chinese or Western, professional or volunteer, gave her pronouncements weight. Haass recognized that to meet new needs, change and adjustment were unavoidable, and new aims and methods necessary.

To Haass, the effects of the war and new trends were inseparable. "In a period of change people are awake, alive, eager to change" – and this was especially true of women. Where formerly women had been confined to the four walls of their homes, and their lives limited to ministering to their families, war had thrown them into the "larger social vortex."

No longer secure, sharing discomfort at close quarters in refugee camps, women were stirred to action. The YWCA found itself the instrument through which they could act.

The new trends were industrial cooperatives, social and mass education, war-relief services, and rural work, some of which built on existing programs. Mass education had its prototype in the industrial night schools. With the destruction of industrial centres, industrial secretaries took up mass education work, but the circumstances were different. The women they now served had no common identity, and were not free to leave home and gather at a YWCA centre, if one was even close. So secretaries brought the classroom to the women, forming small literacy study groups in back streets and alleyways. The national office produced readers for rural women that used rural lives and experiences and thus were more relevant than a standard textbook. Social education was a euphemism for citizenship training because winning the war and building a future in the postwar world depended on "the people."[45]

War had extended the YWCA movement into new areas. Historically, expansion had been ponderously slow. According to Haass, an organization with half a century of experience should be able to respond to an emergency, and this was what had happened, with new associations established without meeting all the specific requirements.

Finally, war had increased the attention devoted to "democracy." In the context of YWCA writings, this meant consensus decision-making with women and girls from every social and economic class, occurring in clubs as well as on committees, in informal as well as formal group gatherings. "Whether clear or chaotic, practical or expedient, feasible or incredible, they *shall be heard.*" In Haass's opinion, cooperation was basic to democracy, but it was not a "heaven sent gift": "it is experience wrought out in countless group tasks." Admitting to mistakes and failure, Haass firmly believed YWCA women would work all this out. And this, she believed, would be the YWCA's greatest contribution during the difficult war years: providing women with direct experience in democratic social action.[46]

Not discussed in Haass's report was the terrible turn the war had taken in the second half of 1940. In August, pressured by both Chiang Kai-shek and the Japanese, the communists launched the Hundred Regiments Campaign. They targeted the rail and supply lines and fought to push the Japanese back to the cities they controlled, leaving the countryside free for the communists to continue their work among the peasants. In retaliation, the Japanese began their "kill all, burn all, loot all" campaign in July 1941, shedding blood over all of north China.[47]

JAPAN "DECLARES" WAR ON THE YWCA

If the Marco Polo Bridge Incident is considered the first day of the War of Resistance against Japan, then China and Japan had been at war for exactly four years and five months when Japan attacked Pearl Harbor on Sunday, December 7, 1941. Even as the United States declared war on Japan, the Japanese marched into the International Settlement and the other foreign concessions in occupied China. The next day, China finally declared war on the country it had been fighting for four years.

The status of foreigners, once privileged and protected within the concession areas, changed immediately. Americans and their European allies were required to wear armbands identifying their nationality – "A" for Americans, "B" for British, and "N" for the Dutch (Netherlands). Movement beyond the settlements was restricted, and a nightly curfew enforced.[48] The Japanese sought control of all organizations, especially those connected to the Americans or British. It was not long before the Kempeitai (Japanese military police) began rounding up prominent citizens and subjecting them to interrogations that regularly included beatings and torture. Eventually, all foreigners would be rounded up and interned.

In the summer of 1942, the national committee chair and national general secretary of the Japanese YWCA visited the Chinese national office. National business secretary Mrs. S.Y. Hsueh; the newly constituted Shanghai committee chair, Mrs. Mason Loh; and vice chair Sheng Zuxin met with the visitors. Two years earlier, similar visitations to the Beijing city association had raised fears that the Japanese YWCA planned to "occupy" the Chinese YWCA, much as the Japanese occupied the city militarily. Now Mrs. Weimura and Miss Hikaru offered their assistance during the current "troubled period." According to the official association history, the Japanese military authorities required that a Japanese secretary be assigned to the Chinese association. Whether it was a genuine offer to help or a requirement imposed by the military command, Japanese YWCA secretary Miss Naito arrived at the end of November, and her service would prove useful.[49]

In the fall, the Japanese informed Mrs. Hsueh that the YWCA national headquarters building at 133 Yuen Ming Yuen Road could no longer be called the national headquarters or be owned by the YWCA because there was neither a national general secretary nor a national board in Shanghai. The Japanese required the YWCA to register the building with the Enemy Property Commission. Thus began an ordeal of meetings and negotiations for Mrs. Hsueh. She was told first to meet with Bishop Abe of the Japanese Methodist Church, who, along with Mr. Suyekane of the Japanese YMCA, had come to "look after" the Christians in Jiangsu Province. The interview took place at the Astor House Hotel on the far side of Suzhou Creek, reached by crossing the Garden Bridge.[50]

Since August 1937, the Garden Bridge had marked the de facto boundary between the International Settlement and Japanese-occupied Hongkou and Zhabei. On one side stood a sentry from the Shanghai Volunteer Corps; on the other stood a Japanese sentry. In the minds of the occupiers, the Japanese sentry personified Emperor Hirohito and thus must be shown utmost respect and deference. Traffic across the bridge was restricted, forcing people to walk across. Foreigners and Chinese alike had to bow to the Japanese sentry or risk being slapped. Mrs. Hsueh had not crossed over the Garden Bridge since 1937.[51] Now, she had no choice.

It soon became apparent to those left in the "national office" that to retain possession of the national headquarters building, not only did Mrs. Hsueh have to provide proof of ownership but the association also had to appoint an "emergency" national general secretary of Japanese-controlled China. When Tianjin general secretary Beatrice Djeng (Zheng Ruquan) visited the national office in October, the staff begged her to accept that position. She almost did, but when the Tanggu district of Tianjin, where her parents lived, was shelled, she dutifully returned to Tianjin to ensure their safety. This left national business secretary Mrs. Hsueh as the most likely person because of her seniority and the fact that she was Chinese, but she was suffering from health problems and facing surgery. The position was then offered to Sheng Zuxin, who accepted on the condition that the "Shanghai committee" accept the responsibility of presiding as the "national board of the occupied area."[52] After her almost quarter-century of service to the YWCA, this proved to be Sheng's gravest hour. Under almost any circumstances, YWCA women would have had implicit trust in her, but this situation disconcerted the national staff in Chengdu because of the spectre of collaboration.

When Cai Kui and the national executive committee in Chengdu received the coded message "Our shop can neither go on as it is nor can it close down" with scant details, Cai cabled back, suggesting that Sheng Zuxin rename the Shanghai committee the "East China regional committee." With communication slowed by the war, her message arrived too late. The Chengdu national office received a second coded message stating that Sheng had been invited to "serve Mother as Hilda did when she was here." "Hilda" was Cai's code name and "Mother" was Sarah

Lyon of the Foreign Division of the YWCA of the USA. Knowing that the Shanghai office was under Japanese surveillance, the Chengdu group was relieved that the very experienced Sheng had been willing to take this new position. However, they feared that the newly constituted emergency national committee in Shanghai might further seek to shield itself by affiliating directly with the World YWCA, or that the latter might even initiate such a step, as it had done in Mukden.[53]

Cai wrote World YWCA general secretary Ruth Woodsmall about her concerns. She pointed out that the China movement was still shocked by the decision taken in 1938 to allow the Mukden association to affiliate directly with the World YWCA after Japan invaded Manchuria in 1931. Cai went as far as to issue a not-so-thinly veiled threat:

> If anything similar should happen with this much greater area involved we would find it extremely embarrassing. From a political point of view it would be absolutely the wrong thing and would involve us all in a very awkward situation. It might even mean such pressure that we would have to suspend our own affiliation with the World YWCA.[54]

Cai's worst fears were never realized. The Shanghai staff's time was consumed with resolving questions relating to the title deed and ownership of the Yuen Ming Yuen Road property and trying to remain financially solvent with little income except the rent from the building. Because of the many layers of occupation authority, each creating its own red tape, they asked Japanese YWCA secretary Miss Naito to help. Very little other work was undertaken during the ordeal of occupation.[55]

"Ordeal" was exactly what foreign residents experienced in Japanese-occupied cities after the United States entered the war. Foreigners from countries allied against Germany and Japan, or holding passports from those countries, found themselves in civilian internment camps beginning in 1943. There were approximately twenty-two camps in China, including one in Hong Kong. There were thirteen camps in Shanghai, created at various times.[56] Two YWCA secretaries were interned: Lydia Johnson at the Zhabei Civilian Assembly Center (the Japanese name for internment camps), seven miles from the Bund on the grounds of the Great China University, and Leila Hinkley at the Weixian Civilian Assembly Center, near the city of Weifang in Shandong Province.[57]

The Zhabei camp commandant claimed they had been interned in response to the internment of Japanese in the United States. President Roosevelt had signed Executive Order 9066 on February 19, 1942,

authorizing the removal of Japanese civilians from the West Coast. The
Japanese began interning Shanghai civilians in spring 1943. One source
described the Zhabei camp as among the "least harsh" of internment camps
because it was under the authority of Shanghai's Japanese consul general
rather than the Japanese military. Families were not separated, a modicum
of self-government was permitted, and food was generally adequate.[58]

A quarter of a century later, Lydia Johnson remembered her experience
there a bit differently. According to her, she was losing weight on a diet
of only 1,200 calories per day. When internees were able to prove that
Japanese civilians in American internment camps received 2,500 calories
a day, they were provided with an egg a week and some fresh, if not quite
ripe, apples. That internees in Shanghai had information on the status of
Japanese internees in the American West is remarkable, but then remarkable things happen even in wartime. Johnson was among the fortunate
ones who were selected for a prisoner exchange in the fall of 1943, as was
Leila Hinkley.[59] Thus, both American YWCA secretaries interned by the
Japanese spent relatively little time in internment camps.[60]

HOPE AND UNITY IN THE INTERIOR: THE WEST CHINA REGIONAL CONFERENCE, JANUARY 15–19, 1942

Just as the YWCA women in Shanghai were dealing with the first shock
waves of occupation, secretaries in the interior met in Chengdu for the
four-day west China regional conference. The report, written by Lily
Haass and very much bearing her imprint, began with the astounding
fact that everyone arrived on time:

> The delegates arrived tired, very dirty, each with a travel tale of days on
> top of an open truck in sunshine and rain, of sitting by the riverside alone
> with one's baggage in the middle of the night, of bus wheels that slip off
> the ferry boat into the water and mud, of accidents to the bus just ahead,
> but proud of the achievement of arriving before the opening date, thanks
> to the help of all the associations at juncture points in finding conveyances
> for the next stage.[61]

The story of war is one of soldiers and fighting, of major battles or large-
scale human drama. The smaller stories, such as women travelling over-
land on almost impassable roads, using all sorts of conveyances, to discuss
ways of serving a refugee population, often go untold. When students

from Beida, Qinghua, and Nankai trekked to Kunming to resume their academic studies, there might have been a sense of adventure. But for YWCA women, the allure of slogging to and from conferences probably wore off quickly.

The conference theme of "The YWCA and the New China" seemed "almost presumptuous": "A nation in turmoil, fighting on several fronts, hemmed in, its coastal areas occupied; internally engaged in the struggle for democracy which for every nation becomes more acute in wartime. What could a few women out of China's millions do in the face of such a crisis?" Haass noted that, to the delegates, it was not presumptuous at all, and after the opening ceremonies, they set out to discuss exactly what a few women could do.[62]

National executive committee president Wu Yifang introduced the theme by stating that there had been talk of a "New China" for many years but that with the outbreak of war between Japan and the United States and her allies, a "new phase" had begun for China. China was no longer a "semi-colonial" country but a partner with the Americans, British, Dutch, and Russians. China's responsibility now required the complete mobilization of women as well as men. The challenge for the YWCA was to make an even greater contribution to nation-building. With the conference opening on such a note of strength and optimism, it would have been unfathomable to participants that, after four and a half years of war, it would still be another three years and seven months from the day of Wu Yifang's address to Japan's surrender.

Long-time friend and YMCA secretary Wu Yaozong added his analysis of the situation from both national and international perspectives:

The will of the people of the democracies is a strong morale ... There is absolutely no chance of China's coming to a compromise with Japan ... There will be a trend toward socialism, the beginning of a new world order, through suffering, a peoples' world rather than a dictators' world; there will be freedom for people.[63]

While Haass's transcription – and her typing – left something to be desired, the core of Wu Yaozong's message was not only clear but eerily prophetic.

With opening formalities completed, discussions began. There were three new work emphases: industrial cooperatives, day nurseries, and health education. The delegates from industrial cooperatives generated the most excitement, possibly because they brought gifts. The Chongqing cooperative gave appliqued bags to each city association. The Guiyang city association presented the first fruits of its cooperative: umbrellas with interlocking blue triangles (the YWCA's organizational symbol), representing the link between city associations and the cooperatives.

The second new emphasis was day nurseries. Some may have thought this an unlikely endeavour as it was so far removed from the fundamental aims of the YWCA movement. As a piece of wartime work, however, it was linked to the mobilization of women, as nurseries freed them to serve their country. This wartime work would provide valuable experience for the future as it became a major program after 1949.

The third line of work, health education, also reflected a pioneering effort of the Chinese YWCA. Wartime exigencies made health education critical as people suffered both physical and mental strain from overcrowded conditions, the high cost of food, and so on. This work at least could be carried out in conjunction with other programs, such as hostels and clubs. Besides the three priorities, other programs included adult education, rural work, patriotic services, religious education, student work, and international education. There was no shortage of work to be done.

Although not a national convention, and thus not able to make decisions that were national in scope, the conference served many of the same purposes. New secretaries and those who had not been around for the last national convention in 1933 were able to experience first-hand the YWCA's "democracy in action." They worked through problems together and came to their own conclusions rather than having decisions presented to them as *faits accomplis*. The process created a sense of unity among the pioneering associations in west China.[64] Cai Kui held those thoughts in her heart when she gave the final benediction, quoted in Chapter 3 but given additional meaning in the context of war:

> We thank Thee for the vision of the New China and New World we have seen these days. In the New China our task is to help to create an enlightened people – to promote social justice ... To build Christian character ... to build World Peace ... Use us to build New China ... Keep us faithful to this vision.[65]

THE CONTINUING TOLL OF WAR

The tone of the reports written in 1942 was upbeat compared with those written in subsequent years. The initial optimism of what Wu Yifang called a "new phase" of the war waned as 1942 turned into 1943 and then

1944. The tone of Lily Haass's report on personnel and training submitted in August 1944 revealed the strain of seven years of war. The lack of trained secretaries thwarted efforts at both association-style character building and emergency war-relief programs. The lack of consistency in administration compounded the difficult experience of those thrust into positions they had not been properly trained for. By way of example, and without mentioning specifics, the report noted that since 1939 one city association had had five general secretaries. Another had gone through three general secretaries and three acting general secretaries, and still did not have a permanent appointment.[66]

Attracting promising secretaries then training and retaining them had been a problem since the earliest days of the YWCA movement in China. It was, and was not, the same problem as the association had experienced since its inception. Those overseeing personnel matters in the interior faced a variety of problems and often had to improvise solutions.[67] In 1943, out of fifty secretaries, half were new to their assigned job. Another problem was that the YWCA recruited from college graduates, and the quality of college students was lower than before the war, although this was not necessarily the fault of the students. War had created a crisis for all colleges and universities in the interior, not only those that were campuses-in-exile. In Haass's opinion, the lack of books and supplies, government restrictions on what was taught, and the resulting cynicism of both professors and students stultified learning.[68]

Graduating students also tended to look for work that was close to family. With wartime inflation, contributing to the family income and being an emotional support to parents were increasingly important. The latter point is often missed by those unfamiliar with the Chinese psyche. It was seen in the decision of Beatrice Djeng to turn down the position of emergency national general secretary in Shanghai in order to return to Tianjin in 1942 to care for her parents. Marriage remained the problem it had been for decades. Women began marrying earlier during the war, a serious enough development that it was listed as a problem in a postwar report.[69]

There was competition for educated and capable women from government agencies such as the Bureau of Social Welfare and the Women's Advisory Council, as working for them provided the official recognition missing from YWCA work. This had also been true in the 1930s, but the wartime capital of Chongqing proved to be more competitive than the prewar capital of Nanjing.[70]

Despite its overall tone of discouragement, the last section of Haass's report bore the simple title "Encouraging Aspect":

This picture of leadership would not be true without including a hymn of thanksgiving for staff who are working efficiently, loyally and indefatigably, who take hardship in their stride, climate, hard living conditions, travel wrecks, losses, bombings … and whose vision and faithfulness are an inspiration to all who touch them. Of them it may be said "On such women the Kingdom may yet be built."[71]

POSTWAR PLANNING IN THE MIDST OF WAR

A year and a half before Japan surrendered and before she left for a year-long trip to India and the United States, Cai Kui authorized a postwar plan. The plan outlined three basic tasks for the postwar YWCA movement in China. First, as part of the worldwide struggle for democracy, the YWCA movement committed itself to functioning as a democratic organization. Second, it recognized its responsibility for building a "New World Society," an echo of the pledge of women after the First World War. Finally, it reaffirmed its Christian foundation and emphasized the need for spiritual growth for individuals and for the YWCA movement.

It was not surprising that the first aspect of postwar work on the minds of YWCA women was the rehabilitation of associations in occupied areas. Nine associations had been closed. Wuchang, Guangzhou, Hangzhou, and Taiyuan would have to be rebuilt or repaired and totally re-equipped. Shanghai, Beijing, Yantai, Hong Kong, and Tianjin had never closed entirely, but staff had been reduced, staff morale sorely tested, and programs curtailed or suspended since 1942. It was not assumed that all the associations in occupied areas would reopen immediately or reopen at all. The plan devoted very few words to the new interior associations except to acknowledge that they would be thrown into crisis as much of their leadership migrated back to the coastal provinces. Because of this, more emphasis needed to be placed immediately on developing leadership in the new associations in the interior so there would not be as severe a leadership vacuum.

Priority was placed on assisting those returning to homes they had fled, especially in formerly occupied areas. They would need travellers' aid in the form of hostels, information services, and employment bureaus. Women would also need counselling and legal aid as they faced heartbreak and disillusionment over missing family members, economic hardship, and so on. The plan recognized that the trauma of war did not end with a declaration of peace.

The longest section dealt with the association's place in the "New China," in which government departments and new women's organizations would take over social service work pioneered by the association. The YWCA would not attempt to compete unless it was serving its own constituency. It would not engage in social service as one group *serving* another group. Getting women to work together to better themselves would be the focus, since this approach supported the aims of the YWCA movement:

> We should recognize anew that the YWCA is a democratic movement in which members participate in the making of policies and programs; that it aims at development of members through the exercise of the initiative and responsibility involved in such participation; and that it aims further at individual character building and social reconstruction on a religious basis – the Christian motivation, philosophy of life and way of life.

The discussion on personnel included the need to re-staff associations in formerly occupied cities as they were rehabilitated, find leadership and staff to maintain work in the interior, and, during the transition period, provide staff trained in case work, hostel management, information services, and other forms of travellers' aid. Not to be forgotten was current staff working long hours in stressful environments. They needed physical rest, mental stimulation, and spiritual nurture.

Possibly, the most delicate part of the postwar plan dealt with Western staff. The leadership wanted the association to be an organizational citizen of China, run by Chinese women actively building the new China. This needed to be reflected in the status of Western secretaries. Instead of taking a lead position, they must now work alongside Chinese colleagues or even simply act in an advisory capacity. The fear was that, given the ability of the Western women who came to China with hopes of making a personal contribution, over time a supporting role might become inhibiting, and even unsatisfactory to both sides. To prevent this, future Western secretaries should be carefully selected for specific jobs requiring specific expertise not available locally. They should be younger women, remain in China for a limited term, and at any given time comprise no more than 10 percent of the total staff. In hindsight, the wording of this section bears the distinct stamp of Cai Kui. In October 1949, she expressed similar thoughts regarding the role of Western secretaries.

The postwar plan's section on international relations addressed four issues: 1) overcoming the isolation of the war years and becoming educated about the new world order; 2) planning for the World YWCA council meeting; 3) having a Chinese secretary on the World YWCA staff; and 4) having Chinese secretaries representing China at international conferences.

The final section, on finances, dealt with all the financial needs. Every activity and program listed in the plan needed funding. The rough estimate for reconstruction was USD$1,000,000.[72]

There was a time when no one would have questioned the unity of the YWCA movement in China in a general sense. There had been policy disagreements over when and how fast to implement devolution. Different generations of Chinese women sometimes had conflicting visions of China's future direction. But the movement itself, its fundamental goal of giving women "abundant life" mentally, physically, and spiritually as symbolized by the blue triangle, had never been challenged. Now, however, the leadership understood that YWCA women had undergone vastly different experiences in occupied and free China. To heal the breach, the postwar plan called for a national convention within two years. This group of YWCA women, however, were not destined to ever hold another national convention.

THE END IS NEAR

In early April 1945, veteran American secretary Marion Dudley wrote World YWCA general secretary Ruth Woodsmall from Chengdu about how the strain of the long conflict wore on the spirit: "It is nothing like the early war years, now it is grim, dull, and more like an endurance contest." Contributing to her doldrums was the pace – or lack of it – of life in that city: "This is a dull academic town, almost without a feeling of the war."[73]

Cai Kui had just returned "in great form" from her trip to Geneva and the United States. Dudley's letter implied that Woodsmall had conspired to get Cai away for a prolonged period as the strain on her had been particularly great. Cai had returned impressed at how well the three "big" associations were functioning. The three big associations in the interior were Chongqing, Kunming, and Chengdu. Dudley viewed the local Chengdu YWCA as only superficially doing well, and its situation would be further compromised if the national office moved to Chongqing[74] – which it did shortly after Dudley wrote her letter, believing it needed to be where all other national organizations were headquartered.[75]

After the United States dropped atomic bombs on Hiroshima on August 6 and Nagasaki on August 9, a shocked Japanese nation heard their emperor announce Japan's surrender on August 15. On September 2, the Japanese leadership signed the articles of surrender on the *USS Missouri*. As fall edged toward winter, Cai Kui noted that "the war atmosphere still exists everywhere even though the international war is over."[76] Postwar life in all countries that had been battlefields with massive physical destruction and huge loss of civilian lives was difficult. But in China, rife with political strife before the war, the re-emergence of political polarization in the months following Japan's surrender augured a troubled future. Cai Kui wrote Woodsmall from Chongqing on November 10, while preparing to leave for a visit to Shanghai: "The common people in China strongly protest against both political parties involved in the present conflict but how much can the public opinion accomplish still remain to be seen. For a social worker like myself, I feel even this process of protesting gives me the hope of a better future."[77] If Cai had been able to see into the future, that feeling of hope would have faded quickly.

INTO THE BREACH, 1946–47

The year 1946 dawned on a relatively hopeful note, as by late February General George C. Marshall had managed to get thirty-eight delegates representing the GMD, CCP, and several small political groups to agree to the framework for a new government. The spirit of cooperation dissipated, however, when the GMD's central executive committee gutted the framework of any pretence of shared governance. As if that were not enough to jeopardize a united government, fighting between GMD and CCP forces broke out, and the GMD continued its campaigns against leftists. It assassinated poet Wen Yiduo in Kunming on July 15, 1946. Continued vocal attacks on the United States by radicals infuriated by the US military presence in China further eroded the possibility of compromise. Despite his efforts to bring all parties back to the negotiating table (accompanied by President Harry Truman's threats to withdraw US aid if Chiang Kai-shek was recalcitrant), Marshall's mission ended in failure, and he left China at the beginning of 1947.[78]

It was in that environment that American YWCA secretary Esther Morrison arrived in Shanghai in June 1946 to rehabilitate national programs aimed at middle school girls. The lapse of work with middle school

and college students had made recruitment of new secretaries extremely difficult. Morrison described this period as one of "adjustment and
struggle, of upheaval, confusion and uncertainty."[79] Her words were not
hyperbole.

What Morrison felt was shared by her national office colleagues who
had experienced seven and a half years of war and dislocation and now
wanted to focus on reviving the YWCA movement in China. Many
of the challenges they faced were caused by an inept, corrupt government. Hyperinflation depleted association finances. Increased censorship
forced YWCA leadership to resume the wartime practice of using code
names in their foreign correspondence. Secret police activities hit home
when a teacher at one of the industrial night schools was kidnapped and
tortured.[80]

Other challenges were more internal. The departure of Lily Haass
in 1945 left a power vacuum: not only was she the most experienced
YWCA secretary and a mentor to Chinese leadership, but there was no
one trained to replace her. There was also lingering concern about recon-
ciliation and the unity of the China movement as those who had survived
under Japanese occupation must now face their YWCA sisters returning
from exile in the interior. China was not alone in facing the question of
unity. When the World YWCA's enlarged executive committee met in
May 1946, those from countries brutally occupied by Germany, such as
the Netherlands, initially found it difficult to think of forgiveness.[81]

The Chinese YWCA's enlarged executive committee met in the summer of 1946. Based on decisions taken at that meeting, Cai Kui and
the national executive staff developed a rehabilitation budget for 1947
through 1949.[82] Why a three-year budget and why 1949 is curious given
that the enlarged executive committee had agreed to schedule a national
convention for 1948. The format of the document suggests that, in the
new democratic fashion, staff had a voice in setting priorities and may
also have developed their own departmental budgets. The eighteen-page
report certainly demonstrated the determination of YWCA women to
continue their work, in order to serve their God, their country, and the
women of China.

There was some overlap with Cai's 1944 plan. A significant addition
was a program for "spiritual rehabilitation" to revitalize the religious emphasis of the association: "In these immediate postwar years of rehabilitation, the combined emphasis of Christianity and Democracy is one of
the most fundamental contributions the YWCA is called upon to make
to its membership and to the country."

The linking of these two – Christianity and democracy – was a legacy of the war years. The Chinese YWCA concept of democracy harked back to Ding Shujing's emphasis on "the power of the group" in the 1920s and her insistence that YWCA women were not above the women they served. Deng Yuzhi and other progressive secretaries had broken down the social barriers to YWCA membership in the 1930s. During the war years, the association leadership stressed consensus decision-making at all levels. Now, Christianity and democracy would be central to the association's identity as a citizen of China.

A major part of the budget was for reopening city associations that had closed during the war. Buildings in eight cities had been destroyed, damaged, or stripped of equipment by Japanese troops. The city department budget of USD$652,000 for 1947 was over three times larger than the next largest budget item. Some of the expense reflected the dire state of those associations. Allocation for rebuilding, repairing, and replacing equipment was USD$230,500 for 1947 and nearly USD$60,000 more for 1948 and 1949.

Considerable sums were budgeted for personnel and maintenance, costs usually borne by local associations. The national office recognized it would be years before city associations would again become self-sustaining. The amount of USD$100,000 was set aside for "strengthening" key associations in Beijing, Shanghai, Nanjing, Hangzhou, Hong Kong, Guangzhou, Xian, Chongqing, Chengdu, and Kunming.

The next largest budget item, USD$200,000, was for the industrial and mass education department, which, in addition to industrial and mass education work, included industrial cooperatives. The budget, estimated at 12.6 percent of the total, was justified because of the association's expansion into the fields of mass education and industrial cooperatives. Mass education included classes and clubs for women and girls in handicraft industries and those peddling food and other items of daily necessity in the big cities with war-swollen populations in the interior. Industrial cooperatives were livelihood programs in both cities and rural areas that also included educational work. The enlarged national committee considered this work as a component of its efforts to educate "intelligent citizens" to practise democracy, and of critical importance to women and girls in the lowest economic strata.

The largest section of the budget report in number of pages concerned training of current staff and recruiting and training of new Chinese secretaries. The latter was critical for the continued development of Chinese leadership, and was to include projects to recruit and train additional personnel, to hold brief training conferences, to expand opportunities for the reorientation and "refreshment" of experienced, tested, and carefully selected staff, and to conserve current staff. The work would be guided initially by Talitha Gerlach, who returned to China in July 1946 to temporarily assume the responsibility for the national city department.[83]

Student and girls' work suffered during the eight years of war and, as a result, China's young women knew little about the association and its work. While both were critical areas for the future of the YWCA movement in China, the fact that the student department budget was thrice that of the girls' work department suggested the former's priority. This was logical: college-age women would be available for employment in a few short years. Thus, student work doubled as recruitment. A third of the USD$100,000 student department's three-year budget was targeted at student centres in government universities. This would cement the effort to develop student-initiated and student-led YWCAs and, in turn, foster Christian fellowship. There was another side as well. According to the report, universities provided few facilities for students to gather. During the war, the YWCA had set up student centres at universities in the interior, and its efforts had been appreciated by school authorities. Here was an opportunity to transfer work done at campuses-in-exile back to the campuses that were also in the process of rebuilding. The YWCA student centres could thus be viewed as part of that process. Money was also allocated for building up student centres in private and Christian universities.

Whether optimism or pragmatism was their guiding principle, it seems clear that these women were focused on the future. Developing such a plan was most likely also a way to reconcile women from occupied and free China, to integrate newer secretaries into the unique bureaucratic world of the YWCA, and to restore some sense of normalcy. This last point would be increasingly difficult as the civil war intensified and as those who had just survived the divisions of war found themselves once again defining their lives by which forces controlled the area where an association was located.

Secretaries got right to work, even those newly arrived like Esther Morrison. Morrison's task was to rehabilitate national girls' work. The work had lapsed during the war, and she was essentially starting from scratch. She even had to recruit and train a national girls' work committee from among the few volunteers. Then, she had to recruit and train girls' work secretaries for city associations as they reopened and, in most cases, this involved on-the-job training. She even had to produce her own program materials. At the same time, she was doing some on-the-job training herself: learning the language and trying to avoid "cultural imperialism" by adapting "western ideas to the Chinese scene." The importance of adapting to local needs must have been impressed on her at some point after she arrived. Morrison took the concept of "local" and truly made it local. She did not try to impose a national approach on city associations but trained local girls' work secretaries to respond to the needs of girls in their city association. In very democratic fashion, ideas came from the girls themselves; the successful ideas were written up at the national office, and then shared with other city associations. Morrison's report gives every impression of an exceptionally thoughtful and organized secretary. Girls' work, however, would not extend into 1949, as it would be absorbed by the Maoist state. Morrison would be an expert without a job after 1949. She would be the first of the remaining secretaries to leave China after the revolution.[84]

Deng Yuzhi was also hard at work. While there are few documents that record her activities once she returned to China after completing her master's degree at New York University, her report at the February 1947 setting-up conference indicated her complete grasp of her department's current situation. Setting-up conferences literally set up the agenda for the following year and are usually held late in the fall. It is not clear why this one, which was clearly setting up the work for 1947, was held after the start of the year.

Industrial work had come to a standstill as the Japanese-occupied industrial cities and those in free China suffered bombardment. Industrial night schools remained open in Shanghai's International Settlement until the Japanese took over that enclave in 1941. At the beginning of the war, the national industrial department then took on mass education work and was tasked with overseeing industrial cooperatives. Deng Yuzhi's report at the setting-up conference dealt with the national office's revival of industrial work and the continuation of its two wartime fields. The report demonstrated her thorough knowledge of the current state of these fields and clear vision for how they should be developed in the near – and distant – future.

For industrial work, Deng noted that the previous emphases had been on leadership training and "quality over quantity." She was convinced that this approach should be maintained. Developing an educated, articulate leadership, however small, for a women's labour movement remained the goal. Service work, mainly welfare work, which many factory owners would rather have seen prioritized, would be secondary. For this reason, YWCA work would be carried out independently "on the outside" rather than inside factories, to avoid giving the appearance of the YWCA's working under the authority of management instead of simply in cooperation with them. Deng developed a chart that listed eight major cities, the type of work they focused on (industrial or mass education), their needs, and how the national office could meet those needs. All cities needed visits from the national staff, six needed money, and four needed personnel.[85]

WORLD YWCA COUNCIL MEETING, OCTOBER 1947

During the war years, or "emergency period," as the World YWCA often referred to it, the World headquarters were relocated to Washington, DC. Once headquartered outside of Europe, the association became more aware of its international standing. The war also ended the former rivalry between the United States and Great Britain, the two dominant and wealthiest members of the World YWCA, as these countries were now war allies. It was partially due to the World YWCA executive committee's desire to make their national constituents equally aware of their membership in a truly international organization, and partially due to Ruth Woodsmall's vision for the future, that the decision was made to hold the first postwar World YWCA Council meeting in China in 1947.[86] In particular, it was the hope of World general secretary Ruth Woodsmall that the meeting would provide an opportunity for Chinese and Japanese women "whose nations had been divided by war to meet again, to reaffirm the fellowship between them and to face together the problems created for the whole movement by the tragic events of the past years."[87]

That the World YWCA Council meeting in China went ahead despite the civil war is testimony to the tenacity of women. Or it could simply reflect the fact that these women, many of whom had lived through the tumult of war, saw few hurdles as insurmountable. One of the few concessions made to the current civil war was the choice of Hangzhou over Beijing as the meeting's location because of military activity in the north.[88] Although the World meeting did not begin until October 15, Ruth Woodsmall and two other World staff arrived in Shanghai in July, and executive committee members American Elizabeth Palmer and Finnish Sylvi Visapää arrived in August.[89] The latter two women would become intimately involved with the Chinese YWCA.

Palmer would be named secretary for Southeast and East Asia during the meeting, a position she held until she was named World YWCA general secretary in 1957. Visapää became very popular among the Chinese and was welcomed back in 1957 as a member of a two-person World delegation, the first to visit China since the Hangzhou meeting.

YWCA delegates from thirty nations attended the meeting. Not among them were delegates from the Japanese YWCA. They had been denied exit visas by three of the eleven members of the Allied Powers' Far Eastern Commission, one of which was China. Presumably, another was the Philippines. Their reason was that Japan had not yet signed a peace treaty. There had been strong resistance from the Chinese YWCA as well.[90] While that thwarted Woodsmall's plan to reconcile the Chinese and Japanese associations, the World YWCA planned to send a fourteen-member delegation to Japan after the World Council meeting. Among the women approved by the Supreme Commander for the Allied Powers (SCAP) was Cai Kui. Due to opposition from her own YWCA colleagues in China, however, Cai did not join the delegation.[91]

The keynote speaker was Dr. Tu Yuqing (Du Yuqing) of St. John's University.[92] Song Meiling also spoke. Their words became strangely prophetic, although certainly in Song's case not as she had foreseen. Dr. Tu said they were living in a time of revolution and "spiritual anarchy." The women of the YWCAs faced issues of unprecedented scale and complexity. "Therefore, we must take every means possible to strengthen our spiritual power ... in order to show our faith in action." Song Meiling recalled the YWCA-led child labour campaign in which she had participated in the early 1920s as an example of "the social effectiveness of the YWCA in action," without noting that the campaign had ended in failure. She went on to challenge the YWCAs to lead the pursuit of peace: "In this post-war era the YWCA, and all kindred organizations who are fighting for moral values in a cynical war-mutilated world, have a hard fight before them ... They must be sustained by the fires of inner faith and purpose."[93]

Within a few short years, the Chinese association would emerge from its "war-mutilated" world and, for the most part, cast away its cynicism and embrace a new set of moral values by committing itself to Mao's China. And it would embrace the cause of peace, but peace as seen through the prism of a polarized world in which the struggle for peace would be waged against the enemy of peace: imperialistic America.

The 1947 World Council meeting was productive. It issued eight official statements. One in particular resonated with its Chinese audience.

It had to do with the importance of involvement in the political life of
a nation:

> Almost every problem relating to the daily life and welfare of the com-
> munity is a matter of political decision. Hence it follows that it is a part
> of the vocation of the Christian to accept responsibility in political life.
> The Association needs to have its leadership and membership accurately
> informed on current political issues. All political systems must be studied
> in the light of Christian principles. Those principles must be the basis of
> our decisions and actions both as Christian individuals and as a Christian
> movement.[94]

Just two years after the World YWCA Council met in Hangzhou, Mao
Zedong announced the creation of the People's Republic of China. Deng
Yuzhi and like-minded YWCA women accepted their responsibility to be
involved in the political life of China as part of their Christian vocation.

Ruth Woodsmall retired after the Hangzhou meeting. She had envisioned a World YWCA that truly centred the worldwide YWCA
movement rather than just existing as a node in a network of national
associations, some of which had many times the World's budget and resources. Some credit a change in leadership in the Foreign Division of
the YWCA of the USA from Sarah Lyon to Margaret Forsyth for the
fruition of Woodsmall's vision. Forsyth used her budget to support the
World office rather than following the former "scheme of relationships"
and supporting American YWCA secretaries in China.[95]

Unknown to some, Cai Kui also tried to retire after the World YWCA
Council meeting but was talked out of it; it is not clear by whom. It may
have been her Chinese colleagues as they may have wanted her continued
leadership to plan for the fourth national convention scheduled for 1948.
It was possible the change in leadership in the World and US associations made it prudent for China to wait to install new leadership in its
organization.

Once the Hangzhou meeting was over and the delegates had departed,
the national office returned to work. Financial matters, staff shortages,
and overwork dominated correspondence between Chinese secretaries
and their overseas colleagues. In September 1948, increasing government
surveillance led Cai Kui to request the Foreign Division of the YWCA of
the USA to address future letters to "Hilda Smith," her code name during the war with Japan.[96] Over the years, the YWCA national office had
largely escaped suspicion, but as the momentum of the civil war shifted

toward the communists, no one was safe. In the following months, communist victories in Manchuria heralded the imminent fall of the north. Still, Cai expressed quiet but firm faith that no matter what life was like under a new regime, women would find a way to serve. "There is a willingness to modify, to change and adjust – and willingness is the important thing!"[97]

This chapter has examined how the war with Japan transformed the Chinese YWCA from an organization with hierarchal decision-making into a more consensus-driven, democratic organization whose leadership often sought input from rank-and-file staff. In many ways, the disruptions caused by the war forced that transformation, and some of the previous patterns of decision-making, such as the power invested in the executive committee, would not only return after the war but continue into the Maoist era. Still, the democratization of the association was seen in the extensive plans drawn up after the war that were the handiwork of many secretaries, including some Western secretaries new to China but experienced in their fields. This chapter has also emphasized the wedding of Christian service to national salvation and the ideal of building a new China as a Christian duty. That trend would continue as the YWCA crossed the 1949 divide.

5

Embracing the Maoist State,
1949–50

For the first time in the history of the YWCA a gathering of national importance was led entirely by Chinese. The time has now come when the Chinese must assume complete responsibility.
                    – Report, Enlarged Executive Committee, March 1950

American secretary Esther Morrison described her sojourn in China from 1946 to 1950 as a time of "adjustment and struggle, of upheaval, confusion and uncertainty." When Shanghai fell to the communists, there was relief. Morrison observed that "the general attitude of the people seemed to be either 'the first impression is good and we are willing to be shown more,' or 'this is a time of great hope for building up our country and we want to do our part.'"[1] The one thing that Morrison did not observe was indifference.

This chapter covers the completion of the long process of the Sinification of the YWCA as Chinese women committed their organization and themselves to Mao Zedong's state-building project. It examines the mood, motivations, and actions of YWCA women to reveal how both Chinese and the few remaining Western secretaries came to grips with regime change. It seeks to understand and explain the decisions of senior staff and tease out what accommodations they made to comply with the new political reality. As a Christian organization, the YWCA assumed a leadership role, partnering with its male counterpart, the YMCA, to preserve a place for a liberal, conforming Christian community in the avowedly atheist state. This discussion is particularly important as the role of the YWCA is left out of, or seriously marginalized in, histories of Christianity in the formative years of the People's Republic of China (PRC).

CROSSING THE 1949 DIVIDE

The year 1949 is a watershed year in China's history, a historical marker that divides the Nationalist from the communist era. Over the past decade and a half, scholarship has examined similarities between the two eras at the state and local level, and argued that the years from 1949 to 1953, the period of Mao's New Democracy, were a period of transition and gradual if meaningful and sometimes violent change before the full-out thrust to create a socialist state began with Mao's first five-year plan.[2] While the argument is persuasive, in terms of YWCA history it makes more sense to divide the association's first decade under communism between the two years in which the association committed itself to following the new regime and the subsequent years, in which it made both painful and pragmatic adjustments to life under communism.

On January 22, national general secretary Cai Kui wrote World YWCA general secretary Helen Roberts a letter that used the rhetorical "we" throughout. She described the situation in China as "uncertain," confessing that "first and most important" the country simply wanted peace. She hoped an agreement was near. She could not have known that Chiang Kai-shek had resigned the presidency the day before, opening the possibility for the new president, Li Zongren, to negotiate with the CCP. Li accepted Mao's eight terms of surrender as the basis for peace talks and withdrew the Nationalist army from Beijing. Cai realistically acknowledged that the communists would be in the dominant position in any future government. For that reason, the national office monitored the broadcasts from the "other side" and studied CCP literature in secret to formulate a plan for the future.[3]

Despite these efforts to fathom the "other side," few anticipated the disjuncture that would develop between past practices and the future. As Cai described her vision of the future, her ideas were thus a mix of realism, optimism, and naïveté. Her words conveyed such a strong conviction that the YWCA would move forward that she would have been surprised to know that at year's end she would resign.

Cai revealed her concerns for the YWCA movement in China in what she described as a "godless" future. She emphasized the Christian nature of the YWCA movement: the "C" must remain in the association's name and be emphasized in its work. Cai's remark may have been a reference to the tendency in the late 1920s and early 1930s to drop the word "Christian" in the association's Chinese name, referring to it only as the "Young Women's Association" to broaden its appeal.[4] The acute question for Cai was what would become of that Christian identity under an avowedly atheistic and anti-religious regime. She accepted that there would be modifications in how the association expressed its identity and approached its work, but in her mind, the association's Christian identity was the "only justification for its existence."[5]

Cai also stressed that the association would work with any future government from a neutral position – "as we have in the past" – cooperating but neither violating its principles nor surrendering its independence. She admitted that the YWCA had always been influenced by the political life of its community, but in a crisis that polarized the nation, neutrality was the only course. Cai appeared to be unaware or refused to see that in the brave new world they were about to enter, there would be no such thing as political neutrality.[6]

The north was "liberated" shortly after Cai wrote her January 22 letter, and Li Zongren attempted to negotiate the communists' terms of surrender. Mao's agreed-upon peace talks were scheduled to begin on April 1, giving him time to prepare to invade the south. Several high-level meetings were convened to discuss the possibility of the United States entering the war if that happened. Stalin had cautioned Mao not to cross the Yangtze River, because of that possibility. Up to that point, Mao had sought to balance American and Soviet influences in order to remain independent. President Truman's somewhat ambiguous foreign policy toward China – on the one hand, stating he would not intervene in China's civil war; on the other, continuing to send aid to the Nationalists – finally led to Mao's decision to "lean to the left" toward the Soviets. Nonetheless, he disagreed with Stalin. The promised peace talks began as scheduled, but new terms were added, including the elimination of the Nationalists from a coalition government. Li was given an ultimatum to accept but he refused. The communists crossed the Yangtze River on April 19 and took Nanjing five days later.[7]

Even with such grave developments, very mundane concerns occupied the minds of women at the national office. Were the Nationalists defending Shanghai going to confiscate their station wagon? The government had already taken thousands of Jeeps and trucks to transport troops and supplies, but it needed cars for the officers.[8] The fate of the station wagon was never revealed. Word that the communists were advancing brought a joint meeting of the national and Shanghai city association staffs to an abrupt end on the afternoon of May 24. That night, those living in the national headquarters building heard cannon fire and saw fires across the Huangpu River in Pudong. Fighting reached the street behind the national building, and bullets shattered several windows. Julia Cheng observed that everyone had thought the YWCA building on Yuan Ming Yuan Road would be a safe place. Not so. The battle had arrived right at their doorstep.[9]

The national staff had been preparing for life under a new regime by studying what British secretary Margaret Garvie referred to as "new modes of thought." Garvie noted that if it had been known how seriously they took their weekly study sessions, they would have been branded as "revolutionaries."[10] In the weeks immediately following the takeover of Shanghai, however, there was no consensus on their future in yet another "New China." Some saw the regime change as the solution to all of China's problems; others believed it was just another adjustment in their lives. They would compromise where they could and tolerate the rest. Between those who were optimistic and those who were simply resigned were a range of women with other perspectives.[11]

No complete or even partial staff or committee lists exist for either the war or postwar years or the first years of the People's Republic, so there is no way to determine who among lay or professional YWCA women stayed and who left, let alone what motivated their decisions. From the names that appear in official documents, it is clear that many experienced Chinese staff remained, as they can be traced back to staff lists compiled in the 1930s. The only national committee member who appears in post-1949 documents was national committee chair Wang Guoxiu.

The communists liberated Changsha, capital of Hunan Province in central China, in August. Guangzhou fell in October, securing the south. Chongqing in the southwest and Xiamen on Fujian's east coast were both liberated in November. Amid those final thrusts, and with victory assured, Mao Zedong formally declared the founding of the People's Republic of China on October 1. Among the dignitaries in the viewing stand for that event was Deng Yuzhi.

Deng believed that the communists provided the most workable solutions to China's problems. Her close ally in this belief was YMCA secretary Wu Yaozong. Wu's 1948 article "The Present-Day Tragedy of

Christianity," a scathing critique of the foreign mission establishment's refusal to acknowledge the exploitive nature of capitalism, had identified him as a leader among left-leaning Christians.[12] Both Deng and Wu had been invited to a meeting organized by the communist leadership in Beijing in January 1949. The purpose of the meeting and the identities of the other participants remain unknown. This was the first indication that ranking CCP officials recognized Deng Yuzhi as a leader among Christians and a potential ally of their cause.

Deng also attended the inaugural meeting of the All-China Democratic Women's Federation (ACDWF) on April 3, 1949.[13] The ACDWF was originally "a united front strategy to gain support from different women's organizations."[14] Another Christian women's organization whose support was sought was the Chinese Women's Christian Temperance Union, led by Liu-Wang Liming.[15] Deng's presence was thus most likely due to her connection to the YWCA. The ACDWF's first president, Cai Chang, had been a student at Zhounan Girls' Middle School in Changsha at the same time as Deng, so there is a possibility they knew each other. Also, Deng was not the sole representative of the association, as YWCA twenty-year veteran secretary Gao Renying also attended.

It was not automatically assumed that the YWCA would join the ACDWF. In one of her earliest efforts to mediate the association's relationships with the new political reality, Deng developed a set of questions to guide deliberations. As it turned out, joining became a moot point as city associations in liberated areas took the matter into their own hands and began joining the city branches of the federation, leading the national office to affiliate with the national Women's Federation in October.[16]

Another and even more serious effort to mediate the new relationship took the form of an article Deng published in August in the *YWCA Magazine,* "The Responsibility of the YWCA in the Reconstruction of China in the New Democracy." At that time, and in the months to come, the communist leadership continued its wartime policy of creating a "populist cross-class coalition" of peasant workers and those "bourgeois" who had deserted Chiang Kai-shek or who were willing to support Mao.[17] This was the basis for the first stage of the political revolution after the civil war, described as the "bourgeois-democratic revolution."[18] The revolution was realized through the Chinese People's Political Consultative Conferences: the preparatory one that began on June 11 in Beijing and the full conference in September. Deng attended both as a delegate with the religious group.

Deng intended her article to educate YWCA women. She noted that the YWCA was the creation of bourgeois capitalistic society. It had entered China as part of the "imperialist invasion," but it had not been an instrument of imperialism or capitalism, because the association became progressive. Now, it could use its "progressive power" to meet the needs of the New Democracy. The New Democracy was an entirely new society, with workers and peasants at its base. It would unite all classes with one mind to "suppress feudalism, the exploitation of capitalism, to destroy imperialism" and wipe out the remnants of the GMD. Women and the women's movement had a responsibility to help complete the revolution and build a new country.[19]

Although part of a Christian society, Deng continued, the association functioned differently from a church. It nourished Christian character, "the spirit of public good with no private selfishness and served all classes of women." Facing a new age, "we want to continuously show a spirit progressive with the times, use the experience and the struggle of the time; we want to thoroughly understand the new conditions, thoroughly scrutinize and change ourselves, use new methods of work and accept the responsibilities which the new age lays upon us in order to express our message."[20]

After the publication of this article, there was no doubt among those in the YWCA or larger Christian community as to where Deng stood regarding the revolution. Within the walls of the national office, however, uneasiness prevailed. In a letter written that same month to former China national secretary Talitha Gerlach, now at the YWCA of the USA national office in New York City, Chinese secretary Jean Kao described the situation as "the turning of upside down" and emphasized the adjustments that everyone was having to make. She anticipated a long period of hardship and lower living standards until China overcame its economic problems. Kao's wording suggested that she, at least, was braced for the future. However, in answering Gerlach's inquiries about YWCA jobs for Chinese students returning from studies in the United States, Kao expressed uncertainty that those returning from several years of study abroad would be able to adjust. And YWCA jobs would be difficult to find: Kao noted that with the loss of traditional service work with factory women, students, girls, and business and professional women, all of whom now had their own mass organizations, there would be fewer jobs overall.[21]

On September 21, 1949, the Chinese People's Political Consultative Conference convened. It produced the Common Program, which served as China's interim constitution for the next four years. On October 1, Deng Yuzhi stood on the viewing platform in Tiananmen Square to witness Mao Zedong's proclamation of the People's Republic of China. She had been a member of the religious delegation to the consultative conference along with Wu Yaozong, theologian Zhao Zichen, scholar Zhang Xueyan, and musician and YMCA leader Liu Liangmo. In her article in *Christian Weekly* magazine, Deng noted that all five accepted the New Democracy and wished to work with its political leadership. They believed that the social revolution was an important part of the gospel of Jesus, and that their Christian beliefs mostly aligned with those of the CCP. Christians and communists were headed in the exact same direction. She was adamant that the five Christian representatives did not and could not represent Christians whose beliefs differed from those of the official Christian representatives.[22] It is interesting, given the prominence of the other delegates, that Deng was chosen to deliver this message to the Christian community. It is also important because histories of Christianity in China, especially during this period, largely overlook her leadership role in negotiating a place for Chinese Christians in the evolving communist state.

Just days after Mao's proclamation, Cai Kui wrote a personal letter to World YWCA general secretary Helen Roberts, confessing that she felt both unqualified and inarticulate to interpret the situation in China, as her thoughts were still very immature. Despite her protestation, she was quite articulate. She referred to the "New Revolution," clearly recognizing that it was different from all the other revolutions she had experienced in her lifetime. She described it as fundamental, not just political, and acknowledged that although "in any revolution maladjustments are unavoidable and some groups or individuals suffer," in this revolution it would be the formerly privileged who would "pay the price." YWCA women for the most part wanted to cooperate because they had sympathy for the long-range plans of the new regime. This early in the revolution, Cai saw positive results: the willingness to sacrifice for the betterment of others, the desire of the majority to meet problems head-on rather than passively evading them, and a "missionary spirit" of willingness to contribute to society.[23]

Cai expressed cautious optimism about the prospects for the YWCA movement in China. She was convinced that the association should continue with its work but proceed in a humbler manner, forgoing "flashy" programs that attracted those with superficial interest in the YWCA's Christian work: "We can lose those who have come into the YWCA circles without much conviction, but those who stay on will be the real strength and pillars of our movement." Cai believed that the association's future work should focus on the cultivation of small groups resembling the fellowship of Jesus's disciples. She acknowledged, however, that the large groups they formerly worked with, such as students and factory women, now had their own mass organizations. Cai believed there might still be a place for Christian welfare work as an expression of Christian truth, not as an end in itself.[24] It was unlikely that the association would continue welfare programs in the future, since at least private charity organizations in Shanghai were slowly being subsumed by the CCP.[25]

Since January 1949, the Christian nature of the YWCA work had been very much on Cai's mind, but so had her own religiosity. In September, she confided to a Quaker missionary that although she believed Christianity had deep roots in China, she had concluded that in the Chinese YWCA, Christianity was not "vivid or vital." Among her colleagues at the national office, she considered only four to be "dependable Christians." The rest were Christian in name only. She wondered what would keep the YWCA, with no spiritual foundation, from disappearing.[26] Given the broad tolerance Quakers had for the religiosity of others, it is difficult to know what Cai might have meant by "dependable Christians," or whether she was referring only to staff or to staff and lay volunteers. Four was certainly not many, and it begs the question of whether or not Deng Yuzhi was one of them. Cai never revealed the names of those four women, however.

The politicization of life, the creation of mass organizations, the emphasis on study groups, and the introduction of new vocabulary that compelled new modes of thinking were overwhelming for both Chinese and Western YWCA women, from those in the national office in Shanghai to those in city associations across China. Early in 1950, Margaret Brennecke, an experienced American secretary who had returned from furlough the previous August, wrote that she increasingly feared "the basic values of life in which we believe, thinking of people as persons and not as units in a class or category, each with personal value of each for the other, and having basic freedom to think for themselves and to make their own decisions – are in danger of being swept away."[27]

Cai Kui had come to that conclusion several months earlier. Speaking with her Quaker missionary friend early in the fall of 1949, she had mentioned her own "spiritual awakening" and the need for a "Church life."[28] Seeking relief and a new spiritual home, she resigned as national general secretary. On December 17, she sent a carefully worded letter to Helen Roberts at the World YWCA, simply stating that in this new period, the association needed new leadership. The national committee would announce her successor soon.[29] Cai took advantage of her expiring contract to again submit her resignation, as she had done two years earlier. This time, the national committee accepted it.[30] Her successor, to no one's surprise, was Deng Yuzhi.

Deng was more than just the logical choice. Her seniority, faith, and political acumen enabled her to bridge differences. But that bridge was a narrow one, as there was, in her mind, a single way forward. Local reaction to Deng's appointment was not recorded. Perhaps it did not need to be. Former China secretaries Florence Pierce and Leila Anderson, now working at the YWCA of the USA headquarters in New York City, thought it entirely the wrong choice, but neither Pierce nor Anderson identified whom they believed would have provided better leadership.[31]

EMBRACING SOCIAL REVOLUTION

The Enlarged National Executive Committee Meeting

As 1950 dawned, the most immediate problems for the New Democracy were stabilization and consolidation. The most pressing concern for the Chinese YWCA was its place in the New Democracy. The association's new leadership believed in Mao's state-building project and saw their participation in it as part of their Christian mission. If 1949 was a watershed year for China, 1950 would be one for the Chinese YWCA.

Despite the formal inauguration of the People's Republic the previous year, pockets of resistance remained, and incidents of sabotage were frequent. A tenacious GMD continued to bombard and blockade the coast. For the new regime, centralizing control in a large country accustomed historically to decentralized rule was as challenging as claiming the loyalty of a large, diverse, and yet-to-be-politicized people. Securing the cities was critical as the locus of the revolution had been rural, not urban. Both were essential to stabilizing an economy plagued by hyperinflation and underproduction of commodities. The cities were full of "middle elements" such as the YWCA, whose staff and volunteers were educated professionals or wives of educated professional men, and their sympathies were suspect.[32] Party rhetoric during the first year of state building emphasized inclusion and unity.[33] How the Chinese YWCA experienced the New Democracy during the first half of 1950 needs to be read against that backdrop.

Chinese YWCA women acted quickly to secure a place for their Christian organization in the new and evolving communist society. From March 1 to 10, the enlarged executive committee met for the first time since 1946. "Enlarged" refers to the fact that the national committee was composed of both members who resided in Shanghai and constituted the executive committee of the national committee, and nonresident members representing city associations across China. When the entire committee met as a whole, it was referred to as an "enlarged national executive committee."

More than forty women attended the meeting, including all national committee members, two representatives from each city association, and a few representatives from student and rural branches. The theme "Study, Unite, and Construct" was not just a theme but described how the delegates went about examining issues from all angles to produce a "united pattern" of thought that they used to construct new plans for the association.[34] This approach modelled the consensus-building techniques that were at the heart of the communist "democratic" process, but also reflected the YWCA's wartime practices and were familiar to many of the attendees.

In her opening address, national committee chair Wang Guoxiu noted that the YWCA was both a Christian and a women's association. For fifty years, it had worked for the emancipation of women in China without regard for class or educational level. However, for one hundred years China had been oppressed by imperialism and feudalism, and thus all "people's organizations" had been limited in their "freedom of expression" and "handicapped in their work." They were now in a new era and had gathered to discuss how they could continue their work and contribute to the building of a new society.[35] National general secretary Deng Yuzhi emphasized that in the new era, "life has a political significance in every respect." In the past, it had not been possible for the YWCA to take a political stance, but under the People's Republic, the association was finally able to express its political conviction through its programs. She emphasized that the association had a new opportunity to express love, service, and sacrifice as taught by Jesus.[36]

During the ten-day meeting, delegates reviewed almost every aspect of the association's policies, administrative practices, and programs in the context of the new China. There was a certain urgency to their work because, although it had been seventeen years since the third national convention, changes could not wait for a fourth convention. The Chinese leadership acknowledged that Western secretaries – especially Americans – had worked hard to create an indigenous leadership, and that had been part of the "progressive tendency" in the YWCA movement. Those efforts were now complete, and the Chinese were taking full responsibility.[37]

Many administrative changes were needed. Relationships between secretaries and lay volunteers, and between secretaries and clerical staff, had to become closer in the spirit of the New Democracy. The delegates emphasized cooperation with other Christian organizations in "service to the people." In matters of religious thinking, they reiterated that the association was a Christian organization but that the fundamentals of Christianity were "the Truth express[sed] by Jesus himself, the Fatherhood of God and the Brotherhood of Man." The women who gathered in Shanghai further pointed out that they were an international organization but accepted the "Principles of Foreign Policy" in the Common Program, policies that included safeguarding Chinese sovereignty, peaceful cooperation with peoples of all countries, and opposition to the imperialistic policy of aggression and war.[38] The report reiterated that the association was a member of the World YWCA: "It has in the past, at present and also will continue to have in the future, close international relationships."[39]

Statements and resolutions regarding personnel clearly indicated the extent to which the YWCA was being politicized. The "philosophy of serving the people" and a "clear political standpoint" were added to the list of qualifications for job candidates. To extend democratic principles, a new personnel committee would include the national committee chair, the national general secretary, and representatives from the national committee and secretarial staff.[40] The report also revealed two new policies regarding foreign staff. The first removed Western staff and volunteers from administrative positions so that "indigenous" personnel could assume those responsibilities. Although not stated as policy, the report noted that to avoid any misunderstanding at a time when China was combatting imperialism, Western staff would not contact the membership or be involved in any group work. The second new policy stated that obstructing the association's political position concerning international relations would now be grounds for immediate dismissal.[41] This was a specific reference to Mao's policy of "leaning to the left" (toward the Soviet Union and Stalin) and castigating the United States as the world's most aggressive nation and enemy of peaceful coexistence.

The delegates officially embraced the communist revolution and committed themselves to Mao's state-building project in an "open letter" to the membership that clearly expressed a "political stand," which formerly was "impossible" to do.[42] It concluded with the following statement:

> Dear fellow members! This is the century of the people. There is only one way before us. Let us live in the spirit of Jesus Christ. Let us uphold our principle to stand firm as the people of the New China. Let us follow the leadership of Chairman Mao and the People's Government; work for the realization of the *Common Program;* and build up the new democratic China. Let us go forward![43]

The national office published the open letter in the March 25 issue of *Christian Weekly*. Although the World office did not receive the official report from the meeting until mid-August, national secretary Esther Morrison sent it a translation of the open letter with her final communiqué as she left China.[44]

In mid-March, the PRC Central Committee issued a directive that initiated the Campaign to Suppress Counterrevolutionaries, the first of several mass campaigns that would imprison and kill thousands. It stemmed from the frustrations of rural party cadres sent to "revolutionize" urban society. Initially, the campaign offered leniency to those who cooperated, which further frustrated seasoned party cadres. In May, the PRC leadership reconsidered the policy of leniency, and in late July issued a directive calling for a hardening of the campaign. Still, the violent phase of the Campaign to Suppress Counterrevolutionaries came only when Mao endorsed it in early October.[45] There are no YWCA documents that indicate that YWCA women were accused of counterrevolutionary activities. There are many silences in this period of the history of the Chinese YWCA.

Severing Ties with Foreign Staff

Shortly after the March enlarged executive committee meeting, the Chinese YWCA leadership decided that Western staff could work only at the national office. Then, they decided not to invite Margaret Brennecke, who was in Guangzhou, and Ruth West, who was in Chengdu, to come to Shanghai, because of the travel restrictions on foreigners and because the only role for foreign secretaries was to "interpret the New China to our sister associations abroad" and do some technical work for which they were more qualified than local staff. In other words, there was no work for Brennecke and West to do.[46] By midsummer, the only foreign secretary left was Briton Margaret Garvie. She left the following May.

During tumultuous times and tamer ones, Western women had been
colleagues and friends. That era was over, however. Many younger Chinese
secretaries had never developed relationships with foreign women, as few
of the latter had remained during the war or afterward. Moreover, many
of those younger women possibly felt animosity toward Americans because of US support for the Nationalists during the civil war, and toward
the remaining missionaries, who were entrenched in their conservative
interpretations of Christianity and suspicious if not hostile to the new
government. Still, the decision that Western women no longer had a role
would not have been made lightly by Wang Guoxiu and Deng Yuzhi,
who had enjoyed long and valued relationships with Western women. It
is noteworthy that in April 1950, the YWCA leadership was not being
forced to sever ties with Western secretaries. The rationale given for the
tacit decision to send Brennecke and West home – Morrison had already
decided to leave, and the national committee had no direct control over
Leila Hinkley in Taiwan – was bureaucratic pragmatism.

For the time being at least, senior leadership maintained collegial relationships with their counterparts overseas. A letter from Wang Guoxiu
to Margaret Forsyth in early April is illustrative. The letter, marked "not
for publication" but nonetheless preserved in the YWCA of the USA
files, used Wang's home address rather than the association's address. It
included a mix of personal and association news relayed in conversation-
al tones indicative of long acquaintance. Having served on the national
committee at least since 1934, Wang would have had long acquaintances
with many American and World secretaries.

Wang explained that the long overdue note was the result of her professional obligations at St. John's University and her volunteer service on
the national committee. She emphasized that the delay was not caused by
the situation in China, which she feared would be the common interpretation. She was anxious lest Forsyth had heard all sorts of contradictory
accounts, as many leaving China interpreted events from their personal
experience and not from an objective viewpoint of what was good for her
country's future.

Reasons for the tardy note included the enlarged executive committee
meeting and the other needs of a "changing environment." Wang discussed Cai Kui's resignation, then mentioned that the association was fortunate to have Deng Yuzhi as Cai's successor, "for now." Did the words
"for now" reflect Deng's own thoughts on how long she wanted to be
tied to an administrative position when she appeared more interested in
politics? What mattered was Wang's conviction that Deng was the only

person capable of maintaining "balance" among "the various elements" in the association. Her comments, allusive as they were, provide a glimpse of possible tensions within the association. Some scholars suggest that radicalized Christians joined the YMCA and YWCA because other organizations would not have them, since as Christians they were associated with foreign missionaries and their loyalty was thus suspect.[47] Deng was not the only person providing balance, as a group of experienced senior secretaries emerged who supported her when she was in the office and took over her administrative duties when she was not.

Wang Guoxiu emphasized that the enlarged executive committee meeting had provided a clear understanding of association policies and programs for the near future. She added pointedly that their international relationships had not changed: they maintained their membership in the World YWCA. They appreciated the Western staff, but there was no work for them to do. Ongoing travel restrictions would force those who stayed to lead dull, inactive lives, which was not fair. Forsyth would be receiving an official letter from the association regarding the decisions on this matter.[48]

The official letter that Wang mentioned was sent to Margaret Brennecke, Ruth West, and the YWCA of the USA's Foreign Division on April 17. It was signed by both Wang Guoxiu and Deng Yuzhi. The letter provided tactful explanations of the national committee's decision. While acknowledging the effort of Western secretaries to develop indigenous leadership, Wang and Deng noted that it was now time for Chinese women to assume the entire responsibility. The decision not to place Western secretaries in local associations was due to the difficulty their presence would cause local staff in the new political reality.[49] Although not explicitly stated, foreigners, especially Americans, bore the legacy of imperialism and the taint of counterrevolution.

A letter from Ruth West in Chengdu to former China secretary Florence Pierce illustrates the points Wang and Deng made to Forsyth. She was upset that foreign members were being eliminated from the Chengdu YWCA governing board, as were Chinese nationals considered "reactionary." "Reactionary" meant not being aligned with the party. Those decisions struck "at the heart of the Christian fellowship" of the YWCA, which she had hoped would elevate the association "above the popular movements of the day." West lamented, "It appears a real and complete revolution has taken place within the Association."[50] That would have definitely put her at odds with the leadership in the national office. While Sichuan Province, with its pockets of GMD resistance, might have forced the Chengdu YWCA city association to be more overtly revolutionary, West's description of the Chengdu association's actions, coupled with the revelation that local city associations had begun joining local branches of the ACDWF, was a reminder that city associations had always enjoyed a certain autonomy.

A New China, a New Christianity

The Christian Revolution: Through Western Eyes

Margaret Garvie continued to serve as the primary interpreter of events at the national office for YWCA colleagues overseas. In a long, rambling letter to Elizabeth Palmer in June, she warned Palmer that her point of view differed from what Palmer was hearing from others. She criticized those who left soon after liberation and gave slanted interviews or wrote opinionated articles. Garvie did not claim to be impartial. A year after Shanghai's liberation, she felt grounded in the Chinese point of view. While she had much work to do at the national office, her work included many hours of study. The emphasis on study and reflection had resulted in headquarters staff remaining at the table long after meals, discussing new ideas and programs. The result was a growth in fellowship. Garvie suggested that YWCA women at the national office agreed on the progressive nature of their interpretation of Christianity.[51] She did not elaborate further, however.

Garvie complained that conservative Christian churches in Shanghai and elsewhere were attacking new ideas. Even though Christian fundamentalists were not politically motivated, they were vulnerable as they encouraged divisiveness at the very time progressive Christians were trying to demonstrate that all faiths, Christians, materialists, and so on could unite to rebuild the nation. She criticized pastors who attacked the YMCA and the YWCA for facing the new political reality, recognizing that there was no going back and, most important, trying to find new ways to express Christian life in China's new society. Young people, including young Christians, believed it was impossible to remain politically neutral and that Christian organizations could not transcend politics.[52]

While Palmer would have been interested in these discussions, the most eye-opening and perhaps even startling part of Garvie's letter was her statement that at this time in Chinese history, communism offered the only solution to China's problems and that foreign support of Chiang Kai-shek was "useless":

> There is no doubt but that a new hope came with the new regime. The old order had deteriorated into one of corruption and oppression. After all the propaganda that went out during the world war to promote aid to Chiang and China, it has been difficult to persuade the West that Chiang's regime was really one of debased feudalism with a veneer of modern education and culture.[53]

She described popular fear of the GMD before liberation because of its record of arrests, torture, and execution, which had directly touched the YWCA. Then, there were the GMD's "scorched-earth" policy as its army retreated from Shanghai, and her present circumstance living in the blockaded city. Currently, there was the exodus of foreigners, slow at first but accelerating since the port of Tianjin had opened. She cited the pull-out of the American diplomatic corps, with many American businessmen and missionaries going as well. The departure of American diplomats meant that the United States was no longer a possible destination for refugees. With that "biggest door" closed, Garvie poignantly remarked that a "heterogeneous collection of displaced persons are stranded penniless in a city which was the Mecca some years ago for those seeking refuge from any regime."[54] She was referring to Shanghai's status as an "open" port that many refugees, especially Jewish refugees, had fled to.

Garvie's interpretation of the division in the Christian community was not the only Western perspective that Palmer and others in the World YWCA office had to consider. Another view came from Robbins Strong. Strong had been an Oberlin-in-Shanxi representative from 1934 to 1937 before returning to the United States to attend divinity school. He returned with his wife to north China as an American Board of Commissioners for Foreign Missions (ABCFM) missionary. They were interned at the Weixian Civilian Assembly Center in Shandong from 1941 to 1943, where it is likely they met Leila Hinkley, as all three were part of the prisoner-of-war exchange in 1943. In 1947, Strong returned as a YMCA secretary serving in Nanjing.[55] He would thus have known both Wu Yaozong and Liu Liangmo and been familiar with their thinking and activities.

In May 1950, he wrote a report that his father forwarded to the World YWCA. In it, he noted that Christians were approaching life under the communist regime from "two schools of thought." The smaller group regarded themselves as "progressive and liberal" and, while not communist, accepted the Marxist interpretation of history. They believed Christians had been too closely associated with the bourgeoisie and too tied to "democratic individualism." They blamed themselves for their previous lack of interest in government, and thus blamed themselves for the economic and social harm caused by the GMD. Now that they had been politically awakened, they planned to help implement the Common Program to guarantee that the regime lived up to its promises. In sum, Strong wrote, this small but vocal group was attempting a synthesis of communism and Christianity.[56]

The other group included most of the church leadership Strong described as conservative, which meant "not sympathetic to the new regime." They were not thinking through the implications for Christianity in the new society, but maintained the "old Christian faith" with its Western overtones. He saw the two groups as a corrective for each other but feared their differences could not be bridged. Strong noted that the principle of religious freedom was being upheld insofar as there was no systematic persecution, although there had been "stories" from rural areas.[57]

Garvie's interpretation reflected those Christians who believed communism was the solution to China's problems at that historical moment. Christian leaders such as Deng Yuzhi and Wu Yaozong had come to that conclusion years earlier. Thus, it was not just their immediate circumstances that led liberal Christians to conclude that the essentialist form of Christian faith – the life and message of Jesus – worked within China's new Marxist economic framework. That message had inspired Deng to pursue social justice when she was a teenager and later as a YWCA industrial secretary. Garvie's remark that progressive Christians were trying to demonstrate that all faiths, Christians, materialists, and so on could unite to rebuild the nation reflected the thinking of Premier Zhou Enlai, who stated that "it doesn't matter whether one is an atheist or a theist, a materialist or an idealist – everyone is able to support the socialist system."[58]

The Christian Revolution: Through Chinese Actions

Garvie's and Strong's descriptions of divisions among Christian leaders in China provide context for efforts by liberal Christian leaders to set the tone for an ongoing, meaningful relationship between the state and Chinese Christians. After the conclusion of the Chinese People's

Political Consultative Conference that produced the Common Program in September 1949, Wu, Deng, and the other delegates had returned to Shanghai to deliberate on how to get word of Article Five, the statement on religious freedom in the Common Program, to Christians throughout China and bring them in union with the government. They decided to send "teams" that included the Christian delegates to the consultative conference and representatives from the National Christian Council, the YMCA, and the YWCA to visit select cities and towns in liberated areas. The teams discovered serious problems in many areas where the social revolution, especially land reform, allowed peasants to vent decades of anger at those who had oppressed them. Christian churches were often targeted or simply got caught in the middle. Foreign missionaries and mission stations, as much as pockets of GMD soldiers, stood as reminders that Mao's revolution was not yet complete. Many cadres and even ranking party members may not have anticipated, or even now supported, the principle of religious freedom, at least for Christians. Revolutionary cadres had little reason to interfere when churches were broken into, robbed, or destroyed.[59]

Wu Yaozong gathered letters describing the situation at different churches. He and others requested a meeting with the government to discuss the implementation of Article Five and other matters, such as the theoretical differences between Christianity and communism and the dependence of Chinese churches on financial support from abroad. The Christian representatives even brought a prepared statement with them.[60] Article Five of the Common Program had guaranteed freedom of religion, but that was the sum of its statement on religion. How to interpret that statement, let alone how to implement it, was left up to others. Religious policy was slow to develop, but as it did, it took shape based on the concept of the "united front" and remained part of United Front work.[61] Zhou Enlai was a particular proponent of the United Front policy during the first phase of the state-building project.[62] It was under the aegis of this policy that the indigenous church movement developed.

On May 2, Wu Yaozong, Deng Yuzhi, and seventeen others held the first of four lengthy meetings with Zhou Enlai and other officials.[63] Given the number and length of the meetings, a number of the topics the Christians wanted addressed may have been addressed. Zhou had a more fundamental matter on his mind, however. He was a pragmatist, not a theorist. He was interested in the social fabric of the new communist state and how Chinese Christians were going to be woven into that fabric. His fundamental issue was the relationship between Christianity and imperialism, and his question was about their patriotism, expressed in the Chinese term *ai guo* (love of country). How would Chinese Christians demonstrate *ai guo*?[64]

According to Deng, if they had expected Zhou to suggest an answer, they were mistaken. While he promised that the government would do "what was required," in Deng's words, Zhou pointed out that many had formed their opinion of Christianity because imperialists had used it as a tool to invade China, which had created a gap between Christians and "the people" that *only* Christians could bridge.[65] They had to convince the Chinese people they were loyal to Mao. This was *not* a suggestion, although Deng's rendering of it thirty-five years later made it seem as if Zhou was only pointing out the obvious.

What the progressive Christian leadership did was exactly what the YWCA had already done in March: issue a statement of loyalty to Mao's New Democracy. The statement that the Christian leaders had brought with them to the first meeting with Zhou was thrown out. A new statement was shown to Zhou at the last meeting, on May 20. Subsequent drafts were also shared with party officials. Among the Christian leadership, it was a contested process, reflecting the diversity of opinion and strong sentiments Garvie and Strong spoke about. When the Christian Manifesto[66] was published in the *Christian Weekly* on July 28, Wu Yaozong's handprint was all over it. However, it was accompanied by a letter signed by forty prominent Christians, including Deng Yuzhi and Wang Guoxiu. The manifesto was subsequently published on the front page of the *People's Daily*, indicating that it had been endorsed by the party. Over the next few years, over 400,000 Christians would sign, although there were prominent Christians who did not. Those numbers reflected the fact that after China's entry into the Korean conflict, signing the letter became a patriotic duty for Chinese Christians.[67]

The Christian Manifesto was a political statement meant to disavow any connection to Western imperialism and unequivocally avow Chinese Christians' support for the communist regime. It explained the contributions Christianity had made to Chinese society. It acknowledged that the first Christians came from imperialist countries and that this made people believe Christianity was also imperialistic. This belief was compounded by the fact that imperialist countries would not accept the revolution or new China. To demonstrate the position of Christianity in the new China, Christian leaders wanted to establish a self-governing Chinese Church.[68]

The manifesto went on to confirm that a Chinese Church and its organization would support the Common Program and would work with the government to oppose imperialism, feudalism, and bureaucratic capitalism, and to build an independent, democratic, free, and united China. Further, the Chinese Church and its organization would "purify" the imperialist influence from their midst. In addition to becoming self-supporting as soon as possible, Chinese churches needed to promote self-criticism to evaluate all their work in order to carry out the "revolutionary aims" of Christianity. The Chinese Church should also unite all denominations, thoroughly reorganize the church system, and build up its own leadership.[69]

The manifesto made news overseas. The *London Observer* noted in an October 2 article:

> The danger of a serious rift among Christians in China over their relations with the Communist regime is foreseen by London Missionaries Societies as the result of a manifesto issued by an important Chinese Christian group last week. The rift threatens to develop between those who are prepared to use Christianity to further Communist doctrine and those who maintain that Christianity has nothing to do with politics.[70]

The paper attributed the manifesto to a group (with whom British missionaries have no connection, the article's author, O.M. Green, pointed out) headed by the "powerful YMCA and YWCA."[71] In a 1986 interview regarding this manifesto, Deng Yuzhi was asked whether she realized that many foreigners who "are against China" believed that the communists had initiated the Three-Self Patriotic Movement, whose momentum had begun with the manifesto. In response, the octogenarian Deng laughed and commented that such a belief was contrary to the facts. Zhou Enlai had simply identified the problems and pointed out that Christians had to resolve them. For Deng, Zhou had demonstrated confidence in people of faith.[72]

What Deng's interpretation of those long-ago events reveals is her faith and confidence in both Zhou and the communist state. As noted earlier, Zhou acted out of pragmatism and interest in political unity. He wanted to make common political ground with Christians, which is why he put so much emphasis on patriotism. On the question of "love of country," there could be no differences. Unlike some other communists, he did not see Christianity withering in China: "Religion will continue to exist for a long time, and its future development will depend upon the future condition. But as long as there are questions which people are not able to explain and resolve on an ideological level, the phenomenon of religion will be unavoidable."[73] That Zhou saw Christianity enduring for some time (although perhaps not forever) made Chinese Christians' embrace of the revolution an important matter.

While the Christian Manifesto was being drafted, North Korea invaded South Korea. Although Mao Zedong was aware that Kim Il-Sung planned to use military force to reunite the peninsula, he did not know the date and did not think the invasion imminent. He had only one army in the northeast, with two in the south poised to invade Taiwan. Thus, he and other party officials were caught off guard when North Korean troops crossed the 38th parallel on June 25, 1950.[74] Two days later, the United Nations Security Council passed Resolution 83, condemning North Korea as the aggressor, insisting that it withdraw its forces, and recommending that assistance be given to the Republic of Korea. The resolution passed by a vote of 7–1, with Yugoslavia voting no. Ironically, the Soviets were not present, as they were boycotting Security Council meetings since the Nationalist Chinese were still occupying the permanent seat designated for China.[75]

Did North Korea's actions, followed by those of the United Nations, influence the final wording of the Christian Manifesto? It is possible but unlikely, as China was not yet involved and the conflict on the peninsula was not at that time relevant to the defined purpose of the manifesto.

INTERNATIONAL CONFLICTS, INTERNATIONAL CONTACTS

In the fall of 1950, peace negotiations floundered and the Korean conflict escalated. General Douglas MacArthur, commander of the United Nations forces in Korea, landed troops behind enemy lines at Inchon on September 15. Seoul was liberated on September 25. From June onward, the PRC aided the North Koreans in any number of ways except for sending Chinese troops. Then, UN forces crossed the 38th parallel. The Chinese leadership was already debating whether to become directly involved. Cogent arguments were made on both sides. On October 2, a consensus was reached that the Chinese People's Volunteer Army (CPV Army) under the command of General Peng Dehuai would enter the war on October 15. This move was cancelled when the Soviets reneged on their offer of air support. After tense negotiations in Moscow, Soviet support was secured and the CPV Army crossed the Yalu River on October 19.[76] The first Chinese offensive was launched on October 25 and the second a month later. The success of the first two offensives encouraged Mao to order a third one on December 31, in time to greet the new year.[77]

Despite the war, Deng Yuzhi was able to secure permission to travel abroad to attend conferences in countries that had recognized the People's Republic. She attended YWCA conferences with financial assistance from the World YWCA office.[78] The first was in Mussoorie, India, for a YWCA Leadership Training Institute, and the second was the World YWCA executive committee meeting in Nyborg, Denmark. Thirty years later, she recalled being met with suspicion and even hostility in India as other delegates expressed doubt that the Chinese association would or could honour the principles the YWCA represented.[79] On the other hand, her reception in Denmark, at least by the Americans, was warm and cordial. Margaret Forsyth, head of the Foreign Division of the YWCA of the USA, attended the Denmark meeting and had several private conversations with Deng. In a letter to Lily Haass, Forsyth shared those conversations with the long-time secretary who had been Deng's mentor and friend. A different, perhaps more familiar Deng rose from the pages of her brief letter. Forsyth commented that she was in good health ("she is a frail person") and was "just the same friendly person that she has always been," with "a definite bias toward Americans." Deng expressed sadness over the departure of foreign secretaries and sought Forsyth's reassurance that the Foreign Division understood the reasons for the Chinese national committee's decisions. She was convinced that the time for international staff in China was not yet over and that eventually some could return. She was eager for more Chinese staff to attend international conferences if a way could be found to fund such travel.[80]

From Denmark, Deng travelled to Poland to attend the Second World Peace Conference in Warsaw from November 16 to 22, after which she visited Moscow. Her attendance at the Warsaw conference was somewhat in defiance of the World YWCA, or so she recalled.[81] The World's executive committee noted only that they were "surprised."[82] Soviet foreign policy divided the world between peace-loving nations and those promoting war and imperialism, such as the United States and Great Britain. Mao's policy of "leaning to the left" indicated his embrace of that policy. Deng was one of 440 women at the conference, 130 of them Chinese. There were 72 representatives from Christian organizations. China sent 2, both laypeople: Deng from the YWCA and Liu Liangmo from the YMCA.[83]

In her article in the January 1951 issue of the *YWCA Magazine*, Deng emphasized the "elite" speakers among the women leaders of the peace movement. They included Eugénie Cotton, founder and first president of the Women's International Democratic Federation; Pak Chong-ae from the Korean Women's Democratic Union; and Li Dequan, widow of the "Christian general" Feng Yuxiang, who was the PRC minister of health, president of the Chinese Red Cross, and vice chair of the ACDWF. Deng praised these women and noted the thunderous applause each received. She concluded:

> Thus the over 2,000 fighters for peace at the Conference, representing billions of people in 80 countries, showed how they sympathize with the courageous struggle for peace in Asia on the part of the Korean and Chinese people ... Let everyone of us contribute our best to participate in the great movement of Resist-America, Assist-Korea and protect-fatherland, so as to advance with the people of the world.[84]

That Deng Yuzhi was permitted to attend the two World YWCA meetings suggests the fluid nature of international contacts between nongovernmental organizations in the very early years of the PRC. That she was selected as a Christian delegate to the World Peace Conference, along with YMCA secretary Liu Liangmo, tends to corroborate her status as a Christian leader who cultivated a politically conforming mindset. She would continue to do so, and it is quite possible that the extent of her political involvement indirectly served the YWCA.

This chapter has examined the major events of 1949 and 1950, for which considerable documentation exists. The most significant events were Deng Yuzhi's appointment as national general secretary in January 1950, the enlarged executive committee's commitment to the Maoist regime at its meeting that March, and the decision to send Western secretaries home. This period also saw the emergence of Deng Yuzhi in the political sphere, including her role as a religious representative to the People's Consultative Conference, her involvement in the creation of the Christian Manifesto, and her selection as one of China's two Christian representatives to the Second World Peace Conference in Warsaw. Although tension and conflict within the association and within the larger Christian community were acknowledged, by and large Chinese YWCA women would no doubt have looked back on this period with satisfaction, and looked forward to the future with more confidence than they had felt for many years.

6

Cultivating a Socialist Mindset, 1951–57

Because in the past we were so deeply poisoned, therefore today we must even more resolute and thoroughly purge the poison ... The most effective method of purging the poison is renunciation.
— "Denounce!," *YWCA Magazine*, July 1951

Women's history does not always conform to political history, and such is the case with the history of Chinese YWCA women. The year 1950 had been a watershed one for the YWCA, with the completion of the decades-long process of Sinification and the first steps toward cultivating a socialist mindset. In the following year, the process of cultivating a state-conforming socialist mindset continued. The two "bookends" of this chapter are the Christian denunciation campaign, which occurred in the context of the Great Movement to Resist America and Assist Korea in 1951, and the Hundred Flowers Campaign in 1957. The first demonstrates the intellectual remoulding of YWCA women, while the second demonstrates the ongoing, very deliberate process of cultivating the politically correct mindset as the Maoist regime accelerated its own political transformation. Admittedly, between these two bookends the shelf is somewhat bare as there are relatively few archival documents from the national office that describe what life was like for association women or what work they performed. What is preserved is the considerable effort of the World YWCA to maintain its connection to its Chinese constituent.

The year 1951 began benignly with the resumption of the *YWCA Magazine*. In its first issue that January, national committee chair Wang Guoxiu wrote that the magazine had ceased publication in September 1949 because the future was uncertain. New China, however, offered favourable conditions for the association to continue its work. YWCA women were once again renewing their pledge to Mao's state-building project:

> Now the *YWCA Magazine* has been approved for republication, just as the national patriotic movement to resist American imperialism is reaching its crest. From now on, the magazine's mission will be of even greater importance ... All of us must strive together to develop the Association's work according to goals of the Common Program. The magazine must ... enable the members to clearly understand that we must coordinate with the current people's patriotic movement and answer the call of the people's government. Under the leadership of the All-China Democratic Women's Federation, we must strive to transform the face of national womanhood ... By means of this monthly magazine, I hope that each and every member of the YWCA of China will awaken to the great spirit of voluntary sacrifice ... and serve with all their hearts and minds in building a new, happy China.[1]

In her opening statement, Deng Yuzhi wrote that the magazine would encourage the sharing of ideas and experiences between YWCA branches. Such communications had been elevated to a higher purpose as it was now incumbent on everyone to share in the decision-making process and participate in the New Democracy:

> So that the YWCA can adapt to the new environment and better suit the principles of democratization, it is important that a novel set of work methods be developed through research and experimentation. How we should effectively utilize the mass line; how to compile our work experiences through research and analysis; how to improve our work using the weapons of criticism and self-criticism; how to establish a system of frequent work inspections and reports – all of this knowledge can be disseminated to the people via the *YWCA Magazine* so that different issues can be raised and so that solutions to these problems can be explored by all.[2]

World YWCA archival documents indicate the World office received the January, February, and April issues of the magazine. A Chinese friend translated the articles for the World office.[3] Some, such as Wang's and

Deng's opening statements, reflected the reality of new China with the use of the political rhetoric of the state. Other articles hardly differed from those published before 1949. A World staff member compiled a list of excerpts for possible use in the World YWCA's *A Handbook of National YWCAs*, and sent them to Deng for her approval, disapproval, or editing. Deng sent entirely different materials that clearly and concisely described the Chinese association's current standing in very positive terms.[4]

The April issue was decidedly political. Its lead article suggested that the best way to celebrate Labour Day on May 1 was by extending the Resist America and Assist Korea movement. For the YWCA, this meant realizing the Christian Three-Self reform movement and cutting off all ties to imperialists. To accomplish this task meant "helping the government to suppress reactionary activities, especially those carried out under the cover of religion."[5] The April issue's heightened political tone was understandable as it was published after Zhou Enlai's meeting with Christian leaders in mid-month and the commencement of the Christian denunciation campaign.

DENUNCIATION

In January 1951, YWCA women were very forthright in acknowledging that they were finding their way in the first half of 1951 and experiencing many difficulties.[6] Embracing an ideology was easy; living that ideology was often not. Christians would learn that simple fact once the Christian denunciation campaign began in April 1951.

The campaign had its genesis in the central government's effort to control external influences on Chinese culture, particularly in organizations still being funded from abroad. In December 1950, the State Council of the People's Republic of China promulgated Regulations Governing All Organizations Subsidized with Foreign Funds. Organizations that did not comply with the regulations or did not provide full and accurate disclosure were punished or taken over and, in extreme cases, closed. Organizations that could prove they no longer received foreign funds were released from such reporting obligations.[7]

Some Christian organizations responded immediately. On January 5, 1951, Wu Yaozong and twenty-four other Christian leaders announced their support for the regulations, which was followed by similar

statements across China.[8] On January 28, the national committee passed
a formal resolution "not to accept any more foreign aid ... so as not to let
imperialists utilize religion for aggression."[9] This decision, at least in the
minds of committee members, did not apply to Chinese YWCA funds
that had been deposited in New York banks during the war with Japan.
Efforts to have those funds transferred to Swiss banks failed. They were
returned only in 1984.[10]

As the Korean War continued and the Resist America and Assist
Korea campaign accelerated, the State Council held a conference of
Christian leaders in Beijing from April 16 to 21, at which Zhou Enlai
introduced additional regulations specifically aimed at subsidies from the
United States. More than 150 church men and women attended, among
them YWCA secretaries Deng Yuzhi, Wang Xiuqing, and Cai Kui.[11] Lu
Dingyi, deputy chairman of the Committee on Culture and Education
of the State Council, explained that the conference was necessary because of American imperialism. This was the crux of his speech and of
the meeting. Lu spoke about patriotism, how American imperialism
used Christianity, and what was expected of Christians. He praised Wu
Yaozong, the Christian Manifesto, and the Three-Self reform. His tirade
against American imperialists' use of Christianity was well-researched,
detailed, and convincingly stated, as YWCA secretaries later noted. The
final part of his speech discussed Christians' responsibilities vis-à-vis
nationwide movements, especially the Resist America and Assist Korea
movement. He described the movement as an effort to secure world
peace by opposing American aggression. Lu was emphatic that everyone
needed to learn to "wipe out the 'fear America, worship America, fawn
on America' thinking, and learn to hate, despise and vilify American
imperialism."[12]

Wu Yaozong gave what amounted to a "state of Chinese Christianity"
speech, reporting on the status of the Christian Manifesto, the progress
of the Three-Self reform, and how American imperialists and their sym-
pathizers had tried to destroy both. He went on to give examples and cite
statistics of Christian support for the Resist America and Assist Korea
campaign. Wu then turned his attention to the need for a Christian
denunciation movement in order to root out not only the hidden imperialists in their midst but imperialist thoughts in their hearts. In conclusion, he emphatically stated: "Denunciation meetings must be held
everywhere, to expose the various schemes by which imperialism tries to
use the church in aggression against China ... We must be energetic in
cleaning our own house."[13]

April 19 has been given as the date when the denunciation movement began. Before the conference attendees, speakers attacked missionaries (who were mostly absent) or colleagues (who might have been present) for their complicity in or cooptation by American imperialism. They then turned their attention to their own actions or inactions, criticizing their culpability in America's insidious agenda.[14] The large meeting was followed by small study groups to create a new political awareness and genuine commitment to the new Protestant church and new China.[15]

One of the speakers at the April conference was Cai Kui, who accused American secretary Lily Haass of deception:

> Before I became general secretary ... the head of training Ms. Haass told me: "You have the temperament of a scholar. We do not want you busying yourself with all the trivial tasks that regular secretaries deal with. Your work is to study, write essays, and give lectures. We can handle internal matters for you. There's no need to worry yourself." I hated administrative work at the time, I was very happy and unwittingly let all administrative powers fall into Haass's hands. I was general secretary in name, but everything was being controlled by "her lordship general secretary Haass."[16]

Haass was a likely target. Her long service in China and her close work with the National Christian Council during the 1920s meant that she would have been known to most Christian leaders. She had also been the longest-serving foreign secretary and wielded more power than any other woman on the national staff – perhaps, as Cai insinuated, even more than the national general secretary at times. She had held the key positions of national personnel secretary in charge of training and national city secretary responsible for coordinating the work of the more than a dozen city associations. Neither of those offices was ever held by a Chinese woman. As to the truth of Cai's remarks, it is difficult to get at the "truth" of perceptions. Haass's praise of Cai Kui's leadership during the War of Resistance against Japan suggested that Cai was more than general secretary in name only. Accusing Haass could be considered a tactical move by Cai: being among the first to step forward, and the first YWCA woman to do so, and targeting someone prominent and doing so with great sincerity, should have prevented Cai from becoming a target. Except that it didn't. Deng Yuzhi would later denounce her.

After the April meeting, YMCA secretary Liu Liangmo wrote extremely detailed instructions on how to conduct accusatory sessions. Denunciations should be planned. Churches and groups should hold "accusation meetings" that almost amounted to practice sessions, where everyone should be urged to express themselves enthusiastically. "In this way we shall be able to find a few people who accuse with the greatest power and invite them to participate in the larger accusation meetings." Liu elaborated on how to structure an accusation speech, and how to structure an accusation meeting. He also suggested that good speeches be sent to the papers to be published.[17] The Resist America and Assist Korea movement was used for both propaganda against and suppression of imperialists. The Christian denunciation campaign was a lesser part of it. Liu Liangmo's detailed instructions indicate that it also was carefully orchestrated political theatre.

Liu's suggestion that good accusation speeches be published explains two speeches written by Deng Yuzhi, and one each written by Wang Xiuqing and Gao Yuxin, that appeared in the July issue of the *YWCA Magazine*. Deng's "US Imperialists' Criminal Invasion of China via the YWCA" was delivered at the June 10 city-wide denunciation meeting that Liu Liangmo organized in Shanghai.[18] The others were dated July 27. There is some question as to whether the denunciation meeting was actually held on that day, as a news item in the magazine notes that Deng Yuzhi was conducting a government-sponsored tour of several provinces.[19] It can be presumed that the YWCA denunciation meeting was held after the last Western secretary, Briton Margaret Garvie, left in the spring. The YWCA of Great Britain published a very positive article on her work in China in June 1951.[20]

The lead article of the July *YWCA Magazine* was an unsigned statement titled "Denounce!" It provided insight into the intensity of denunciation meetings:

The American imperialists have always used Christianity to carry out their cultural invasion of China, and the YWCA is one of the groups that they have exploited. In the past, however, we could not see this clearly. We thought the YWCA was a progressive organization ... Actually, our so-called "progressive nature" was cleverly used by American imperialism ... actually for more than sixty years our personnel was ever being manipulated by American imperialism; actually, our work, owing to its reformist nature, not only did not serve the people of China, but on the contrary, was used to carry out the American imperialist policy of encroachment, muddling the people's thinking and weakening the revolutionary power of the Chinese people ... Because in the past we were so deeply poisoned, therefore today we must be even more resolute and thoroughly purge the poison, clean house, wash our bodies clean of all the dirt and filth. Only then can we walk toward the light, walk toward a new life. The most effective method of purging the poison is renunciation, because renunciation itself is a very good method of study, and it is also an intense process of ideological struggle.[21]

Deng Yuzhi's impassioned article "American Imperialists' Criminal Invasion of Southeast Asia and China via the World YWCA and the Foreign Division of the YWCA of the USA" must have carried much weight given her years of service, her close relationships with Western YWCA colleagues, and her prominent role as a Christian leader.[22] Unlike her more rambling speech before her YWCA colleagues on June 10, Deng got right to the point:

> Using the YWCA as a means of invasion is part of American imperialist policy. Ever since American imperialist missionaries exported the YWCA to China, they have for several decades maintained a tight grip on the YWCA of China via the US YWCA. The YWCA of China is subordinate to the Foreign Division of the US YWCA. The Foreign Division has great authority. General Secretary of the Foreign Division Margaret E. Forsyth, an advisor to the United Nations non-governmental organization, maintains frequent contact with the US Department of State ... The World YWCA is also tool of American imperialist invasions. It is manipulated by the American imperialist. Eighty percent of the World YWCA's budget comes from the United States.

Deng's tone in the beginning of her denunciation somewhat deviated from Liu Liangmo's advice that accusations should be "first high tension, then moderate, then another high tension."[23] Her initial tone was moderate, reaching a crescendo as she attacked the 1947 World Council meeting and her own former YWCA colleague Cai Kui:

> First I will unveil the conspiracy behind the 1947 YWCA World Council Meeting held by the American imperialists in Hangzhou ... 1947 was a

year not too long after our victory against the Japanese. The American conspirators were planning the reconstruction of Japan to use it as a tool of invasion. At the world council meeting in Hangzhou the World YWCA emphasized its so-called universal-love regardless of race. The World YWCA did everything in its power to invite members of the Japanese YWCA to attend the meeting in China. Yet full light cannot be shed on this conspiracy because Japan was under American military control at the time, and the Japanese YWCA members were not allowed to leave the country. After the council meeting, however, several members of the World YWCA and the US YWCA visited Japan. The American imperialist general secretary of the World YWCA at the time was Ruth Woodsmall. She insisted that Cai Kui, the former general secretary of the YWCA of China, also visit Japan. In the end, Cai Kui did not go due to much protest, nevertheless. It was apparent that Cai Kui was implementing the American imperialist policy of Japanese reconstruction. Cai had even planned to use the YWCA of China to help implement that policy. Comrades! Eight years of torment we suffered in the fight against the Japanese. Every one of us will never forget these eight years. Before a treaty with regard to Japan had been signed, when an eight-year blood debt had not been fully repaid, the World YWCA wanted us to forget the atrocities committed and extend a hand of friendship to the enemy. The World YWCA wanted us to forget our identity as a race. What malicious intent. Comrades! Right now the American imperialists are arming Japan and planning to use Japan in another invasion of the new China. Today we must denounce the American imperialists for their long-planned malicious conspiracy.[24]

It can be assumed that Cai Kui was present when Deng accused her of "implementing the American imperialist policy" by visiting wartorn Japan. Another of Liu Liangmo's directions on holding denunciation meetings was that Christian organizations should study whom to accuse, and who should be the accuser. Thus, it is possible that Cai was aware that Deng was going to accuse her. Liu also said [W]hen the accusations have succeeded in deeply stirring people, clapping and applauding may be used as a form of expression."[25] Unfortunately, the tone and texture of the actual meeting are lost in the provocative language that jumps off the written page, so whether the YWCA denunciation reached the desired fever pitch or ended in clapping and applause cannot be known.

Deng condemned the World YWCA for declaring North Korea an aggressor and supporting the UN police action. She also faulted it for not signing the Stockholm Appeal to ban nuclear weapons or attending the Second World Peace Conference in Warsaw, which she considered a serious failing for an international women's organization. Because of their relationship with the United States, Chinese secretaries believed in many ways that the World YWCA was on the wrong side of history. Although they did not disavow their connection with it, it was obvious that the relationship had become complicated. In the end, Deng's strongest condemnation was for herself and her colleagues:

> In reality, they used us to carry out a cultural invasion, made us work with imperialists to engage in numerous acts aimed at numbing the minds of our fellow compatriots ... As I recall all that has been done, I feel tremendous guilt and must thoroughly repent. We used to think we were "advanced." Because we were so content with ourselves in this regard, we failed to clearly see how closely we had been working with the imperialists. We failed to realize that we had been working hand in hand with counterrevolutionary bureaucracy and capitalists. We also mistakenly thought that we were innocent and had done no wrong. But only today, under the leadership of the people's government, do we finally understand that our homes and our persons are covered in filth; that we must wash away all this disgusting filth before we can become a YWCA that truly serves the people.[26]

In her denunciation, Wang Xiuqing noted that she had been "awakened" at the Beijing meeting. She contended that the Americans had manipulated the Chinese YWCA by controlling its finances and personnel. Internal reports documented the fact that the American YWCA invested more in China than in any other country. American women outnumbered all other foreign secretaries. They were imperialists sent to implement a policy of invasion. American women trained Chinese women to be "slaves" to their imperialist cause. Controlling the Chinese YWCA was part of a larger American conspiracy to turn China into a colony.[27]

Wang reflected on how she had been influenced by her Western-style Christian education, the time she had spent in the United States, the YWCA training conferences she had attended, and her friendships with American secretaries. She had idolized America

and been blinded to its imperialist intent. She had believed in the
YWCA doctrine. She had believed that all her work, even her fundraising work, genuinely served society. She now recognized that she
had been "exploiting the people and using that money to perform
reformist work. I was working for them, aiding reactionary forces,
and acting counter to the revolution. Recalling all of this, I am truly
ashamed."[28]

She said she had been most deceived in believing that American
secretaries were truly friends. Wang saved her most virulent attack for
one of those secretaries, Margaret Brennecke. Wang and Brennecke had
worked together in Yantai from 1932 to 1937, when both were reassigned to the national staff. Home on furlough in 1949, Brennecke had
insisted on being sent back to China even as the civil war continued.
Wang criticized Brennecke's words and actions, such as stating that the
People's government was all right but it was best not to ally with the
Soviets, and that she hoped China would follow Yugoslavia and not be
drawn into the Soviet orbit. Wang was especially angry because, despite
Brennecke's having the air of an imperialist, Wang herself had never
been able to recognize Brennecke as one but simply regarded her as a
friend, even travelling to see her off in Hong Kong when she returned
to the United States.[29]

Cai Kui, Deng Yuzhi, and Wang Xiuqing all denounced close friends
and colleagues. For that reason, their denunciations were dramatic and,
thus, they met Liu Liangmo's expectation. Were they authentic or merely
political theatre? The answer cannot be known, but it does go to the core
of these women's Christian identity as they sought to overlay it with a
socialist mindset.

RECONCILIATION

The World YWCA had an unpolished translation of Wang Xiuqing's
denunciation. It was marked "confidential," which does not necessarily
mean that it was not read by many.[30] How did YWCA women outside of
China understand the virulent tone of this denunciation? Did they know
of the Christian denunciation movement? Or did they attribute Wang's
words to the nationalistic fervour and anti-American sentiment caused
by China's entry into the Korean conflict?

After Mao's victory in 1949, the World YWCA leadership realized
that their relationship with the Chinese association would change. They

might not have immediately realized how great that change would be. It is quite possible the "open letter" and the decision to send Western secretaries home surprised the World office as much as Wang's speech might have shocked or saddened them. Since the end of the Second World War, however, the World YWCA leadership had tried to heal the wounds of war among its constituents from formerly combatant nations. They remained committed to maintaining their relationship with the Chinese YWCA, and sent China all documentation for it to attend the World YWCA's council meeting in Beirut in October 1951. It was only on the meeting's opening day that the Chinese cabled that they would not attend. World YWCA general secretary Helen Roberts interpreted the timing of that cable as a message of greeting. Her positive reaction was perhaps due to the fact that China had earlier indicated that it wanted to continue receiving materials from the World headquarters, which meant that, despite the harsh words Deng and others had uttered in their denunciations, the Chinese association intended to maintain the relationship with the World YWCA staff.[31] So World publications, including its monthly magazine, continued to be sent. World staff kept somewhat abreast of the goings-on of their Chinese constituent through their broad social network.

The connection between the two organizations and their women had changed, however. For one thing, meaningful correspondence all but stopped. Official and personal letters sent and received before 1951 had provided scholars with insight into the daily operation of the Chinese national association, into the goals and ideologies of its Chinese leadership, and into complex cultural exchanges between and among YWCA women. Without such correspondence, that vital avenue to understanding the past closed. From the contemporary perspective of the World YWCA, the voices of their Chinese colleagues had fallen silent.

The silence was not always deafening. Here and there, directly or indirectly, a Chinese voice was heard. This happened in 1953, when the World office sent observers to the Women's International Democratic Federation (WIDF) Congress held in June in Copenhagen. It was a large meeting, with a total of 1,990 women from sixty-seven countries. There were 613 delegates and 65 observers, among them women sent by the World YWCA. The remainder of the participants were recorded as guests.[32] Deng Yuzhi attended as part of the All-China Democratic Women's Federation (ACDWF) delegation. The ACDWF had joined the WIDF in 1949. According to historian Zheng Wang, the women's federation "became the most important international channel for the Chinese government, largely via the WIDF, and organized many international cultural exchanges."[33] Deng's inclusion as a member of the delegation was not by happenstance. The ACDWF had recognized the Chinese YWCA as a responsible member of the federation, and the association had priority status for its delegates.[34]

Deng and the World YWCA observers had several opportunities for brief talks and, on the last day, a longer talk at Deng's hotel.[35] Their discussions were preserved in a document titled "Summary of Conversations with Cora Deng and Some Impressions of the Congress," marked "strictly confidential" and "notes by E.P." (Elizabeth Palmer). There were points on which Deng and the World YWCA women disagreed. Deng, in fact, spoke with two voices: that of the national general secretary of the Chinese YWCA and that of a delegate representing the ACDWF and, indirectly, all Chinese women. And with both voices, she sparred with her World colleagues.

Speaking as the national general secretary, Deng made it clear that as a Christian organization, the YWCA was completely free as a "religious movement," but that there was a clear distinction between religion and politics. Her former World colleagues could not understand how religion and politics could be separated, as "it was a function of Christians to make judgements on the state." Their remark suggested that they were not listening closely to what Deng was saying about the position of Christians in China. Deng not so subtly tried to point this out by reiterating her basic message: in matters of religion, Christians in China were free. No one, however, was free to criticize the state. At least not in 1953.

When asked to send news from the Chinese association for the World monthly magazine, Deng said she would have to check with the national committee, making it clear that, as it had done before the revolution, the national committee set policy. Deng did assure her World colleagues that they could publish the fact that they had met if they made it clear that she had attended the WIDF Congress as a delegate from the women's federation, not the YWCA. She welcomed any news from them, noting that while her secretary opened all second-class mail, she herself opened her first-class mail. On the possibility of writing personal letters to friends in China, she cautioned that women in the West should wait for Chinese women to initiate any correspondence.

Then, speaking as a delegate, Deng turned her attention to the congress. She was gratified that the World office had sent observers. If they sincerely wanted to understand what was happening in the world and in China, attending such meetings was critical. She considered the congress to be of historical importance. She pressed her former colleagues on their thoughts. They responded that they had found it "sobering and over-whelming the accumulative picture of the problems of women around the world." Palmer's notes made it clear, however, that when it came to solutions, each side had difficulty understanding the assumptions of the other. This was most apparent in their discussion of world peace. Deng felt that women should make peace a paramount goal and that there should be no problem finding common ground: "We all want the war in Korea to stop, don't we? We all want people to live together in a relation-ship of equality rather than dependence and dominance, don't we? We all want an end to imperialism, don't we?" When the World staff said that they agreed with her in general but that people in "different halves of the world" had different ways of looking at things like imperialism, Deng retorted, "The truth is one." Trying not to explicitly disagree with Deng, the World staff claimed that any view was a partial view and people had to come together to find the truth "or to come nearer to it." The women evidently did not pursue the discussion. The process of decolonization around the world had just begun. Time would prove Deng right.

The World staff pressed Deng on the key position the Chinese YWCA held because it was the only functioning YWCA in the "East." Their "East" was ideological rather than geographical, "East" as juxtaposed with the "West," the communist versus noncommunist halves of the world. Some YWCA associations, the World women noted, did not even know the YWCA in China still operated, an interesting claim as the World YWCA handbook of national associations continued to list the YWCA in China as a constituent. This was not the point the World staff were making, however. Many YWCAs would not be interested in the WIDF, but they would be interested in the Chinese YWCA and would "give thought to ideas coming from a fellow YWCA." In her notes, Elizabeth Palmer stated, "We said that the association in China had a great respon-sibility for opening windows to the 'East' for other YWCAs."[36] This per-haps is the best explanation of why the World YWCA leadership would spend the next four years searching for a way to send a personal delega-tion to China.

The many questions Deng Yuzhi fielded on the "religious situation" in China while in Europe prompted her to publish an article in the November/December issue of *China Reconstructs,* the English-language magazine Song Qingling had started the previous year.[37] The magazine's target audience was international. It was the only publication coming out of the People's Republic of China allowed in the United States. Deng's article "Christian Life and Activities" probably repeated what she had told the many people who had queried her in Europe; now, however, her audience was worldwide. She emphasized that Christian life remained vital. Churches were growing in number, congregations were full, and many of them had been in continual service. She mentioned that her own pastor was about to celebrate his golden jubilee.

Deng particularly emphasized that for the first time in China's history, all people were taking a "real part" in government affairs. Christians were treated on an equal basis. She used her own experience as an example. She was a delegate to the nationwide Chinese People's Political Consultative Conference and the Shanghai municipal People's Representative Conference. Everyone shared a single goal, but this did not preclude a variety of opinions. But "the basic attitude is cooperation, not of opposition as in the party system in the West. All differences, even on very small matters, are discussed until agreement is reached on the action to be taken." This was a message Deng certainly wanted the readership of *China Reconstructs* to hear.[38]

Much of what Deng claimed in her article was confirmed by the Reverend Marcus James, a member of a British youth delegation that visited China in July 1954. He met with Deng Yuzhi and observed how engaged she was both within the YWCA and in public life, and how she was looked to for leadership. He further observed how active local YMCA and YWCA associations were "playing their part in helping people ... cooperate in the Government programs for vocation, education, etc." Probably in answer to a question upon his return from China, he mentioned that personal letters were not advisable at that time.[39]

The communication of news to the World YWCA office by James was the type of indirect contact that kept the World staff informed about the Chinese association. Whenever relevant, such information was forwarded to the World's executive committee. Sometimes, a news item was brief, such as a note sent in September 1955 to the general secretary of the British YWCA by Lena Jeger, a Labour Party member of the House of Commons, after her return from China. Jeger had visited both the Beijing and Shanghai associations and found them very active. She had met with Deng Yuzhi, who indicated that she had little news from abroad and would welcome knowing about the work of YWCAs in other countries. Jeger's closing lines might have piqued the curiosity of her correspondent: "I think there is no doubt that in spite of the difficulties in China, the YWCA is carrying on a great work of witness and of social service."[40]

A British Quaker delegation to China sent a lengthy report to the World office after its visit in 1955. It was the first visit by a Western Christian denomination since 1949. The group included four men and two women.[41] The reports that were circulated to the World executive committee were written by William Grigor McClelland and Janet W. Rees. McClelland, who would become a successful retailer, was a dedicated Quaker and participated in other such delegations in the 1950s.[42] He reported on a discussion he and a fellow delegate had with Shanghai Christian pastors involved in youth work. Rees had lived in China with her Methodist missionary husband before the war with Japan forced them to return to England. She visited eight of the thirteen city YWCAs. About her visit to the national office, she commented that "about a dozen members of the staff were gathered to greet us, many of them old friends." Those friends included Deng Yuzhi, Shi Baozhen, and Shi Ruzhang. Rees knew those women because in the 1930s her husband had worked for the National Christian Council in Shanghai. Her second daughter was born there in 1931. She noted that the YWCA was carrying out its activities with "energy and devotion," and that its Christian spirit had grown stronger.[43]

What were the activities that YWCA women engaged in with "energy and devotion"? The only documents that testify to them are the 1951 and 1957 issues of the YWCA Magazine, and the former existed merely as excerpts translated by Sui-May Kuo Ting, a friend of the World YWCA who was residing in Geneva with her husband at that time. The 1951 materials are sketchy. As suggested earlier, it seems that the World office was attempting to find newsworthy items about China for its bulletin. What can be gleamed from the excerpts was that there were fifteen city associations with membership figures ranging from a few hundred to almost a thousand. There were 269 staff members, of which only 80 were trained YWCA secretaries. The remainder were teachers, literacy teachers, nurses, and general staff.[44] Labour and education work was being conducted in ten cities. Industrial night schools operated only in Shanghai. Work continued in two schools until they were shut down in April 1952.[45] The only other city conducting labour education for industrial women was Guangzhou, and there, it had been combined with education for non-industrial women. Many other types of women were included under the category of "women's education," including middle-class housewives. As part of the YWCA's commitment to help build the Maoist state, political awareness lessons and activities were included.[46]

The four issues of the *YWCA Magazine* published in 1957, on the other hand, carried a political tone, although often very subtly. For example, the chair of the Beijing YWCA committee, Yu Xiu'ai, wrote about the uniqueness of its fortieth-anniversary celebration. Unlike the thirtieth anniversary, when mostly YWCA staff, volunteers, and members gathered to celebrate, pastors and members of Beijing churches attended the fortieth anniversary. Yu noted that the Three-Self Patriotic Movement had united all Christians into a single movement. "The churches will spread the gospel, while the YWCA, in the spirit of Jesus, serves society and the greater good for the benefit of all. This will put more people in touch with God, and give glory to His holy name."[47]

The theme of service was amply represented: service to women, service to the association, and service to the state. The YWCA served women through formal programs, and not just by bringing them into the YWCA sisterhood. The Nanjing YWCA educational department wrote at length about its literacy classes for girls and housewives and how they integrated service to women with socialist instruction. In the previous eight years, it had graduated fourteen classes, each of which had received three years of training in basic literacy. Of the 516 graduates, approximately 132 were employed. Instead of entering the workforce immediately, other graduates went on to complete secondary school or teacher training schools and nursing schools. Not satisfied with these achievements, the department wanted to enlarge the scope of its program: "In this way we can create more effective work methods to mobilize any of our sisters who have clouded awareness, who are afraid of facing difficulties, or who are not resolute in pursuit of their studies ... This will improve their culture and open opportunities for them to serve socialist construction."[48]

The themes mentioned in the article from the Nanjing YWCA aligned very well with the work of the ACDWF up to 1957, which also focused on housewives and on teaching political awareness.[49] The focus of the ACDWF, however, shifted during 1957, when it was incorporated into the party structure. It dropped the word "Democratic" from its name and became the All-China Women's Federation, which would henceforth serve as a formally organized mass organization within the party.[50]

Understandably, all the accounts of the Chinese YWCA given by foreign visitors were positive. It must be assumed that all such visits had been arranged in advance and that permission had been obtained from the appropriate authorities. Janet Rees's visit would have been the most meaningful, as she knew the women she was visiting in Shanghai. The World office still lacked a direct contact, however. It came close in the spring of 1956, when Finnish national committee member Inga-Brita Castrèn visited China as part of a Finnish youth delegation.[51] World YWCA general secretary Roberts asked Castrèn to contact the Chinese YWCA and inquire into the possibility of a visit to China by World YWCA women.

Castrèn more than obliged Roberts. She met several times with Deng Yuzhi and other Chinese YWCA leaders in Beijing and Shanghai. They expressed their hope that the World YWCA would send representatives to the World Federation of Democratic Youth (WFDY) delegation that planned to visit China in the fall of 1956, especially as the fall was a better time for them. This did not preclude a separate World YWCA visit later, but Chinese YWCA leaders urged that the World leadership take advantage of the current openness. When asked who should be sent, they specifically mentioned World executive committee member Sylvi Visapää. Visapää had been a missionary for the Finnish Missionary Society in Hunan from 1931 to 1937, and thus would have been known to some YWCA secretaries.[52] Castrèn also learned that the Chinese national office had received very little news from World headquarters. The Chinese recommended sending everything by airmail if possible, including personal letters.[53]

The suggestion that the World YWCA take advantage of the current "openness" described the actual situation in China from 1955 to early 1957. Starting with the signing of the Korean Armistice Agreement, China became more outward-looking and conciliatory. Premier and foreign minister Zhou Enlai remade the image of the People's Republic from that of an isolationist and bellicose nation to that of a nation pursuing peaceful coexistence with the world family of nations. He attended numerous international conferences, most notably the Bandung Conference in Indonesia in 1955. Among its other accomplishments, this conference produced resolutions on mutual aid and cooperation among Asian and African countries and created a "third world" coalition of non-aligned nations.[54]

That openness was reflected in a YWCA pictorial brochure that covered important association activities in 1956 and 1957. Captions in English and Chinese indicated that it was aimed at an international audience. One photo showed Xian general secretary Wang Cunyi and her staff greeting the Dean of Canterbury, Hewlett Johnson, and his family at the Xian airport in September 1956. A photo dated October

1956 showed Mrs. H.W.K. Mowill, wife of the Primate of the Anglican Church in Australia, seated with Wang Guoxiu and Deng Yuzhi in the reception room at the national headquarters with nine other members of the national staff. Finally, a photo from the following spring featured the president of the Ceylon (Sri Lanka) YWCA, Mrs. F.B. de Mel, seated in the same reception room surrounded by national staff.[55]

Key events in 1956 and 1957 eventually brought the more open and conciliatory era to an end in China. In February 1956, Nikita Khrushchev attacked Stalin's dictatorship in his "On the Cult of Personality and Its Consequences" speech before the Twentieth Congress of the Communist Party of the Soviet Union. Although de-Stalinization had begun immediately after Stalin's death in 1953, Khrushchev's speech resulted in a literal purge of Stalin from the Soviet Union's historical memory. In attendance at that speech were Chinese vice premier Deng Xiaoping and vice party chairman General Zhu De. Senior party members, especially Mao Zedong, mulled over Khrushchev's speech and its implications for them. In response, Mao made two speeches, one to party cadres, the other to party leaders, neither of which was published. In April 1956, he encouraged party cadres to include non-party members among their social relationships and to respect their "reasonable" views. He even urged them to "study" the West. During a speech in May, Mao uttered the famous lines from a traditional poem "Let a hundred flowers bloom, and a hundred schools of thought contend," seeking to engender new efforts in cultural production and scientific research. Mao's stance did not please party hardliners. Fissures in party leadership were beginning to appear. In an increasingly unsettled atmosphere, Hungarian dissidents revolted in late October and the Soviet Union intervened.[56]

Months before the failed Hungarian revolt, the World YWCA executive committee discussed the possibility of a visit to China during its meeting in Crêt-Bérard, Switzerland. After much back and forth, Visapää moved that the World YWCA, along with other Christian organizations, visit China as early as possible the following year.[57] Deng Yuzhi was also told that the delay was caused by the World executive committee plan to send two people, and it would take time to get them released from their primary work responsibilities.[58]

In an October letter, World YWCA general secretary Elizabeth Palmer brought Deng up to date on plans for the visit. There had been some complications with the original plan, and it now appeared that the delegation would be travelling alone. What most concerned Palmer, however, was that the World executive committee wanted its delegation to come at a time best for the Chinese association. She also informed Deng that the World representatives would be World executive committee vice president Sylvi Visapää and Ivy Khan, general secretary of the YWCA of India. She ended by stating: "I admit that I am looking forward to the day when I shall bring my own greetings to you and to all the other[s]. In the meantime, they are not less warm because they are on paper."[59] Palmer would never bring those greetings in person, although she served as World general secretary for another twenty years.

The long-planned meeting finally took place in the fall of 1957. After being met at the border, Visapää and Khan visited seven associations in a slow journey up the east coast. They noted the frenetic pace of building construction, the improvement in public health and overall standard of living, and a new respect for manual labour. They observed that almost all married women worked outside the home, and the association staffs reflected this as most of them were married women. In her presentation to the World staff in Geneva after her return, Visapää spoke of a new "love of country" and enthusiasm for the government and for its achievements. "The YWCA is part of China in a new way, and also part of the Christian community who nowadays are a united front." Visapää ended her report by saying that while the YWCA and other Christians did not deny that they had experienced difficult years, they felt that what they had achieved had been worth the price. Above all, they supported their government and believed that its people "live as they teach."[60]

Visapää's report mentioned that the Chinese YWCA had encountered difficulties and paid a price, but it is not clear what these were. Was she was referring to the past eight years, or perhaps the previous eight months? The year 1957 would have been a difficult, if not a tragic, year for many in the People's Republic. The brief period of openness ended abruptly in mid-year. The ideological fissures that appeared in 1956 continued, with hardliners trying to usurp Mao's authority and Mao trying to increase the momentum of his Hundred Flowers Campaign. Mao was disappointed at the mediocre response to his initial call the previous spring. A key speech, and its later revision, shaped events between February and July. On February 27, Mao delivered the original iteration of "On the Correct Handling of Contradictions among the People" to a select private audience at the Eleventh Session of State Council. He rhetorically explored what had caused the repudiation of Stalin in the Soviet Union and the revolt in Hungary. He claimed that China had never been more united or had a brighter future. The speech was not published, but in other public appearances and by publishing his poems for the first time, Mao got the message out: he wanted the flowers to bloom. Specifically, he wanted criticism of the party for its shortcomings. Finally, in late April and early May, not only party cadres but also intellectuals took Mao at his word. Such a torrent of criticism was unleased that by June Mao was forced to side with the hardliners. The February speech was edited to make it an attack on critics of the party, and that version became the definitive one. It was published by the *People's Daily* on June 19, signalling the demise of the flowers, which were now considered weeds to be pulled up by their roots. The Anti-Rightist Campaign had been launched. Well-known party figures, intellectuals, writers, and scientists, along with lesser-known figures, were arrested by the thousands and sent to re-education camps or sentenced to hard labour. Some were executed.[61]

It has already been noted that the World YWCA delegation visited China in the fall. Does this indicate that the Chinese YWCA was unaffected by the Anti-Rightist Campaign? No, it does not. True to the commitment it made in March 1950, and perhaps influenced by its politically engaged national general secretary, the association supported it. Deng Yuzhi had been a delegate to the People's Political Consultative Conference since its inception in 1949. When it was succeeded by the National People's Congress in 1954, Deng was elected as one of its representatives. In June 1957, Deng Yuzhi addressed the fourth session of the First National People's Congress. She spoke about how Christians loved their country. She emphasized that most Christians rejected rightist ideas and supported socialism and the party. According to her, imperialists were spreading absurd rumours about Christians in China, as well as Christians in other socialist countries, but Christians were ever vigilant and determined to resist rightist influences. With her usual political acumen, she also noted how Christians were working to transform China from an agricultural society to one based on industrial production. "We Christians, under the leadership of the communist party, will strive to produce economic results and work hard, making China a great shining beacon of socialism."[62]

The following month, at the very beginning of the Anti-Rightist Campaign, the *YWCA Magazine* published an article titled "Studying Chairman Mao's 'On the Correct Handling of the Contradictions among the People' – Excerpts of Discussions." It reported on a meeting of the association's study group led by veteran secretary Gao Yuxin. This particular session included at least fifteen women. The format of the article was unusual. Although described as "excerpts of discussions," it was made up entirely of quotes, three from the chair and one from each of the other fifteen women. Nonetheless, there was a sense of the back and forth typical of discussions, as some woman raised questions and others attempted to answer them.

Gao Yuxin asked whether the Hundred Flowers Campaign had been set as a trap.[63] Gao Tao Yong stated, in what must have been an emphatic tone:

> I don't think the Communist Party is setting a trap to snare them. Rightists in fact do exist; they've taken advantage of the rectification campaign to come out of hiding. They believe that can make use of the opportunities provided by "contending" and "blooming" to rouse a portion of the people to overthrow the Party. But they have misjudged the situation.

Another interlocutor asked what type of rightists had been exposed. Two names were given, leading government official and politician Zhang Bojun, labelled the "number one rightist," and poet and translator Sun Dayu. The last woman quoted in the article was Ma Zhongjie, who described the battle against rightists from a Christian vantage point. She observed that some religious circles maintained that their Christian beliefs "transcend politics," which left them open to being exploited by rightists. "By way of study and increasing our understanding, we can stymie the rightists and do an even better job of mobilizing religion's power, constructing socialism." But Ma also had a warning. "At the outset of the anti-rightist campaign, we could not differentiate right from wrong, which shows we were not firm in our convictions. If we do not continue to reinforce what we have learned and increase our ideological understanding, we will most likely be taken prisoner by right-wing ideology and fall from the ranks of those walking the socialist path." But that was unlikely to happen, she believed, noting that even in the 100-degree heat of summer, everyone was studying diligently.[64]

Throughout most of this book, the YWCA women's voices that have been heard belonged to women whose identities were known. Except for the chair of the study group just described, however, none of the women are at all familiar. They were truly grappling with this new situation, in essence actively "cultivating their mindset," which suggests the degree to which that had been an ongoing process. And as Ma Zhongjie's final statement makes clear, there was fear of falling off the "socialist path." There was a lot at stake. It could not be assumed that any one was above suspicion. Liu-Wang Liming, the head of the Chinese Women's Christian

Temperance Union (WCTU), had been accused of being a rightist. Although she was only stripped of her titles and positions and not jailed, it was still a warning.[65]

The fact remains that the YWCA's commitment to the communist state stemmed from genuine dedication to, and even adulation of, Mao Zedong. Associate director of the Shanghai YWCA Chen Jieshi attended a speech delivered by Mao in Shanghai on July 8, 1957. The iconic images of young Red Guards cheering and waving their *Little Red Books* when Mao appeared over the Gate of Heavenly Peace during the Cultural Revolution make it easy to visualize Chen's exhilaration when Mao entered the Sino-Soviet Friendship Building:[66] "I was unable to hold my excitement and started uncontrollably waving my hands high in the air. I cried out 'Chairman Mao, ten thousand years!'" Her article in the *YWCA Magazine* captured her rapture, which was not that of a schoolgirl but that of an adult. She wrote of her deep understanding of the correctness of the suppression of the rightists and of how difficult it was to "remold" bourgeois intellectuals. She closed by exhorting YWCA members and "our Christian sisters" to deliver crushing blows to the rightists. She also tacitly admitted that even for them, this was a process of learning to understand the problem and how to be guided by the chairman: "So long as YWCA members and our Christian sisters temper themselves and improve their awareness, any bourgeois mindset will gradually be remolded so that we may all march forward in the great socialist revolution together."[67] The fact that Chen's article was not published until December again suggests that cultivating this newest version of the socialist mindset was an ongoing process.

As mentioned at the beginning of this chapter, it is at this point that the documentary trail falters and is not picked up until the 1970s. Those familiar with the history of China know that the subsequent years were very difficult and, at times tragic, especially during the Great Proletarian Cultural Revolution from 1966 to 1976, in which thousands died or were sent to labour camps. Among them would be Deng Yuzhi.

EPILOGUE

Deng Yuzhi was arrested after Red Guards going through her personal papers found a receipt for land sold by her family many years earlier and declared her a member of the landlord class and thus an enemy of the people. Even after her release around 1972, she remained under house arrest on the eighth floor of the YWCA building in Shanghai and was allowed no visitors. This restriction applied even to Maud Russell, former YWCA secretary and staunch supporter of the People's Republic.[68] It also applied to another former YWCA secretary, Talitha Gerlach. Gerlach had been forced to retire from the YWCA after twenty-five years of service, partially because of her political beliefs, which included support for the communist regime in China. She returned to China in 1952 at the invitation of Song Qingling to work at her Child Welfare Institute. During the Cultural Revolution, friends in high places protected her, and a chauffeured car took her to and from work.[69] In a 1975 letter, Gerlach wrote that she had still not seen Deng, although this was on Deng's advice. Gerlach's housekeeper visited Deng in her stead.[70] Finally, in 1978 Deng was "rehabilitated," that is, exonerated of her alleged crimes. Friends like Gerlach were now able to see her.[71] The rehabilitation of the YWCAs of China began in 1980. At eighty years of age, Deng Yuzhi once again became national general secretary.[72] She was still listed as an "honorary national general secretary" in 1995, a year before her death.[73]

Conclusion

This book has asked what made it possible for a Christian women's organization that arrived on Chinese soil as a foreign transplant at the turn of the twentieth century to embrace Mao Zedong's revolution a half-century later. It has argued that the YWCA gradually became wholly Chinese, a process called "Sinification." It made the distinction between "Sinification" and "indigenization," defining "indigenization" as putting something (a process, institution, etc.) under native control. Indigenizing leadership was a World YWCA policy; indigenizing the YWCA movement and defining its own goals independent of the World YWCA were not. In this context, Sinification meant making the YWCA "the stuff of Chinese life" – in other words, not just Chinese in leadership but Chinese in policy, programs, and institutional culture. That is why it took five decades, and why it was accomplished only under Chinese leadership. This book has also argued that it was YWCA women on the ground in China who drove Sinification. It has examined the four most important of those women: Grace Coppock, Ding Shujing, Deng Yuzhi, and Cai Kui.

The process of Sinification began in 1908 when Grace Coppock insisted that a Chinese associate general secretary be appointed to assist her when she became the general secretary of the newly established Shanghai city association. Another advance occurred in mid-1919 when Chinese women became the officers of the national committee. Thereafter, with rare exceptions, Chinese women would continue to serve as national committee officers. The first national convention in 1923 was a major marker of Sinification, as its delegates passed a constitution that officially empowered the national committee to make policy, approve programs, and confirm staff appointments. The work of the national committee was conducted behind the scenes for the most part, but when its leadership raised their voices, as they did after the May Thirtieth Incident in 1925 or during Lord Lytton's visit after the Shanghai War in 1932, they articulated the association's "Chineseness," especially in the matter of China's right to national sovereignty. The most dramatic assertion of their Chinese identity was made at the March 1950 enlarged national executive committee meeting, when they declared the association "wholly Chinese" for the first time in its history, and declared their support for Mao Zedong.

With regard to indigenizing the association's professional staff, at the national level the major advance came when Ding Shujing was appointed national general secretary in 1925, an office she assumed in January 1926. Several months later, the national committee hired Deng Yuzhi as a national student secretary after her graduation from Jinling College, and the following year, they hired Cai Kui as a member of the editorial department. Thus, by 1927, the three most important women in the history of the YWCA movement in China were working together at the national office.

Ding was groomed for leadership by Western YWCA women almost from the time she joined the staff of the Beijing city association in 1916. The Beijing association sent her on a tour of the United States in 1919 and welcomed her back as its general secretary in 1920. The national committee brought her to the national office to serve as secretary for the first national convention, and then made her associate national general secretary. She assumed the office of national general secretary after a year of formal training in the United States. Her successors would not enjoy that type of deliberate preparation, but both Deng and Cai would have the benefit of serving for almost ten years under a highly respected Chinese national general secretary. While both Deng and Cai were befriended and mentored by Western secretaries, Ding Shujing's influence on their future success as leaders cannot be ignored.

Sinification was also a historical process subject to institutional realities and buffeted by historical forces. Although by the mid-1920s a decidedly Chinese identity had begun to emerge, in reality the association's dependence on foreign staff and foreign financial support meant that many continued to consider the association a Sino-Western hybrid until it embraced Mao's revolution in 1950 and sent its Western secretaries home. In the 1930s, however, Western staff was already much reduced and served almost exclusively in the national office. In 1934, there were only three Western women in city associations, and in the following year, only two. In 1934, twelve of the twenty-three secretaries in the national office were Chinese. Five of the nine executive positions were held by Western women, as Lily Haass served simultaneously as executive of the city and personnel departments, so it appears that either Western expertise was still being prioritized or such positions were being used to justify the retention of foreign secretaries to the home boards that supported them. The executive positions held by Chinese women included Ding Shujing as national general secretary, Deng Yuzhi as industrial executive, and Cai Kui as editorial executive. In 1935, there were eleven Western and ten Chinese secretaries on the national staff. A comparison of who held which executive positions cannot be made, however, as both Ding Shujing and Cai Kui were on furlough and this led to much shuffling of responsibilities.[1]

During the association's first decades in China, Western YWCA women defined the goals for association work and developed programs using Western models recognized as the "association way." Some programs emphasized the goal of individual moral and material uplift typical of mission work, while a few reflected the increasingly progressive agenda the British, American, and World YWCAs adopted to meet societal needs on a larger scale. As Chinese women advanced into leadership positions, they mitigated the foreignness of the association, domesticating the association way as they prioritized programs that made sense in a Chinese context and to a Chinese mindset. In a cultural tug-of-war, the Chinese leadership won. Still, working through those changes often caused tension. The national committee did not approve of the industrial secretaries' goal of developing a leadership for a self-directed women's labour movement, but the industrial secretaries pursued this goal anyway. Lily Haass objected to Ding Shujing's insistence on concrete programs; concrete programs were developed anyway.

Woven throughout this book is the identity of Chinese YWCA women as Christian New Women. Their identity as "new women" is more readily seen, as being "New Women" meant they had received modern educations and either pursued careers, involved themselves in social or political campaigns, or otherwise led lives of public service. It is much more difficult to get at what it meant to be a Chinese Christian woman. It cannot be assumed that the evangelical Protestant Christianity of Western and mostly American YWCA women, with its insistence on Christianity's overriding universal truth and assumptions of cultural superiority, was the Christianity professed by Chinese Christian YWCA women. Nor can it be assumed that the spiritual and lived experience of being Christian was the same for any two Chinese women. Thus, it is critically important to understand the individual religiosities of Ding Shujing, Deng Yuzhi, and Cai Kui. Ding's and Deng's conversions were essentially "social conversions" as children, in stark contrast to Cai's conversion to Quakerism as an adult. Cai's choice of the Society of Friends suggests that she sought both a human community and a spiritual home. The fact that Ding's conversion experience in the most spiritual sense came from witnessing her mother at prayer before a Buddhist altar also explains her broad understanding of the truth in all religions, even if her personal faith was Christianity. It also helps explain her abiding belief in internationalism, which has as its foundation the ability to overcome differences. Without Jesus's gospel of social revolution – as Deng seemed to understand the message of his life – Christianity might not have remained her life's animating principle after 1949. As for Cai, the degree to which Quakerism centred her life can be seen in her profound belief that the war with Japan was a "spiritualizing experience," but also in her decision to resign from the YWCA in order to seek her own spiritual renewal free from the distractions and demands of leading the association.

As it is clear that their religiosity informed their social views and their visions for the YWCA movement in China, it is also clear that Ding and Cai became somewhat disillusioned when the association did not accept their visions for the YWCA movement. Ding Shujing's desire that international staff be retained so the association could promote itself as an international community was rebuffed at the third national convention as the delegates supported the departure of Western staff as a natural part of the process of devolution. Internationalism remained the touchstone of her vision for the YWCA movement in China, Japanese aggression notwithstanding. Her death spared her from witnessing Japan's invasion of China and the enormity of pain and suffering that war would inflict on her people.

Cai Kui believed deeply that association women should model the essence of the Christian spirit. By mid-1949, she could not find even a half-dozen YWCA women who fit her model. Although she understood the historical circumstances that were reshaping the YWCA organizationally, her resignation in order to seek her own spiritual renewal spoke to her disappointment. Of course, it is possible that the problem lay in her model, and not in her Christian colleagues. It is also possible that, having tried to retire in October 1947, Cai recognized that she had the opportunity to make that request again and this time no one would dissuade her.

The discussion of the evolution of the YWCA's nationalism and its nationalistic identity may have not been anticipated by readers unfamiliar with Chinese history. It has been repeatedly noted that the association was buffeted by historical events. From the time of the May Fourth Movement, it was difficult for Chinese YWCA women to remain politically neutral as imperialism became a major impediment to China's search for modernity. Chinese voices were mainly silent in early YWCA archival documents. The first anti-imperialist, nationalistic voice that was recorded was that of industrial secretary Cheng Wanzhen during the closing months of the child labour campaign. The next voices heard were those of the officers of the national committee after the May Thirtieth Incident. The delegates to the second national convention expressed their desire to contribute to the building of a "new China." The leadership of the national committee again asserted China's claims to national sovereignty in their address to the Lytton Commission after the Shanghai War. But it was Japan's invasion of China in 1937 that sparked its nationalism as the association threw itself into war-relief work. The War of Resistance against Japan was the catalyst for the fullest expression of the association's nationalism, which came at the enlarged national executive committee's meeting in March 1950.

It was at that meeting that the association's leadership committed itself to the Maoist regime. The reasons behind this decision included the abject failure of the Nationalist government during the postwar period, the belief that the association's Christian-inspired social goals aligned with Mao Zedong's revolutionary aims, and the association's dedication to the Chinese nation-state. Deng Yuzhi was the guiding force behind the embrace of the Maoist state even before she became national general secretary in January 1950. But if she was the guide, the force behind her was a collective one. Just as during its first five decades, during its first years under Mao the association was buffeted by historical forces beyond its control. Between 1949 and 1957, it was forced to accommodate itself to party policies that were continually changing, often rapidly and drastically. It is likely that not all YWCA women were able to adapt, although an experienced leadership core made up of Deng Yuzhi, Wang Guoxiu, and a half-dozen others remained steadfast in the national office.

This book has not attempted to provide a comprehensive history of the Chinese YWCA from its inception to the mid-1950s. It has examined what transpired during six turbulent decades of war and social revolution that allowed a Christian women's institution to survive, which it has done to the present day, in the People's Republic of China. It has focused narrowly on the lives and work of four women at the national office located in what was originally Shanghai's International Settlement: Grace Coppock, Ding Shujing, Deng Yuzhi, and Cai Kui. That their leadership was transformational cannot be disputed. Collectively, their efforts made a Christian organization relevant to Chinese women, Chinese society, and the Chinese state during the first half of the twentieth century. This book has also focused narrowly on YWCA industrial work in Shanghai as emblematic of YWCA programs that were also relevant to certain Chinese women and certain segments of Chinese society. These were deliberate decisions to make this book manageable. Admittedly, those women, and that one program, are not the entire story, and there is room for much future scholarship.

Glossary: YWCA Women, YMCA Secretaries, Christian Leaders, and Related Terms

Note: Chinese names are given in traditional characters as they appear in period documents.

YWCA WOMEN AND ASSOCIATES

Cai Kui 蔡葵 (*Tsai Kwei*) – National editorial secretary after 1927; national general secretary, 1936–49.

Cheng Wanzhen 程婉珍 (*Zung Wei Tsung*) – YWCA editorial secretary in the early 1920s; wrote about the child labour campaign. Cheng's married name was Mrs. W.Y. Chiu (Qiu)裘程婉珍.

Dan Dexing 單得馨 – National industrial secretary in the 1920s.

Deng Yuzhi 鄧裕志 (*Deng Yu Chih, Cora Deng*) – National industrial secretary after 1930; national general secretary after 1950.

Ding Shujing 丁叔靜 (*Ting Shu Ching*) – First Chinese general secretary of the Beijing city association in 1920; first Chinese national general secretary, 1926–36.

Gao Renying 高仁瑛 – Joined staff of Tianjin YWCA in 1929; on national staff at least by 1949.

Gao Yuxin 高毓馨 – Listed on national staff in late 1930s; listed as rural secretary in 1951.

Gong Hezhen 梅華銓夫人 (*Mrs. H.C. Mei*) – Long-standing member of the national committee; chair of the national committee for most of the 1920s.

Gong Peizhen 龔佩珍 – Shanghai city association industrial secretary.

Hu Binxia 胡彬夏 – First Chinese chair of the national committee.

Mrs. Jin Longzhang 金龍章夫人 – Long-standing member of national committee.

Mrs. Mason Loh 陸梅僧夫人 – Long-standing member of the national committee.

Mrs. S.Y. Hsueh 薛韋增佩夫人 – Long-standing member of the national committee.

Qian Cuige 錢萃格 – Shanghai city association industrial secretary in the 1920s.

Sheng Zuxin 盛祖新 (*Mrs. C.C. Chen*) – Long-standing member of the national committee.

Shi Baozhen 施葆真 – National student secretary in the 1930s; on the national staff in the 1950s; wrote memorial tribute in Deng Yuzhi commemorative volume.

Shi Ruzhang 施如璋 (Phoebe Shi) – Long-time national secretary; assistant general secretary of the national YWCA in 1984.

Song Meiling 宋美齡 – Former YWCA secretary; participated in child labour campaign; wife of Chiang Kai-shek.

Sui-May Kuo Ting (*Guo Siumei*) – Wife of the Reverend K.H. Ting (Ding Guangxun) 丁光訓 and long-time friend of the YWCA; vice chair of the national committee in 1984.

Wang Guoxiu 王國秀 (*Mrs. J.H. Sun*) – Member of the national committee from at least 1934; national committee chair from at least 1950.

Wang Xiuqing 王秀卿 – Secretary from 1930, first in Yantai and then at the national office; national staff after 1937; listed as national financial and operations secretary in 1951.

Wang Zhijin 王知浸 – Author of oral history on communist infiltration of YWCA night schools, dated 1953.

Wu Yifang 吳貽芳 – President of Jinling College; in 1942, chair of the national committee after it relocated to Chengdu.

Xu Peiling 徐佩玲 – YWCA worker in industrial night schools who joined the Communist Party, as mentioned in Wang Zhijin's oral history.

Yang Shuyin 楊樹因 – Along with Shi Ruzhang, Shi Baozhen, Gao Renying, and Gao Yuxin, member of the administrative committee 行政員會 in the national office that was in charge when Deng Yuzhi was out of town; editor of the *YWCA Magazine* in 1957.

Zhang Yuezhen 張嶽偵 – Nanjing city association education secretary; wrote article on her association's education programs for *YWCA Magazine* in 1957.

Zheng Ruquan 鄭汝銓 (*Beatrice Djeng*) – General secretary of the Tianjin city association in 1937; still in that position in 1942.

YMCA Secretaries, Christian Leaders, and Other Important Men

Chen Wangdao 陳望道 – Translated Marx's *Communist Manifesto;* college professor; sources suggest he was Cai Kui's husband.
Chiang Kai-shek 蔣介石 (*Jiang Jieshi*) – Leader of the United Front; president of the Republic of China from 1927 to 1949, when he fled with his government to Taiwan.
Liu Liangmo 劉良模 – YMCA secretary; member of the religious delegation to the Chinese People's Political Consultative Conference; wrote instructions on how to conduct a denunciation session.
Wu Yaozong 吳耀宗 (*Y.T. Wu*) – YWCA secretary and close friend of YWCA secretary Deng Yuzhi; radical leader of liberal Christians after 1949; religious delegate to the Chinese People's Political Consultative Conference; primary author of the Christian Manifesto and leader of the Three-Self Patriotic Movement.
Zhao Zichen 趙紫宸 – Prominent Chinese Christian theologian who sought to indigenize Christianity to make it authentically Chinese; religious delegate to the Chinese People's Political Consultative Conference.

Terms

YWCA Magazine – *Nüqingnian bao* 女青年報
Christian Weekly – *Tian feng zhoukan* 天風週刊
"Mr." Deng Yuzhi Commemorative Volume – *Deng Yuzhi xiansheng jinian wenji* 鄧裕志先生紀念文集
National Southwestern Associated University – Xinan lianhe daxue 西南聯合大學, Lianda 聯大
Mt. Lu – Lushan 廬山
gymnastics (calisthenics) – *ticao* 体操
To Build a New Society – *jianzao xin shehui* 建造新社会 (theme of the third national convention)
League for the Promotion of Women's Rights – Shanghai nüquan yundong tongmeng hui 上海女權運動同盟 Women's group Ding Shujing organized to meet the Lytton Commission.

Notes

1 The May Fourth Movement began on May 4, 1919, when Beijing University students marched through the streets of the capital to protest the Paris Peace Conference's decision to award German concessions in China to Japan instead of returning them to China. The nationalist and anti-imperialists protests spread across the country. Deng, a middle school student at the time, actively participated. This topic is addressed in Chapter 1.

2 Helen Thoburn, "General Report," *Annual Report of National Committee*, December 1, 1925 (hereafter Annual Report/1925), 7, Box 403, World YWCA Archives, Geneva, Switzerland (hereafter World/China).

3 Marshall Sahlins, "Structure and History," in *Islands of History* (Chicago: University of Chicago Press, 1985), 136–56.

4 James E. Sheridan, *China in Disintegration: The Republican Era in Chinese History, 1912–1949* (New York: Free Press, 1975), 215–20.

5 Aihua Zhang suggests that it was introduced in China in 1918 directly or indirectly as a result of the New Culture Movement: *The Beijing Young Women's Christian Association, 1927–1937: Materializing a Gendered Modernity* (Lanham, MD: Lexington Books, 2021), 2.

6 Zhang, *The Beijing Young Women's Christian Association, 1927–1937*, xv.

7 Ibid., ix.

8 Ibid., 25.

9 Jane Hunter, "Introduction: 'Christianity, Gender, and the Language of the World,'" *Journal of American–East Asian Relations* 24 (2017): 305–6.

10 In my doctoral dissertation, I used the term "social feminism." The more accepted term is "maternalism," and that is the term I have used in all my subsequent scholarship.

11 "Going Public: The YWCA, 'New' Women, and Social Feminism in Republican China" (PhD diss., Carnegie Mellon University, 2002); "Negotiating a Space of Their Own: The YWCA, Women's Institutions, and the 'Female Public Sphere' in Early Republican China" (unpublished paper, History Society for Twentieth Century China, University

of Singapore, June 24, 2006); "Claiming Citizenship: The Chinese YWCA, War Relief Work, and Institutional Identity" (unpublished paper, International Conference on Gender Studies, co-sponsored by the University of Michigan and Fudan University, Fudan University, Shanghai, June 26–29, 2009); "Gospel of the Body, Temple of the Nation: The YWCA Movement and Women's Physical Culture in China, 1915–1925," *Research on Women in Modern Chinese History (Jindai Zhongguo funü shi yanjiu)* 16 (December 2008), 168–206; "Ding Shujing: The YWCA's Pathway for 'New' Women," in *Salt and Light: Lives of Faith That Shaped Modern China*, vol. 1, ed. Carol Lee Hamrin and Stacey Bieler (Eugene, OR: Pickwick Publications, 2008), 79–97; "Localizing the Global: The YWCA Movement in China, 1899 to 1939," in *Women and Transnational Activism in Historical Perspective*, ed. Erika K. Kuhlman and Kimberly Jensen (Dordrecht, The Netherlands: Republic of Letters, 2010), 63–87; "Caught in the Crossfire: Women's Internationalism and the YWCA Child Labor Campaign in Shanghai, 1921–1925," *Frontiers: A Journal of Women's Studies* 32, 3 (December 2011); and "Engendering a Class Revolution: The Chinese YWCA Industrial Reform Work in Shanghai, 1927–1939," *Women's History Review* 21, 2 (April 2012).

12 Li Ma, *Christian Women and Modern China: Recovering a Women's History of Chinese Protestantism* (Lanham, MD: Lexington Books, 2021), ix.

13 Ibid., ix.

14 Daniel H. Bays, *A New History of Christianity in China* (Chichester, UK: Wiley-Blackwell, 2012), 127.

15 Pui-lan Kwok, *Chinese Women and Christianity, 1860–1927* (Atlanta: Scholars Press, 1992).

16 Literature focused on Western YWCA women includes Alison R. Drucker, "The Role of the YWCA in the Development of the Chinese Women's Movement, 1890–1927," *Social Science Review* (September 1979); Nancy Boyd, *Emissaries: The Overseas Work of the American YWCA 1895–1970* (New York: Women's Press, 1986); Robin Porter, *Industrial Reformers in Republican China* (New York: M.E. Sharpe, 1994), which includes a chapter on YWCA industrial reform; Karen Garner, "Redefining Institutional Identity: The YWCA Challenge to Extraterritoriality in China, 1925–30," *Women's History Review* 10, 3 (2001); and Sarah Paddle, "The Limits of Sympathy: International Feminists and the Chinese 'Slave Girl' Campaigns of the 1920s and 1930s," *Journal of Colonialism and Colonial History* 4, 3 (Winter 2003).

17 Karen Garner, *Precious Fire: Maud Russell and the Chinese Revolution* (Amherst: University of Massachusetts Press, 2003). Russell was a YWCA secretary in China from 1917 to 1943. During those years and because of her experiences in China, she became an avowed Marxist. She was one of several YWCA secretaries with radical leanings. After the People's Republic of China was established in 1949, Russell became one of its most outspoken supporters in the United States.

18 Christina Wai-yin Wong, "Expanding Social Networks: A Case Study of Cora Deng and Y.T. Wu on Their Roles and Participation in the National Salvation Movement of 1930s China," in *Great Faiths of Our Times: Wu Yaozong and 20th Century Chinese Christianity* [Dashidai zongjiao xinyang: Wu Yaozong yu ershiji Zhonghua Jidujiao], ed. Na Fuzeng (Hong Kong: Chinese Christian Religious Culture Research Center [Jidujiao Zhonghua zongjiaowenhua yanjiushe], 2011), 291–339.

19 Xia Shi, *At Home in the World: Women and Charity in Late Qing and Early Republican China* (New York: Columbia University Press, 2018); and Margaret Mih Tillman, "Mediating Modern Motherhood: The Shanghai YWCA's 'Women's Work for Women,' 1908–1949," in *Spreading Protestant Modernity: Global Perspectives on the Social Work of the YMCA and*

YWCA, 1889–1970, ed. Harald Fishcher-Tiné, Stefan Huebner, and Ian Tyrell (Honolulu: University of Hawaii Press, 2021), 119–46.

20 I thank Republic of Letters for allowing me to use material from my "Localizing the Global: The YWCA Movement in China, 1899 to 1939" in this book. I also want to acknowledge the Institute of Modern History in Academia Sinica for allowing me to include excerpts from my "Gospel of the Body, Temple of the Nation: The YWCA Movement and Women's Physical Culture in China, 1915–1925" in Chapter 1. I extend the same thanks and acknowledgment to the University of Nebraska Press for its permission to use material from my "Caught in the Crossfire: Women's Internationalism and the YWCA Child Labor Campaign in Shanghai, 1921–1925" in Chapter 1.

21 I extend my thanks and acknowledgment to Wipf and Stock Publishers for allowing me to use material from my "Ding Shujing: The YWCA's Pathway for 'New' Women" in Chapter 2.

22 I thank the editors of *Women's History Review* for allowing me to use material from my "Engendering a Class Revolution: The Chinese YWCA Industrial Reform Work in Shanghai, 1927–1939" in Chapter 3.

23 I thank Dr. Michael Cole, editor of the Florida Conference of Historians *Annals* for allowing me to use material from "'Denounce!' – The Chinese YWCA and the 1951 Christian Renunciation Campaign in the People's Republic of China," *FCH Annals* 29 (publication pending) in Chapter 6.

CHAPTER 1: CREATING A YWCA MOVEMENT IN CHINA, 1899–1925

Epigraph: Helen Thoburn, "General Report," Annual Report/1925, 7.

1 Helen Thoburn, "General Report," Annual Report/1925, 7.

2 Ibid.

3 Cassandra Ponto, "The Search for Grace in China" (master's thesis, Southern Oregon State University, 1993), 1–11.

4 See Joseph W. Esherick, *The Origins of the Boxer Uprising* (Berkeley: University of California Press, 1988), for the most cogent analysis of this event.

5 Bays, *A New History of Christianity in China,* 108.

6 Ibid., 107–10.

7 Most YWCA histories, including those written by YWCA women in 1930 and 1947, date the beginning of the Chinese YWCA to 1890, when a student YWCA was established at a Presbyterian mission school in Hangzhou. I believe the creation of the first YWCA national committee in 1899 marks the beginning of the YWCA as a women's association.

8 Anna Rice, *A History of the World's Young Women's Christian Association* (New York: Women's Press, 1947), 1–10.

9 Ibid., 68–69, 90, 106–9, 143–45.

10 Ibid., 116–17.

11 Ponto, "The Search for Grace in China," 7.

12 For YMCA statistics, see Shirley S. Garrett, *Social Reformers in Urban China: The Chinese YWCA, 1895–1926* (Cambridge, MA: Harvard University Press, 1970), 77 and 175; Kenneth Scott Latourette, *A History of Christian Missions in China* (London: Society for the Promotion of Christian Knowledge, 1929), 589; and H.G.W. Woodhead, ed., *The China Yearbook: Year 1916* (Tientsin and Shanghai: North China Daily News and Herald, 1912–36), 465, and *Years 1920/1921,* 812. For YWCA statistics, see "The Young

Women's Christian Association of China," National Board of the YWCA of the USA, September 1914, and "The Blue Triangle in China: Annual Report and Directory of the Young Women's Christian Association of China," National Committee of the YWCA, 1921, File 164-1 – YWCA of China 1914–23, Historical Records Collection (HRC), Yale Divinity School Library, New Haven, CT (CRP/YDSL).

13 Latourette, *A History of Christian Missions in China,* 620.

14 Boyd, *Emissaries,* 69–70.

15 Ponto, "The Search for Grace in China," 30–31.

16 "Gateway to Progress for Women: A Report of the Work of the Young Women's Christian Associations of China," YWCA of China, Shanghai, 1915, 5, File 222-1708, Record Group 46 – World Student Christian Federation Collection (WSCF), CRP/YDSL.

17 "Report of the Third Secretarial Conference, Shanghai, February 5–14, 1916," 15–17, and "Report of the Fourth Secretarial Conference 1919," 63–64, File 164-1, HRC, CRP/YDSL.

18 Grace Coppock to Mrs. G.E. Bretherton, May 9, 1919, Box 396, World/China.

19 Ponto, "The Search for Grace in China," 114–15.

20 Ibid., 22; Clarissa Spencer, Shanghai, Private, 1907, "The Chinese Mill Women" and "Mission and Gentry Scholars"; and Harriet Taylor, "Report of Work in China, April 24 – May 10, 1907," Box 396, World/China.

21 Ponto, "The Search for Grace in China," 25–26. Ding Mingyu had graduated from the mission school of St. Mary's Episcopal Church in Shanghai and spent two years training at the China Inland Mission School in London. The actual level of her educational attainment is not known. Archival documents and early histories spell her name as "Mary Ting."

22 "The YWCA of China" (Zhongguo Jidujiao nüqingnianhui), stamped "received 14 Dec. 1957," Box 416, World/China.

23 In addition to the work of middle- and upper-class women with poor urban women, a separate student YWCA movement sprang up on college campuses. The two eventually merged.

24 Ponto, "The Search for Grace in China," 22.

25 Estelle Paddock, "Shanghai – A Sketch," *Association Monthly* (National Board of the Young Women's Christian Association of the United States of America) 5, 11 (December 1911): 435.

26 "Gateway to Progress for Women," 15.

27 "News Items, Young Women's Christian Association of China," Shanghai, February/March 1919, 6, Ruth White Carr papers, Boxes 36–38, Record Group 8 – Miscellaneous Personal Papers (MPP), CRP/YDSL.

28 "News Items, Young Women's Christian Association of China."

29 "Gateway to Progress for Women," 15.

30 Ibid., 14.

31 "Association Life Around the World," Foreign Department of the National Board YWCA, 1914, 25, File 310-2918, and "Chinese Women Working Together through the YWCA, The Story of 1916 as Told through the Chinese Women of the YWCA of China," National Committee of the YWCA of China, Shanghai, 1917, 16, File 222-1709a, WSCF, CRP/YDSL; and "Gateway to Progress for Women," 11–12.

32 "Report of the Fourth Secretarial Conference," 33; "Gateway to Progress for Women," 11–12; and "Chinese Women Working Together," 15.

33 "A 1915 Message from the YWCA of China," 19, File 222-1709a, WSCF, CRP/YDSL; and "Report of the Fourth Secretarial Conference," 34.

34 Kwei Tsai (Cai Kui) and Lily K. Haass, "A Study of the Young Women's Christian Association of China: 1890–1930" (YWCA of China, 1930), reprinted in *Chinese Studies in History* 11, 1 (1977): 46; and "Report of the Fourth Secretarial Conference," 34.

35 "The Present State of Protestant Missions in Tientsin," *Chinese Recorder* 48 (September 1917): 583.

36 "Jindai zhongguo nüquan yundong dashi ji" [Chronology of the modern Chinese women's rights movement], in *Jindai Zhongguo nüquan yundong shiliao, 1842–1911* [Documents on the feminist movement in modern China, 1842–1911], vol. 2, ed. Li Yuning and Chang Yü-fa (Taipei: Biographical Literature), 1531; and Yü-fa Chang, "Women – A New Social Force," *Chinese Studies in History* 11 (1977–78): 31–32.

37 "Chinese Women Working Together," 19.

38 Charles Andrew Keller, "Making Model Citizens: The Chinese YMCA, Activism, and Internationalism in Republican China, 1919–1937" (PhD diss., University of Kansas, 1996), 35–36.

39 "Gateway to Progress for Women," 19; and "The Widening Circle, a Record of Growth," National Committee of the YWCA of China, Shanghai, July 1919, 24, Folder 222-1709a, WSCF, CRP/YDSL.

40 "The Widening Circle," 28.

41 "Chinese Women Working Together," 20–21.

42 "News from China," 1909, 1, Box 396, World/China.

43 Ibid.

44 Debora Lynn Cottrell, "Women's Minds, Women's Bodies: The Influence of the Sargent School for Physical Education" (PhD diss., University of Texas at Austin, 1993), 373.

45 Andrew Morris, "Cultivating the National Body: A History of Physical Culture in Republican China" (PhD diss., University of California at San Diego, 1998), 90–91. Dr. Morris's dissertation was published as *Marrow of the Nation: A History of Sport and Physical Culture in Republican China* (Berkeley: University of California Press, 2004).

46 Abby Mayhew to Foreign Division (of the YWCA of the USA), "Combining the Normal School of Physical Education and Hygiene with Ginling College," June 1924, Microfilm 51.1, Record Group 5 – International Work, Record Group 5 International Work, YWCA of the USA MS324, Sophia Smith Collection of Women's History, Smith College, Northampton, MA (hereafter USA/China).

47 Abby Shaw Mayhew, "Physical Education, a Vital Part of the YWCA Programme in China," *International Quarterly* (October 1916): 7.

48 Grace Coppock to Clarissa Spencer, May 19, 1919, Box 396, World/China.

49 Abby Mayhew to Miss Margaret Mead, Chairwoman, Foreign Section, May 8, 1922, Microfilm 51.3; and Norah Jervis, "First Semester, 1923," Microfilm, 52.2, USA/China.

50 Rice, *A History of the World's Young Women's Christian Association*, 106–9; and *World YWCA Statements of Policy Adopted at Legislative Meetings 1894–2019* (Geneva: World YWCA, 2020), 157–58, https://www.worldywca.org/wp-content/uploads/2021/01/World-YWCA-Statements-of-Policies-2019-FINAL-EN.pdf.

51 Lily Haass to Mary Dingman, April 9, 1927, Box 405, World/China; Boyd, *Emissaries*, 134; and Ponto, "The Search for Grace in China," 120–22.

52 Emily Honig, *Sisters and Strangers: Women in the Shanghai Cotton Mills, 1919–1949* (Stanford, CA: Stanford University Press, 1986), 17; and Marie-Claire Bergère, *The Golden Age of the Chinese Bourgeoisie 1911–1937*, trans. Janet Lloyd (Cambridge: Cambridge University Press, 1989), 70–71. These figures refer to Chinese-owned factories that benefited when the war economies of European nations forced those nations to withdraw some of their investments from China. Only Japan and the United States saw their investments in

China grow during the war years. See Bergère, "The Economic Miracle," in *The Golden Age of the Chinese Bourgeoisie.*

53 Grace Coppock to Miss Wathen, May 26, 1919, Box 397, World/China. There was a reference to the 1917 request in this letter.

54 Excerpt from letters to Mrs. Katherine Willard Eddy, June 20, 1919, and October 28, 1919, in "China," May 3, 1926, a later compilation of excerpts from Coppock's letters, Microfilm 52.2, USA/China.

55 Ponto, "The Search for Grace in China," 120. I have no staff lists in either English or Chinese from before 1922, and none in Chinese before 1926. Thus, I do not know the Chinese characters for Fan Yu Jung or what position either secretary held in 1920. However a "Y.J. Fan" appears on the list of National Christian Council (NCC) secretaries on its letterhead in late 1925.

56 Dorothea Browder, "A 'Christian Solution of the Labor Situation': How Workingwomen Reshaped the YWCA's Religious Mission and Politics," *Journal of Women's History* 19, 2 (Summer 2007): 85–110, https://doi.org/10.1353/jowh.2007.0033.

57 Ponto, "The Search for Grace in China," 116–17.

58 *World YWCA Statements of Policy,* 158.

59 Agatha Harrison, "Annual Report, February 23, 1921 – March 23, 1922," Microfilm 51.2, USA/China.

60 Porter, *Industrial Reformers,* 49; and unsigned letter likely written by Miss Wathen to Grace Coppock, December 8, 1920, Box 396, World/China. Jean Chesneaux incorrectly identifies the YMCA as having asked Agatha Harrison to study labour problems, and refers to her as an ardent Quaker. Chesneaux, *The Chinese Labor Movement 1919–1927* (Stanford, CA: Stanford University Press, 1968), 205. According to Robin Porter, Harrison did not join the Society of Friends until 1941. Porter, *Industrial Reformers,* 218n.

61 Agatha Harrison to Miss Wathen and Miss Phillips, November 15, 1921, Box 396, World/China.

62 "National Committee Minutes, October 19, 1922," Box 398, and Mary Dingman to Agatha Harrison, January 12, 1922, Box 396, World/China.

63 Agatha Harrison and Florence Sutton, "Review of the Industrial Work of the YWCA, 1921–1924," 9, Box 398, World/China.

64 "Minutes National Committee, June 16, 1921," Box 398, World/China.

65 Honig, *Sisters and Strangers,* chs. 2–6.

66 Agatha Harrison to Miss Dingman, November 26, 1921, Box 396, World/China; and Porter, *Industrial Reformers,* 49.

67 John Fitzgerald, *Awakening China: Politics, Culture and Class in the Nationalist Revolution* (Stanford, CA: Stanford University Press, 1998), 37.

68 Helen Thoburn, untitled, undated biographical sketch of Cheng Wanzhen, Box 396, World/China.

69 Christina K. Gilmartin, *Engendering the Chinese Revolution: Radical Women, Communist Policies, and Mass Movements in the 1920s* (Berkeley: University of California Press, 1995), 62, 69, 82, 92.

70 Agatha Harrison to Miss Dingman, November 26, 1921, Box 396, World/China.

71 "Minutes, National Committee, January 18, 1923," Box 400, World/China.

72 "Committee of Economic and Industrial Relations, November 1, 1921," Microfilm 51.2, USA/China.

73 Porter, *Industrial Reform,* 74.

74 "Some Work of the Conference," *North China Herald* (hereafter *NCH*), May 13, 1922.

75   Agatha Harrison, "Industrial Statement, November 7, 1921," Microfilm 51.2, USA/China; and "Minutes National Committee, October 20, 1921," Box 398, World/China.

76   Agatha Harrison to Miss Dingman, November 26, 1921, Box 396, World/China.

77   Stationery letterhead, 1925, Box 402, World/China.

78   Agatha Harrison to Mary Dingman, November 26, 1921, Box 396, World/China.

79   Cheng Wanzhen, "The Results of the Second International Congress of Working Women" [Dierci guoji nüzi laogonghuide jingguo], trans. by the author, *Ladies' Journal (Funü zazhi)*, March 1922.

80   Cheng Wanzhen, "The YWCA Industrial Department" and "The Campaign for Labor Legislation" [Laodong lifa yundong], trans. by the author, *YWCA Magazine*, 1922, Record Group U121-0-60-[4], Shanghai Municipal Archives (hereafter SMA).

81   Cheng, "The YWCA Industrial Department," 13.

82   "Child Labour in Factories," *NCH*, April 14, 1923.

83   This was the perspective presented in the 1930 association history, which influenced later YWCA studies (see Boyd, *Emissaries;* and Drucker, "The Role of the YWCA"). Robin Porter also gives considerable credit to the role of the Joint Committee. Porter, *Industrial Reformers*, 101–2.

84   "Women and the Council," Letters to the Editor from Margaret H. Polk, *NCH*, March 24, 1923.

85   "Child Labor in Shanghai: Women's Organizations to Approach the Council," *NCH*, February 7, 1923; and "Child Labour in Factories," *NCH*, April 14, 1923.

86   "Child Labor Commission: Inaugural Address by Council's Chairman," *Shanghai Times*, n.d., Box 399, World/China. For Shi Meiyu, see Connie Shemo, "Shi Meiyu: An 'Army of Women' in Medicine," in *Salt and Light: Lives of Faith That Shaped Modern China*, vol. 1, ed. Carol Lee Hamrin and Stacey Bieler (Eugene, OR: Pickwick, 2008), 50–63.

87   Cheng Wanzhen, "Why We Should Promote the Campaign for Labor Legislation" [Weishemma yingyau tichang laodong lifa yundong], trans. by the author, *YWCA Magazine*, April 1924.

88   "Child Labor Commission – I" and "Child Labour Commission – II," *NCH*, August 9, 1924.

89   "Report of the Child Labor Commission of Shanghai Municipal Council," July, 1924, Box 401, World/China.

90   Ibid.; and "Child Labour in Factories," *NCH*, October 18, 1924.

91   "Child Labour in China," *NCH*, January 10, 1925; and "Correspondence" [Letters to the Editor], *NCH*, January 10, January 17, February 7, March 28, April 11, and April 18, 1925.

92   "The Press By-Law Once More," *NCH*, March 28, 1921; "The Ratepayers Meeting April 14," *NCH*, April 16, 1921; and "Municipal Gazette News: Registration of Printers and Publishers," *NCH*, April 5, 1924.

93   "A Quiet Ratepayers' Meeting," *NCH*, April 18, 1925.

94   "The Child Labor By-Law," *NCH*, May 2, 1925.

95   "Communist and Child Labour: Attempt by Unknown Agitators to Create Class Hatred Out of the By-Law," *NCH*, April 18, 1925; and "Correspondence [Letters to the Editor] – Council, Chinese, and By-Laws," *NCH*, May 30, 1925.

96   *Threads: The Story of the Industrial Work of the YWCA in China, 1925* (Shanghai: National Committee of the YWCA of China), 11, Box 402, World/China.

97   "Correspondence [Letters to the Editor] – W. Bruce Lockhart, 'Some Facts re Child Labour Agitation,'" *NCH*, May 9, 1925; and "Correspondence [Letters to the Editor]," *NCH*, May 9, May 30, and June 6, 1925.

98 "Special By-Law Again Held Up," *NCH,* June 6, 1925.

99 Reports, Eleanor Hinder, "Toward the End of a Two-Year Term, Phases in an Evolution," January 1, 1928, 4, Box 406, World/China.

100 "The Work of the Committee Directed toward the Regulation of Child Labour in Shanghai 1921–1926," Box 404, World/China.

101 *Supplement to "The Green Year" Concerning the Events of and since May Thirtieth in Shanghai,* July 1, 1925, 3, Record Group U121-0-60-[4], SMA. The *Green Year* was the English-language supplement to the *YWCA Magazine.* The name was a play on the Chinese word for "young," which is composed of two characters that literally mean "green year."

102 Hilda S. Murray, "Industrial Work of the YWCA: 1924–1925," 9, Box 402, World/China.

103 *Supplement to "The Green Year,"* July 1, 1925, 3.

104 Karen Garner, "Redefining Institutional Identity: The YWCA Challenge to Extraterritoriality in China, 1925–30," *Women's History Review* 10, 3 (2001): 409–40.

105 https://history.state.gov/countries/issues/china-us-relations#:~:text=1943%3A%20The%20End%20of%20Extraterritoriality,privileges%20long%20held%20by%20foreigners.

106 "A Chinese Social Service Worker" (Women's Page), *NCH,* April 7, 1928.

107 Lily Haass to Rosalee Venable, March 20, 1925, Microfilm 51.2, USA/China.

108 Chiu Zung Wei Tsung (Cheng Wanzhen), "Report to the Industrial Department, National YWCA, December 1925," Annual Report/1925, 34.

109 Ibid., 34–35.

110 Ponto, "The Search for Grace in China," 87.

111 Ting Shu Ching (Ding Shujing), "Message of the China Group from Ting Shu Ching," Correspondence with General Secretaries, Microfilm 50.2, USA/China.

112 Woodhead, *The China Yearbook: Years 1926/1927,* ch. 13; and *The China Yearbook: Years 1924/1925,* "Colleges and Universities."

113 Ponto, "The Search for Grace in China," 100.

114 *International Quarterly* (quarterly magazine of the World YWCA), October 1913, 61.

115 Ibid.

116 "Gateway to Progress for Women," 4; and "Chinese Women Working Together," 5.

117 Littell-Lamb, "Going Public," app. C. Many committee lists are incomplete.

118 Ponto, "The Search for Grace in China," 40; "Gateway to Progress for Women," 48–49; "Report of the Third Secretarial Conference"; and "Report of the Fourth Secretarial Conference."

119 Littell-Lamb, "Going Public," app. A, "Statistics of the YWCA of China."

120 Helen Thoburn, "General Report," Annual Report/1925, 6.

121 Rosalee Venable, "The New Status of the Chinese YWCA," Annual Report/1925, 18–22.

CHAPTER 2: MAKING A CHINESE LEADERSHIP, 1925–36

Epigraph: Rosalee Venable to Miss Harriet Taylor, Foreign Division, National Board, YWCA of the USA, April 6, 1923, Microfilm 50.2, USA/China; and Rosalee Venable to Mrs. Waldegrave, July 2, 1923, Box 399, World/China.

1 Unless otherwise noted, biographical information on Ding Shujing's life is from "Miss Ting Shu Ching," *Chinese Recorder* 67 (September 1936): 578–79; Ruth White Carr, "Some Appreciations of Ting Shu-Ching, Late General Secretary of the Young Women's Christian Association of China 1926–1936," Ruth White Carr papers,

CRP/YDSL; *YWCA Magazine (Nü qingnian bao),* December 1922, 16, Microfilm collection, YDSL; "Ding Shujing nüshi shengping jianlüe" [A summary of the life of Miss Ding Shujing], 1936, in *Ding Shujing nüshi jinian ce* [Memorial of Miss Ding Shujing], Box 410, World/China; Mrs. C.C. Chen, "A Short Sketch of Miss Ting's Life," July 30, 1936 (given at the funeral service), Box 410, World/China; *Who's Who in China: Biographies of Chinese Leaders* (Shanghai: *China Weekly Review,* 1917–50; repr. Hong Kong: China Materials Center, 1982, 3 vols.); and Rosalee Venable, "Ting Shu Ching," October 1936, Microfilm 50.2, USA/China.

2 Unless otherwise noted, information on Deng Yuzhi's life and education is from Emily Honig, "Christianity, Feminism and Communism: The Life and Times of Deng Yuzhi (Cora Deng)," in *Christianity in China from the Eighteenth Century to the Present,* ed. Daniel Bays (Stanford, CA: Stanford University Press, 1996), 243–62; Garner, *Precious,* 49–50; "Some Biographical Notes on Cora Deng" [Deng Yuzhi xiansheng pingjianjie], 1–2; and Deng Zhenying, "Reminiscences and Gratitude" [Mianhuai yu zhixie], trans. Erik Avasalu, in *Mr. Deng Yuzhi Commemorative Volume* [Deng Yuzhi xiansheng jinian wenji] (Shanghai: National Committee of the Chinese YWCA, 2000), 176–78 (hereafter *Deng Commemorative Volume*).

3 Xiang married communist leader Cai Hesen.

4 Patricia Hill, *The World Is Their Household: American Women's Foreign Mission Movement and Cultural Transformation, 1870–1920* (Ann Arbor: University of Michigan Press, 1985); and Jane Hunter, *The Gospel of Gentility: American Women Missionaries in Turn-of-the-Century China* (New Haven, CT: Yale University Press, 1984).

5 Except where noted, details of Cai Kui's early life and education are from Tsai Kui, academic transcripts, Folder 2654, Box 130; alumni questionnaires, Folder 2673, Box 131; and Tsai Kwei, "Miss Tsai Kwei – Ginling (Jinling) College Class of 1927," Folder 2864, Box 144, Record Group 11 – United Board for Christian Higher Education in Asia Records, Series IV China College Files, Ginling College (UBCHEA/Jinling), CRP/YDSL.

6 The Christian women's colleges followed the custom of neighbouring male colleges in their choice language of instruction. North China Union Women's College followed Yanjing University and taught in Chinese, while Jinling followed Nanjing University and taught in English.

7 There is an interesting counter-narrative to this given by a family relative in Deng's commemorative volume. Quoting Deng Shuci: "When she was 13 years old Deng Yuzhi contracted tuberculosis and was cured by a famous Changsha physician surnamed Zhang. To thank Dr. Zhang for healing her granddaughter, Deng Yuzhi's grandmother promised her in marriage to the doctor's son, Zhang Dabing. The wedding took place as soon as Yuzhi graduated from secondary school. Before the marriage Yuzhi expressed her wish to study at a university, and the Zhang family agreed to it. But after the wedding the Zhangs would only allow her to serve her mother- and father-in-law, play mah-jongg with them, and carry out the household duties of a daughter-in-law. It was only after the Deng family interceded on her behalf that the Zhangs acceded and allowed Yuzhi to enroll in Jinling Women's University. Although her relations with her husband Zhang Dabing were good, in order to pursue an education and throw off the shackles of feudalism, Deng Yuzhi left her marriage and never again remarried." Whether this is a result of different versions of the story passed down through generations is an open question. Deng Shuci, "A Life in Pursuit of Social Progress and Equality – Cherishing the Memory of Deng Yuzhi"

[Zhuiqui shehui jinbu yu pingdengde yi sheng huai shiji lao ren Deng Yushi xiansheng], in *Deng Commemorative Volume,* 179–83.

8   Honig, "Christianity, Feminism, and Communism," 130; Garner, *Precious Fire,* 49–50; Deng Yuzhi academic transcripts, Folder 2651, Box 129, UBCHEA/Jinling, CRP/YDSL.

9   "Wartime Experience" survey, Microfilm 130, File 2624, Series IV (Jinling College), UBCHEA Archives.

10 Tsai Kwei, "Miss Tsai Kwei – Ginling (Jinling) College Class of 1927." The Nanjing Fellowship was associated with the Ohio (Three Meeting) branch of conservative Quakerism in the United States. It had its origins in a nursing school and later orphanage established by Esther H. Butler in 1887. Quakers in the World, "Quakers in China," http://www.quakersintheworld.org/quakers-in-action/308/Quakers-in-China.

11 Lin Yutang, *My Country and My People* (London: W. Heinemann, 1936), 98, https://archive.org/details/MyCountryAndMyPeople1936/page/n5.

12 Lily Haass to Ruth Woodsmall, February 3, 1938, Box 411, World/China.

13 Sarah Goodrich to Miss Miner, May 28, 1916, Sarah Boardman Goodrich papers, File 118, Box 89, MPP, CRP/YDSL.

14 Grace Coppock to Miss Ella D. MacLaurin, October 23, 1920, Microfilm 50.2, USA/China.

15 Deng Zhenying, "Reminiscences and Gratitude."

16 Among the most notable were Gao Renying and Shi Baozhen. Gao graduated with a degree in sociology around 1929 and worked for the Tianjin YWCA and then the national office. She remained on the YWCA staff in the early 1950s. Shi was in her third year of middle school in 1926. When she graduated from Jinling is not clear, but in 1934, she was a national student secretary. Shi was still alive in 1996 and wrote a memorial of Deng.

17 In a letter written by Ding Shujing in October 1930, she noted that Cai Kui married a man named Chen Mong Dao in September. I presume that was a transcription error. Ting Shu Ching (Ding Shujing) to the National Committee and Staff, October 1, 1930, Microfilm 50, USA/China. Cai and her husband had one son, Chen Zhenxin.

18 Wong, "Expanding Social Networks," 306–7; and Yang Meiping, "Translator's Former Residence Now a Communist Manifesto Exhibition Center," https://www.shine.cn/news/metro/1805074182/.

19 Tsai Kwei, "Miss Tsai Kwei – Ginling (Jinling) College Class of 1927."

20 Christina Gilmartin, "Gender in the Formation of a Communist Body Politic," *Modern China* 19, 3 (July 1993): 302, 307.

21 Lily Haass to Agatha Harrison and Mary Dingman, February 28, 1929, Box 406, World/China.

22 Shi Baozhen, "Remembering Deng Yuzhi" [Mianhuai Deng Yuzhi dajie], in *Deng Commemorative Volume,* 173.

23 Lily Haass to Ruth Woodsmall, World YWCA, February 3, 1938, Box 411, World/China.

24 Margaret MacKinlay in "Some Appreciations of Ting Shu-Ching, Late General Secretary of the Young Women's Christian Association of China 1926–1936," 3, Ruth White Carr Papers, CRP/YDSL.

25 "Message to the China Group from Ting Shu Ching, under appointment of general secretary of the China National Committee," n.d., Microfilm 50.2, USA/China.

26 Garner, *Precious Fire,* 35, 50.

27 Wangzhi Gao, "Y.T. Wu: A Christian Leader under Communism," in *Christianity in China from the Eighteenth Century to the Present,* ed. Daniel H. Bays (Stanford, CA: Stanford University Press, 1996), 341.

28 "Mrs. Chen Tsai Kwei," in "Brief Review of the Work of the Literature Project Commission: First Project September 1931 to December 1932," April 13, 1933, Microfilm 52.2, USA/China.

29 Tsai Kwei to Miss Sarah S. Lyon, April 4, 1938, Microfilm 50.2, USA/China.

30 Theresa Severin, "Quarterly Report, Peking," April 1920, Box 397, World/China.

31 "The Young Women's Christian Association in China 1922" (Shanghai: National Committee of the YWCA, 1922), Box 398, World/China.

32 Grace Coppock to Miss Ella D. McLaurin, Foreign Division, National Board, YWCA of the USA, October 23, 1920, Microfilm 50.2, USA/China; and Rosalee Venable to Mrs. Waldegrave, July 2, 1923, Box 399, World/China.

33 Mary Cookingham to Margaret MacKinlay, November 29, 1921; and Mrs. H.C. Mei (Gong Hezhen) to "Fellow Workers," March 25, 1922, Microfilm 50.2, USA/China.

34 Ibid.

35 "First National Convention, Hangchow, October 19–25, 1923," xi, Microfilm 50.1, USA/China.

36 "Minutes of the National Committee of China, March 22, 1923," Box 399, World/China.

37 Rosalee Venable to Miss Harriet Taylor, Foreign Division, National Board, YWCA of the USA, April 6, 1923, Microfilm 50.2, USA/China; Rosalee Venable to Mrs. Waldegrave, July 2, 1923, Box 399, World/China; Address Given by Rosalee Venable, March 19, 1924, Microfilm 50.2, USA/China. Rosalee Venable attributed these words to Ding Shujing.

38 Rosalee Venable to Miss McLaurin, Foreign Division, National Board, YWCA of the USA, June 27, 1923, Microfilm 50.2, USA/China; Rosalee Venable to Mrs. Waldegrave, July 2, 1923; and "National Committee Meeting Minutes, September 27, 1923," Box 399, World/China.

39 "National Committee Meeting Minutes, October 1, 1923," Box 399, World/China; and "Miss Ting – Scholarship," May 8, 1924, Microfilm 50.2, USA/China.

40 "Minutes of the National Committee of China, February 9, 1925," Box 403, World/China.

41 "Message to the China Group from Ting Shu Ching, under Appointment of General Secretary of the China National Committee," n.d., Microfilm 50.2, USA/China.

42 "Ting Shu Ching," October 1936, Microfilm 50.2, USA/China.

43 Lily Haass to Mary Dingman and Agatha Harrison, July 6, 1927, Box 405, World/China.

44 Lily Haass to Mary Dingman, September 30, 1927, Box 405, World/China.

45 Gertrude Steel-Brooke to "Dear Friends," February 29, 1928, Box 406, World/China.

46 "National Committee Minutes, March 21 and April 18, 1928," Box 406, World/China.

47 Lily Haass to Agatha Harrison and Mary Dingman, February 28, 1929, Box 406, World/China; Ting Shu Ching to "My Dear Friends," March 6, 1929, Box 406, World/China.

48 Lily Haass to Agatha Harrison and Mary Dingman, February 28, 1929.

49 "National Committee Minutes, June 27, 1930," Box 408; and Lily Haass to "Dear Friends," September 10, 1929, Box 406, World/China.

50 Shu-Ching Ting, "Trends in the Young Women's Christian Association of China," January 7, 1930, Microfilm 50.1, USA/China; and "Brief Review of the Work of the Literature Project Commission, First Project September 1931 to December 1932," April 13, 1933, Microfilm 52.2, USA/China.

51 Lily Haass to Mrs. Cotton, July 29, 1934, Box 410, World/China.

52 "Directory of YWCA of China 1934," Microfilm 50, USA/China.

53 Rosalee Venable, "Ting Shu Ching," October 1936, Microfilm 50.2, USA/China.

54 Lily Haass to "Dear Friends," December 5, 1935, Microfilm 51.2, USA/China.

55 Gioh-fang Dju (Mrs. T.S. Ma), *The YWCA of China, 1933–1947* (Shanghai: National Committee of the Young Women's Christian Association of China, 1947), 19, Box 416, World/China.

56 Ting Shu Ching, "Message to the China Group from Ting Shu Ching."

57 Carrie A. Foster, *The Women and the Warriors: The U.S. Section of the Women's International League for Peace and Freedom, 1915–1946* (Syracuse: Syracuse University Press, 1995), 6.

58 "Miss Jane Addams's Addresses," *NCH*, May 12, 1923.

59 Ting Shu Ching, "For the World Service Council Meeting, May 19, 1925," Ting Shu Ching, Correspondence with National General Secretaries, Microfilm 50.2, USA/China.

60 Translated by James Legge. In Chinese, 大道之行也,天下為公,選賢與能,講信修睦.故人不獨親其親,不獨子其子 (*Da dao zhi xing ye, tian xia wei gong, xuan xian yu neng, jiang xin xiu mu. Gu ren bu du qin qi qin, bu du zi qi zi*). This is a partial quote from a larger passage in a section that describes Confucius's ideal society and was foundational for Sun Yat-sen's philosophy. Ding left out the fourth phrase, 講信修睦 (Their words were sincere, and what they cultivated was harmony).

61 "Give-and-Take: China YWCA, 1926" (Shanghai: National Committee of the YWCA of China), Microfilm 50, USA/China.

62 Ting Shu Ching to Mrs. John Finlay, National YWCA of the USA, January 23, 1931, Microfilm 50.2, USA/China.

63 "The Way Ahead of the China YWCA," November 1929, and "Newsletter," October 1934, YWCA of the USA, Microfilm 50.2, USA/China.

64 "Reports of the Conference of Industrial Secretaries of the YWCA, September 1 and 2, 1927" (this report later became the article "Trends in YWCA Industrial Work in China To-Day"), Box 404, World/China.

65 Ting Shu Ching, "Profession Ideals and Standards," in "Report of the Second Conference of Industrial Secretaries of the YWCA Held at Shanghai, February 20–24, 1930," Box 408, World/China.

66 Cora Deng, "Christianity and Industrial Women," *Chinese Recorder* 65, 2 (February 1934): 76.

67 Dju, *YWCA of China*, 21.

68 Tsai Kwei, "China Speaks," 1937, 3, Microfilm 50.2, USA/China.

69 Ibid.

70 Ibid.

CHAPTER 3: SEEKING A PLACE IN A SOCIAL REVOLUTION, 1926–36

Epigraph: Ruth Woodsmall interview with Mrs. L.C. King (Mrs. Jin Longzhang), vice president of the YWCA national committee and interim general secretary of the Shanghai city association, March 13, 1932, Laymen's Foreign Missions Inquiry 1930–32, Box 29, MS175 Series V – Professional Activities, Ruth Frances Woodsmall Papers, Sophia Smith Collection of Women's History, Smith College, Northampton, MA (hereafter Ruth Woodsmall Papers).

1 R. Keith Schoppa, *Revolution and Its Past: Identities and Change in Modern Chinese History*, 3rd ed. (New York: Routledge, 2011), 181–200.

2 "Hinder, Eleanor Mary (1893–1963)," https://trove.nla.gov.au/people/706060?c=people; and "Hinder, Eleanor Mary (1893–1963)," *Australian Dictionary of Biography*, http://adb.anu.edu.au/biography/hinder-eleanor-mary-6678.

3 "Labor Unions Drive for Funds: More Propaganda Used in Connection with Appeal," *NCH*, January 23, 1926. See also Chesneaux, *The Chinese Labor Movement*, 280–84.

4 Eleanor Hinder to Mary Dingman ("old dear"), September 2, 1926, Box 402, World/China.

5 "Agitators Again Active among Labourers," *NCH*, November 7, 1925.

6 Eleanor Hinder to "My dears," May 16, 1926, Box 402, World/China.

7 Lily Haass to Mary Dingman and Agatha Harrison, September 28, 1926, Box 402, World/China.

8 Jane Addams's Hull-House Settlement project was her personal home but also a community centre that offered social services to Chicago's working-class residents.

9 Lily Haass to Mary Dingman and Agatha Harrison, October 30, 1926, and Lily Haass to Mary Dingman, December 22, 1926, Box 402, World/China; and Eleanor Hinder to Mary Dingman, January 3, 1927, Box 405, World/China.

10 Eleanor Hinder to Mary Dingman, March 29, 1927, Microfilm 51.2, USA/China.

11 Eleanor Hinder to Mary Dingman, April 18, 1927, Box 405, World/China.

12 Eleanor Hinder, "The YWCA Seeks Its Place in a Social Revolution," *"Green Year" Supplement*, Folder 222-1709a, WSCF, CRP/YDSL, May 25, 1927, 23–29.

13 The discussion of the conference is from "Reports of the Conference of Industrial Secretaries of the YWCA, September 1 and 2, 1927," Box 404, and Eleanor Hinder to Mary Dingman, September 15, 1927, Box 405, World/China.

14 Ding Shujing to Agatha Harrison, July 5, 1927, Microfilm 50.2, USA/China; and Lily Haass to Mary Dingman and Agatha Harrison, July 6, 1927, Box 405, World/China.

15 Lily Haass, "Trends in YWCA Industrial Work in China To-Day," Box 404, World/China.

16 "National Committee Minutes, March 19, 1925," Box 403, World/China; Lily Haass to Rosalee Venable, March 20, 1925, Microfilm 51.2, USA/China; and Lily Haass to Mary Dingman and Agatha Harrison, October 7, 1925, Box 402, World/China.

17 Lily Haass to Mary Dingman, November 7, 1927, Box 405, World/China.

18 Mary Dingman to Lily Haass, November 24, 1927, 2, Box 405, World/China.

19 Lily Haass to Mary Dingman, January 5, 1928, Box 406, World/China.

20 Ibid.

21 Deng Yu Chih (Deng Yuzhi), "A Visit to a Silk Filature in Shanghai," *The "Green Year" Supplement YWCA of China: Industrial Number*, November 1928, 9–12, Box 406, World/China.

22 Eleanor Hinder, "Toward the End of a Two-Year Term, Phases in an Evolution," January 1, 1928, 3, Box 406, World/China; and Kyong Bae-tsung (Gong Peizhen), "Education of Industrial Women and Girls," *The "Green Year" Supplement YWCA of China: Industrial Number*, November 1928, 15–17, Box 406, World/China.

23 Hinder, "Toward the End of a Two-Year Term."

24 For a discussion of the Yangshupu social centre, see Dorothy Ko Yin-yee, "Social Reformism in Action: The YMCA-YWCA and the Chinese Labor Conditions, 1917–1927" (unpublished paper, July 1979). I wish to thank Dr. Ko for sharing her paper.

25 Wang Zhijin, "How We Used the YWCA Night Schools for Working Women to Advance Our Efforts prior to the Liberation of Shanghai" [Shanghai jiefang yiqian women zenyang

liyong Jidujiao nüqingnianhui nügong yexiao jinxing gongzuo], trans. Erik Avasalu, October 19, 1953, 1–16, Shanghai Academy of Social Sciences, Shanghai. This handwritten document was found in a random search of documents from 1930 at the Shanghai Academy of Social Sciences by Dr. Lien Lingling of the Institute of History, Academia Sinica, Nankang, Taiwan, in June 2005. Dr. Lien photographed the document and sent it to me.

26 Kyong Bae-tsung, "Education of Industrial Women and Girls," 15–17; and Honig, *Sisters and Strangers,* 218–23.

27 Wang Zhijin, "How We Used the YWCA Night Schools," 3.

28 Ibid.

29 Hinder, "Toward the End of a Two-Year Term."

30 Ibid.

31 Unless otherwise noted, the discussion of the second national convention is drawn from "Second National Convention of the YWCA in China, from Discussion Group Topics, July 1928," Microfilm 50.1, USA/China.

32 "Biennial Report of the National Committee of the Young Women's Christian Association in China, 1927–1929," 5, Microfilm 50, USA/China.

33 Ibid.

34 A. Estelle Paddock, "Shanghai – A Sketch," *Association Monthly,* National Board of the Young Women's Christian Association of the United States of America, 5, 11 (December 1911): 435.

35 "National Committee Minutes, April 21, 1927," Folder – untitled, Box 404, and "Rural Work and the YWCA of China," 1932, 1, Box 409, World/China.

36 See Sheridan, *China in Disintegration.*

37 Tsai and Haass, "A Study of the Young Women's Christian Association of China, II," 67.

38 Tsai and Haass, "A Study of the Young Women's Christian Association of China, II."

39 "Biennial Report of the National Committee."

40 Lily Haass to Mary Dingman, January 5, 1928, Box 406, World/China.

41 Cora Deng (Deng Yuzhi) to "Dear Fellow Workers," May 8, 1931, Box 407, World/China.

42 "Report of National Industrial Department 1929–1930," Cora Deng (Deng Yuzhi) to Mary Dingman, October 16, 1930, and "China – News from Cora Deng, National Industrial Secretary in China" in a letter dated October 16, 1930, Box 408, World/China.

43 "National Committee Minutes, June 28, 1929," Box 496, World/China.

44 Ting Shu-ching, "Profession Ideals and Standards," in "Report of the Second Conference of Industrial Secretaries of the YWCA Held at Shanghai, February 20–24, 1930," Box 408, World/China.

45 Porter, *Industrial Reformers,* 66–68.

46 Shu-Ching Ting to Members of the National Committee and Staff of China, December 9, 1929, Microfilm 50.1, USA/China.

47 Lily Haass to Sarah Lyon, December 2, 1929, Microfilm 51.2, USA/China.

48 Shu-Ching Ting to Mrs. John H. Finlay, January 23, 1931, Microfilm 50.1, USA/China.

49 Shu-Ching Ting to Members of the National Committee and Staff of China, March 1, 1930, Microfilm 50.1, USA/China.

50 One fragile copy of the report is preserved in Box 424, World/China.

51 Lily Haass to Sarah Lyon, December 2, 1929, Microfilm 51.2, USA/China; and "Minutes of the National Committee, October 29, 1930," Box 408, World/China.

52 One very fragile copy of the full report, "A Study of the YWCA of China 1891–1930," is preserved in the World YWCA Archives.

53 "National Committee Minutes, September 19, 1930," Box 408, World/China; Deng Yuzhi to Mary Dingman, October 16, 1930, and "China – News from Cora Deng, National Industrial Secretary in China" in a letter dated October 16, 1930, Box 408, World/China.

54 "Report of Work of Industrial Department, Shanghai YWCA, September to October 1930," and "A Few Facts about the Industrial Department and Its Work," 1931, Box 408, World/China.

55 Most YWCA industrial programs were forced to close when the Japanese invaded China in July 1937 and subsequently occupied industrial cities in eastern China. Industrial night school work continued in Shanghai's International Settlement until December 8, 1941, the day after Pearl Harbor, when the Japanese occupied it. There were plans to resume industrial work after the war ended but, as will be seen, circumstances would prevent that.

56 Deng Yuzhi to Mary Dingman, October 16, 1930, and "National Committee Minutes, June 27, 1930," Box 408, World/China.

57 Mary Dingman to "My Dear Cora," August 3, 1931, Box 407, and Deng Yuzhi to Mary Dingman, March 13, 1933, Box 409, World/China.

58 Deng Yuzhi, "Shanghai YWCA Factory Women's Night School" [Shanghai Jidujiao nüqingnian hui nügong yexiao], in Deng Commemorative Volume, 18–19.

59 Porter, Industrial Reformers, 69–70.

60 Honig, "Christianity, Feminism, and Communism," 136.

61 Wang Zhijin, "How We Used the YWCA Night Schools," 2–3.

62 Ibid.

63 May Bagwell, "May Bagwell," November 7, 1931, Microfilm 51.2, USA/China.

64 May Bagwell, "Industrial Girls' Conference," April 1932, Microfilm 51.2, USA/China.

65 Wang Zhijin, "How We Used the YWCA Night Schools."

66 There is some controversy over whether this was the Marxist-Leninist Study Group mentioned in so many biographies of Rewi Alley and previous studies of YWCA industrial work, including my own. Anne-Marie Bradley states that according to one of its members, there were only four expatriates in that group and Rewi Alley was not one of them, although he later claimed to have been. Anne-Marie Bradley, Friend of China – The Myth of Rewi Alley (London: Routledge, 2003), 29.

67 Garner, Precious Fire, 133–36.

68 Deng Yuzhi, "Shanghai YWCA Factory Women's Night School," 18–19, and "Mr. Tao Zingzhi – The Outstanding Educator I Knew" [Wo suo renshide jiechu de renmin jiaoyujia Tao Xingzhi xiansheng], in Deng Commemorative Volume, 157–59.

69 Deng Yuzhi, "Shanghai YWCA Factory Women's Night School," 17.

70 Honig, "Christianity, Feminism, and Communism," 136.

71 Christian Henriot, Shanghai, 1927–1937: Municipal Power, Locality, and Modernization, trans. Noël Castellino (Berkeley: University of California Press, 1993), 65–73.

72 Ibid., 83–94.

73 Mrs. C.C. Chen (Sheng Zuxin) on behalf of the National Committee of the YWCA of China, "A Statement Recording the Evolving Thinking and Attitudes of a Group of Chinese Women in the YWCA in Respect to International Action, September 1931 – February 1932, for Presentation to the League of Nations Commission of Enquiry Concerning Manchuria," "Green Year" Supplement no. 26, April 1932, 7–8, Box 409, World/China.

74 Ibid.

75 "To the League of Nations Commission of Inquiry, a Declaration of the Chinese Women's League for the Promotion of Women's Rights," March 1932, Box 409, World/China. Attached to the English document was an abbreviated version in Chinese.

76 Ibid.

77 Interview with Miss Ting, general secretary of the YWCA, and Mrs. C.C. Chen (Sheng Zuxin), president of the YWCA national committee, March 13, 1932, Ruth Woodsmall Papers 1930–32, Box 29, MS175 Series V – Professional Activities, Ruth Woodsmall Papers.

78 Ting Shu Ching to Mrs. Cushman, Minneapolis, Minn., April 15, 1932, Microfilm 50.2, USA/China.

79 Ting Shu Ching to "Dear Friends," February 28, 1933, Microfilm 50.2, USA/China.

80 "News for the Month of March," April 3, 1933, Microfilm 50.2, USA/China.

81 Porter, *Industrial Reformers*, 47–72.

82 Ruth Woodsmall interview with Lily Haass and Jane Ward, YWCA Shanghai, March 10, 1932, Ruth Woodsmall Papers.

83 Ruth Woodsmall interview with Mrs. L.C. King, Secretary, Shanghai YWCA, March 1932, Ruth Woodsmall Papers.

84 Ruth Woodsmall interview with Lily Haass and Jane Ward. The term "returned student" (*liu xuesheng*) refers to students who returned from studying abroad in Europe or America.

85 "Report of the Third Conference of Industrial Secretaries," Microfilm 52.2, USA/China.

86 The discussion of the third national convention is taken from Convention Reports 1923, 1928, 1933, Microfilm 50.1, USA/China; "Summer Gatherings: The YWCA Third National Convention," *Chinese Recorder* 64 (October 1933): 678–82 (both draft and published article).

87 "Directory of the YWCA of China, 1934," Microfilm 50.1, USA/China.

88 Ting Shu-jing, "The Way Ahead of the China YWCA," November 1929, and "Newsletter," October 1934, Microfilm 50.2, USA/China.

89 Cora Deng, "Labour Problems," Box 410, World/China; Woodhead, *The China Yearbook 1934–35*, 15–18; and Patricia Stranahan, *Underground: The Shanghai Communist Party and the Politics of Survival, 1927–1937* (Lanham, MD: Rowman and Littlefield, 1998), 103–46.

90 Henriot, *Shanghai, 1927–1937*, 218–25; Ko, "Social Reformism in Action"; Porter, *Industrial Reform*, 46; and Cora Deng, "Industrial Welfare Work in China," 1936, 5–8, Box 410, World/China.

91 Deng, "Labour Problems"; and Deng, "Industrial Welfare Work in China."

92 Cora Deng, "Report of the Industrial Work of the National Committee of the YWCA of China," Box 406, World/China; and "Industrial Work, 1934–1936," Microfilm 52.2, USA/China.

93 Cora Deng, "Christianity and Industrial Women," *Chinese Recorder* 65, 2 (February 1934).

94 Deng Yuzhi, "Shanghai YWCA Factory Women's Night School," 18.

95 Roxanne Witke, *Comrade Chiang Ch'ing* (Boston: Little, Brown, 1977), 82–94.

96 Honig, *Sisters and Strangers*, 220.

97 Witke, *Comrade Chiang Ch'ing*, 82.

98 Honig, *Sisters and Strangers*, 222–23.

99 Ibid.
100 Deng Yuzhi, "Shanghai YWCA Factory Women's Night School," 20–21.
101 Rosalee Venable, "Ting Shu Ching," October 1936, Microfilm 50.2, USA/China.
102 Ibid.
103 Ruth Woodsmall to Lily Haass, January 28, 1936, Box 410, World/China; Venable, "Ting Shu Ching"; and Lily Haass to "Dear Friends," July 10, 1936, Microfilm 50.2, USA/China.

CHAPTER 4: CLAIMING NATIONAL CITIZENSHIP, 1937–48

Epigraph: Lily K. Haass, "Gleanings from the Interior," April 1939, Box 419, World/China.
1 Jonathan Spence, *The Search for Modern ·China* (New York: W.W. Norton, 1990), 444–48.
2 Map: "Refugee Camps in 1937," Virtual Shanghai, Virtual Cities Project, Institut d'Asie Orientale, http://www.virtualshanghai.net/Asset/Preview/vcMap_ID-303_No-1.jpeg. This map shows the location of all refugee camps. No camps are identified by name.
3 "Wartime Activities of the Shanghai YWCA with the National YWCA Co-operating," 9/3/1947, Box 411, World/China.
4 "Annual Report, YWCA of China, 1938–39," 2, Box 411, World/China.
5 Stephen R. McKinnon, *Wuhan, 1938: War, Refugees, and the Making of Modern China* (Berkeley: University of California Press, 2008), 14.
6 See McKinnon, *Wuhan, 1938.*
7 Lily Haass to Ruth Woodsmall, February 3, 1938, Box 411, World/China.
8 Tong Ren, trans. Erik Avasalu, "Interview with an Elder of the Three-Self Patriotic Movement – Deng Yuzhi" [Fang sanzi yuanlao zhiyi Deng Yuzhi xiansheng], *Christian Weekly,* 9 (1986), reprinted in *Deng Commemorative Volume,* 62–64; and Honig, "Christianity, Feminism, and Communism," 259. It is noteworthy that these interviews were only a year apart. Also, Honig's interview with Deng was in English at Deng's request.
9 Tsai Kwei, "Report on Trip to South Central and West China, January – March 1938," Microfilm 50.1, USA/China.
10 Tsai Kwei and Lily K. Haass, "Report on Trip to Central, West, and South China – Conclusions," January–March 1938, Microfilm 50.1, USA/China.
11 Marion Dudley to Ruth Woodsmall, April 17, 1945, Box 417, World/China.
12 See John Israel, *Lianda: A Chinese University in War and Revolution* (Stanford, CA: Stanford University Press, 1998).
13 Tsai Kwei, "Report on Trip to South Central and West China."
14 Ibid.
15 Ibid.
16 McKinnon, *Wuhan, 1938,* 47–49.
17 Tsai Kwei, "Report on Trip to South Central and West China."
18 Leila Hinkley to "Dear friends," December 20, 1938, Box 411, World/China; and "General Questions – Annual Report, September 1938 – August 1939, National Committee Y.W.C.A. of China," Box 411, World/China.
19 Haass, "Gleanings from the Interior."
20 Schoppa, *Revolution and Its Past,* 266.
21 Haass, "Gleanings from the Interior."
22 "Annual Report, YWCA of China, 1938–39," 6, 13.

23 Tsai Kwei to Miss Elizabeth M. McFarland, June 29, 1939, Microfilm 50.2, USA/ China.

24 "Facts about City Associations 1938–1939," part of annual report to the YWCA of the USA, with a cover letter from Tsai Kwei to Elizabeth McFarland dated September 9, 1939, Box 419, World/China.

25 For a detailed description, see C. Peter Chen, "Tianjin Incident," World War II Database, https://ww2db.com/battle_spec.php?battle_id=250.

26 Haass, "Gleanings from the Interior," 1.

27 Dju, *YWCA of China*, 86–87.

28 Garner, *Precious Fire*, 163.

29 Dju, *YWCA of China*, 86–87.

30 "International Education Commission Bulletin, National Committee YWCA of China, April 30, 1940," Record Group U1-121-0-19-[2], SMA.

31 Helen M. Schneider, "The Women's Advisory Council, Resistance and Reconstruction during China's War with Japan," *European Journal of East Asia Studies* 11, 2 (2012): 214.

32 "City Department Committee Minutes, April 1939," and Tsai Kwei to "Dear Co-workers All," October 18, 1939, Microfilm 50, USA/China.

33 "The YWCA of China Industrial Cooperative Work 1941," Box 420, World/China; and Garner, *Precious Fire*, 165.

34 Wilfred Burchett and Rewi Alley, *China: The Quality of Life* (Baltimore: Penguin, 1976); Bradley, *Friend of China;* and Garner, *Precious Fire*, 165–66.

35 Ruth Packard to "Dear Friends," November 9, 1939, and Ruth Packard, "Nations Must Act as Friends: A Letter from Ruth Packard American YWCA Secretary in China, Written from Kunming, Yunan," Microfilm 51.3, USA/China; and "The YWCA of China Industrial Cooperative Work."

36 Garner, *Precious Fire*, 165.

37 Ibid.

38 "International Education Commission Bulletin, National Committee YWCA of China, May 1939," Record Group U1-121-0-19-[2], SMA.

39 Tsai Kwei to Ruth Woodsmall, World YWCA, May 11, 1940, Box 420, World/China.

40 Ibid.

41 Tsai Kwei to Miss Sarah S. Lyon, November 6, 1940, and "Minutes Staff Meeting, November 1, 1940," Microfilm 50.2, USA/China.

42 Ibid.

43 Tsai Kwei, to Australia, Canada, Great Britain, India, Burma, Ceylon, Malayan Committee, Honolulu, Philippines, and New Zealand, December 31, 1940, Microfilm 50.2, USA/ China.

44 Lydia Johnson to Ruth Woodsmall, World YWCA General Secretary, August 13, 1941, Box 418, World/China.

45 Lily K. Haass, "New Trends in the Young Women's Christian Association," reprint from the *Chinese Recorder* (January 1941), Box 418, World/China.

46 Ibid.

47 Schoppa, *Revolution and Its Past*, 264–66.

48 Lydia Johnson Interview, January 29, 1970, China Missionaries Oral History Project, Claremont University Graduate School Oral History Program, Claremont, CA; BBC Southern Counties Radio, "Internment in Shanghai," Article ID: A5730464, WW2

People's War: An Archive of World War Two Memories, http://www.bbc.co.uk/history/
ww2peopleswar/stories/64/a5730464.shtml. Note: this website has been archived.

49 "Report from December 1942 – August 1945 by Emergency General Secretary Mrs. C.C.
Chen," 1–2, Box 417, World/China.

50 Ibid.

51 Ibid.

52 Ibid.

53 In 1931, the Japanese invasion of Manchuria cut the Mukden YWCA off from the national
office in Shanghai. The World YWCA allowed the Mukden city association to affiliate
directly with it, an action that angered the Chinese national office.

54 Tsai Kwei to Ruth Woodsmall, January 26, 1943, Box 418, World/China.

55 "Report from December 1942 – August 1945 by Emergency General Secretary Mrs. C.C.
Chen."

56 For a list and description of each, see "Captives of Empire: The Japanese Internment of
Allied Civilians in China and Hong Kong, 1941–1945," https://captives-of-empire.com/
the-camps. This website lists thirteen camps in or near Shanghai. A diary by an internee
at Lunghwa camp inspired Steven Spielberg's movie *Empire of the Sun*.

57 Historically, it is commonly referred to as the Weihsien (pinyin: Weixian) Internment
Camp.

58 "Internment: Internment of Civilians," The Pacific War Online Encyclopedia, http://
pwencycl.kgbudge.com/I/n/Internment.htm.

59 Lydia Johnson Interview; and Boyd, *Emissaries,* 207–8. Boyd mistakenly states that the
camp was closed in 1943. Among those interned at Weixian along with Leila Hinkley was
British Sinologist Paul Thompson, who was my undergraduate adviser at the University
of Wisconsin. Thompson and his missionary parents were released at the end of the war.
His brother was accidentally electrocuted in the camp. Olympian Eric Liddell, immortal-
ized in the movie *Chariots of Fire,* who became a missionary to China, also died in the
camp. See Langdon Gilkey, *Shantung Compound: The Story of Men and Women under
Pressure* (New York: Harper and Row, 1966).

60 The actual exchange took place in Murmugao, a seaport in south Goa, India, on October
16, 1943. Goa was at that time a Portuguese colony and thus a neutral port. A Japanese
troop ship brought more than 1,500 prisoners from Japanese-occupied territories, and they
were exchanged for Japanese prisoners from the United States and South America. The
former American prisoners returned on the *MS Gripsholm,* a Swedish cruise ship leased
by the United States for this purpose. Evelyn Iritani, "The Gripsholm WWII Exchanges,"
Densho Encyclopedia, https://encyclopedia.densho.org/The%20Gripsholm%20WWII%20
Exchanges/.

61 Lily K. Haass, "Toward Building New China: West China Regional Conference of the
YWCA, January 15–19, 1942," 1, Box 418, World/China.

62 Ibid.

63 Ibid.

64 Ibid.

65 Ibid.

66 "Annual Report, National Committee YWCA, August 1, 1943 – August 1, 1944, Personnel
and Training," 1–4, Box 418, World/China.

67 Ibid.

68 Ibid.

69 "Present State of the Young Women's Christian Association in China: Answers to Questions Proposed by the World's YWCA in Preparation for the World's Council Meeting in 1947," 7, Box 416, World/China.

70 "Annual Report, National Committee YWCA, August 1, 1943 – August 1, 1944."

71 Ibid.

72 "Post War Work Plan of the China YWCA," January 10, 1944, 1–8, Box 417, World/China.

73 Marion Dudley to Ruth Woodsmall, April 17, 1945, Box 417, World/China.

74 Ibid.

75 Dju, *YWCA of China,* 22.

76 Tsai Kui to Ruth Woodsmall, November 10, 1945, Box 417, World/China.

77 Ibid.

78 Spence, *Search for Modern China,* 464–66.

79 Esther Morrison, "Survey Report on China Experiences 1946–1950: A – Introduction," 1, Microfilm 50, USA/China.

80 Chang Lien-Hua, "I Accuse!," *China Weekly News,* April 19, 1947; and Esther Morrison, "Survey Report on China Experiences 1946–1950: B – June 1946 – May 1949," 2, Microfilm 50, USA/China. On March 5, Chang was arrested while teaching at a night school on charges of being a communist, imprisoned in Shanghai and Suzhou, and released on March 18 only after she finally signed a confession and was ordered to "forget" the incident.

81 Carole Seymour-Jones, *Journey of Faith: The History of the World YWCA 1945–1994* (London: Allison and Bushby, 1994), 31.

82 Tsai Kwei, "Rehabilitation Budget 1947–1949," Microfilm 50, Finance, USA/China.

83 Tsai Kwei to Margaret Forsyth, April 1, 1947, marked "confidential," Microfilm 50, USA/China.

84 Morrison, "Survey Report on China Experiences 1946–1950: B – June 1946 – May 1949," 8–10.

85 Cora Deng, "Industrial Department and Mass Education," in "Minutes of the National Staff Setting Up Conference, February 10, 1947," 7–9, Box 417, World/China.

86 Seymour-Jones, *Journey of Faith,* 35–36.

87 Karen Garner, "Global Feminism and Postwar Reconstruction: The World YWCA Visitation to Occupied Japan, 1947," *Journal of World History* 15, 2 (June 2004): 209n46.

88 Tsai Kwei to Ruth Woodsmall, December 31, 1946, 1, Box 417, World/China.

89 Seymour-Jones, *Journey of Faith,* 35–36.

90 Ibid., 39.

91 Garner, "Global Feminism and Postwar Reconstruction," 211–13.

92 York Lo, "Yu-Ching Tu: Physicist, College President and Christian Leader," China Comes to MIT: MIT's First Chinese Students, 1877–1931, http://chinacomestomit.org/yc-tu. Tu had also worked with the YMCA and resigned his presidency in 1948 to rejoin the YMCA after the St. John's administration criticized his sympathetic attitude toward students protesting the corrupt GMD. He remained in China after 1949 and became a Christian leader.

93 Seymour-Jones, *Journey of Faith,* 40.

94 *World YWCA Statements of Policy,* 150.

95 Seymour-Jones, *Journey of Faith,* 44–45.

96 Tsai Kwei to Margaret Forsyth, September 1, 1948, and October 15, 1948, Microfilm 50, USA/China.
97 Tsai Kwei to Margaret Forsyth, November 30, 1948, Microfilm 50, USA/China.

CHAPTER 5: EMBRACING THE MAOIST STATE, 1949–50

Epigraph: "Report of the Enlarged Executive Committee Meeting of the Young Women's Christian Association of China and Extracts from the Minutes, Shanghai, March – 1950," 4, Box 416, World/China (hereafter "Report of the Enlarged Executive Committee").

1 Morrison, "Survey Report on China Experiences 1946–1950: A – Introduction," 1.
2 Jeremy Brown and Paul G. Pickowicz, "The Early Years of the People's Republic of China: An Introduction," in *Dilemmas of Victory: The Early Years of the People's Republic of China*, ed. Jeremy Brown and Paul G. Pickowicz (Cambridge, MA: Harvard University Press, 2007), 1–18.
3 Tsai Kwei to Helen Roberts, January 22, 1949, Box 416, World/China.
4 This was important, as in Chinese the word "Christian" came first: Jidujiao nü qingnian hui, which is literally translated as the "Christian Young Women's Association."
5 Tsai Kwei to Helen Roberts, January 22, 1949.
6 Ibid.
7 Spence, *Search for Modern China*, 510–11; Yufan Hao and Zhihai Zhai, "China's Decision to Enter the Korean War: History Revisited," *International History Review* 19, 1 (February 1997): 96–97, https://www.jstor.org/stable/654064; and "Chinese Civil War," *Encyclopedia Britannica*, https://www.britannica.com/event/Chinese-Civil-War.
8 Julia Cheng to Madeline Roden, May 12, 1949, Microfilm 50, USA/China.
9 Ibid.
10 Margaret Garvie to Florence Sutton, July 29, 1949, 1, Box 416, World/China.
11 Ibid.
12 Gao, "Y.T. Wu."
13 Margaret Garvie to Florence Sutton, July 29, 1949. The federation's name is sometimes given as "All-China Women's Democratic Federation."
14 Zheng Wang, *Women in the Chinese Enlightenment: Oral and Textual Histories* (Berkeley: University of California Press, 1999), 142.
15 Ibid.
16 Cai Kui to "Dear Friends," October 6, 1949, Loose-Leaf Binder China I, World/China.
17 Nara Dillon, "New Democracy and the Demise of Private Charity in Shanghai," in Brown and Pickowicz, 80, 82.
18 Ibid., 82.
19 Deng Yuzhi, "The Responsibility of the YWCA in the Reconstruction of China in the New Democracy," Box 416, translation by unknown translator from article in *YWCA Magazine*, August 1949, 1–3, World/China. The magazine ceased publication in September.
20 Ibid.
21 Jean Kao to Talitha Gerlach, August 24, 1949, Loose-Leaf Binder China I, World/China. Jean Kao most probably was Gao Yuxin.
22 Deng Yuzhi, trans. Erik Avasalu, "Our Experiences at the Chinese People's Political Consultative Conference" [Women canjia jenmin zhengxie huiyide jingguo], *Christian Weekly*, no. 10 (October 1, 1949), reprinted in *Deng Commemorative Volume*, 37–39.

23 Cai Kui to Helen Roberts, October 6, 1949, 1–2, Loose-Leaf Binder China I, World/China.
24 Ibid., 2.
25 See Dillon, "New Democracy and the Demise of Private Charity in Shanghai."
26 "From a Quaker Missionary in Shanghai," receipt date stamped June 8, 1950, Box 416, World/China.
27 Margaret Brennecke to Margaret Forsyth, February 23, 1950, 1, Microfilm 51, USA/China.
28 "From a Quaker Missionary in Shanghai."
29 Cai Kui to Helen Roberts, December 17, 1949, Box 416, World/China.
30 Cai Kui to Margaret Forsyth, December 20, 1949, Microfilm 50, USA/China.
31 Honig, "Christianity, Feminism and Communism," 260. Their whereabouts were identified by the address on their correspondence.
32 Spence, Search for Modern China, 489–94, 507–13; and Julia C. Strauss, "Paternalist Terror: The Campaign to Suppress Counterrevolutionaries and Regime Consolidation in the People's Republic of China, 1950–1953," Comparative Studies in Society and History 44, 1 (2002): 80–84, http://www.jstor.org/stable/3879401.
33 Strauss, "Paternalist Terror," 84. These principles also underlaid much of Zhou Enlai's thinking. Philip L. Wickeri, Seeking Common Ground: Protestant Christianity, the Three-Self Movement, and China's United Front (Eugene, OR: Wipf and Stock, 2004), 107.
34 "Report of the Enlarged Executive Committee Meeting," 5.
35 Ibid., 9.
36 Ibid.
37 Ibid., 5.
38 Ibid., 1–3.
39 Ibid., 10.
40 Ibid.
41 Ibid., 16.
42 Ibid., 2.
43 Ibid., 6–7.
44 Morrison, "Survey Report on China Experiences 1946–1950: B – June 1946 – May 1949."
45 Yang Kuisong, "Reconsidering the Campaign to Suppress Counterrevolutionaries," China Quarterly 193 (2008): 104–5, https://www.jstor.org/stable/20192166; Spence, Search for Modern China, 489–94, 507–13; and Strauss, "Paternalist Terror," 80–84.
46 "National Committee of YWCA of China, Statement by Committee of National Staff," April 10, 1950, Box 416, World/China.
47 Wickeri, Seeking Common Ground, 125.
48 K.S.W. Sun (Wang Guoxiu) to Margaret Forsyth, April 8, 1950, Microfilm 50, USA/China; and Margaret Brennecke to Margaret Forsyth, April 6, 1950, Microfilm 50, USA/China.
49 Mrs. J.H. Sun (Wang Guoxiu) and Cora Deng to Ruth West, April 17, 1950, Box 416, World/China; and similar letter to Margaret Brennecke, Microfilm 51, USA/China.
50 Ruth West to Florence Pierce, May 1, 1950, 2, Microfilm 51, USA/China.
51 Margaret Garvie to Elizabeth Palmer, received July 7, 1950, 5, Box 416, World/China. This letter is not dated. In it, Garvie noted that airmail could reach her from England in as little as ten days. Her reference to "a year after liberation" suggests that this letter was written in June. It is the last letter from Garvie in the World YWCA Archives.
52 Ibid., 4–5.

53 Ibid., 2.
54 Ibid., 3–4.
55 "Robbins Strong Papers, 1934–1989, n.d. | Oberlin College Archives," http://oberlinar chives.libraryhost.com/index.php?p=collections/controlcard&id=240&q=robbins+str ong (see "Administrative/Biographical History").
56 Robbins Strong, "Report on China," May 18, 1950, Loose-Leaf Binder China I – Visapää Visit 1957, World/China.
57 Ibid.
58 Zhou Enlai, "Several Questions on China's Nationalities Policies," August 4, 1957, *Selected Writings of Zhou Enlai on the United Front* (Beijing: People's Publishers, 1984), 383–84, quoted in Wickeri, *Seeking Common Ground*, 107.
59 Wickeri, *Seeking Common Ground*, 127–28.
60 Ibid., 129.
61 Ibid., 70; and Fuk-Tsang Ying, "The CPC's Policy on Protestant Christianity, 1949–1957: An Overview and Assessment," *Journal of Contemporary China* 23, 89 (June 2014): 887.
62 Ying, "The CPC's Policy on Protestant Christianity," 885–87; and Wickeri, *Seeking Common Ground*, 107.
63 Tong Ren, "Interview with an Elder of the Three-Self Patriotic Movement"; and Wickeri, *Seeking Common Ground*, 95.
64 Wickeri, *Seeking Common Ground*, 95, 114–15.
65 Tong Ren, "Interview with an Elder of the Three-Self Patriotic Movement."
66 Full name: "Direction of Endeavor for Chinese Christianity in the Construction of New China" [Zhongguo Jidujiao zai xin Zhongguo jianshe zhong nul tujing].
67 Wickeri, *Seeking Common Ground*, 129; and "Manifesto of the Chinese Church," July 28, 1950, Box 416, World/China.
68 "Manifesto of the Chinese Church."
69 Ibid.
70 O.M. Green, "Split Feared among China's Christians," *London Observer*, October 2, 1950, Box 416, World/China.
71 Ibid.
72 Tong Ren, "Interview with an Elder of the Three-Self Patriotic Movement."
73 Zhou Enlai, quoted in Wickeri, *Seeking Common Ground*, 108.
74 Hao and Zhai, "China's Decision to Enter the Korean War," 99–100.
75 "Resolution 83 (1950) [Adopted by the Security Council at Its 474th Meeting], of 27 June 1950," United Nations Digital Library, https://digitallibrary.un.org/record/112026?ln=en.
76 Hao and Zhai, "China's Decision to Enter the Korean War," 100–11.
77 Allan R. Millett, "Korean War, 1950–1953," *Encyclopedia Britannica*, https://www.britannica.com/event/Korean-War. Millett, a renowned expert on the Korean War, is director of the Eisenhower Center for American Studies at the University of New Orleans.
78 Jean Kao Wu to Miss Palmer, January 19, 1951, Box 416, World/China.
79 Honig, "Christianity, Feminism, and Communism," 261.
80 Margaret Forsyth to Lily Haass, December 21, 1950, Microfilm 51.2, USA/China.
81 Honig, "Christianity, Feminism, and Communism," 262.
82 Margaret Forsyth to Lily Haass, December 21, 1950.
83 Cora Deng, "Religious Representatives at the 2nd World Peace Conference," World YWCA translated excerpts from 1951 issues of *YWCA Magazine*, February excerpts, 3, Box 416, World/China (hereafter World excerpts/1951).

84 Deng Yuzhi, "My Thoughts on Attending the Second Peace Conference" [Canja erjie head de yi xie ganxiang], trans. Erik Avasalu, *YWCA Magazine*, January 1951, 10, U121-0-60-[4], SMA.

CHAPTER 6: CULTIVATING A SOCIALIST MINDSET, 1951–57

Epigraph: "Denounce!" [Kongsu!], trans. Erik Avasalu, *YWCA Magazine*, July 1951, 1, U121-0-61, SMA.

1 Wang Guoxiu, "Hopes for the Re-establishment of *YWCA Magazine*" [Dui nüqing fukan qiwang], *YWCA Magazine*, January 1951, 1.
2 Deng Yuzhi, "The Re-establishment of the Magazine" [Fukanci], *YWCA Magazine*, January 1951.
3 The friend was Sui-May Kuo Ting. Her name was handwritten at the top of one issue. I have not found her Chinese name. She was the wife of the Reverend K.H. Ting (Ding Guangxun). Thus, Ting (Ding) was her married name, Kuo (Guo) her surname, and Sui-May her given name. In 1951, the Tings were living in Geneva, where he worked for the World Student Christian Federation. They returned to Nanjing in 1952. In 1956, K.H. Ting was an Anglican bishop and principal of the Theological College, and Sui-May Kuo Ting was a member of the Nanjing YWCA city association committee. He became the leader of the China Christian Council and the Three-Self Movement in 1980. Sui-May maintained relations with the YWCA, and in 1984 was vice chair of the YWCA national committee.
4 Mary Sullivan to Deng Yuzhi, March 15, 1951 (cover letter to excerpt documents), and Deng Yuzhi to Mary Sullivan, April 2, 1951, Box 416, World/China.
5 "Announcement on How to Commemorate May 1st," April excerpts, 1–2, World excerpts/1951.
6 YWCA Labor and Education Department, "An Overview of Labor and Education Work for the First Half of 1950" [Xiehui laogong ji minjiao, yijiuwuling shangbannian laogong ji minjiao gongzuo gaikuang], trans. Erik Avasalu, *YWCA Magazine*, January 1951, 4–8.
7 "Peking Edict of December 29, 1950: Regulations Governing All Organizations Subsidized with Foreign Funds," in *Documents of the Three-Self Movement: Source Materials for the Study of the Protestant Church in Communist China*, ed. Francis P. Jones (New York: National Council of the Churches of Christ in the USA, 1963), 22–24.
8 "Y.T. Wu's Report," in Jones, *Documents of the Three-Self Movement*, 36.
9 Translated excerpts from *YWCA Magazine*, February 1951, 1, Box 416, World/China.
10 Seymour-Jones, *Journey of Faith*, 344.
11 "Methods for Dealing with Christian Bodies," in Jones, *Documents of the Three Self Movement*, 27–28.
12 "Lu Ting-yi's Speech," in Jones, *Documents of the Three Self Movement*, 29–33.
13 "Y.T. Wu's Report," in Jones, *Documents of the Three Self Movement*, 34–40.
14 Wickeri, *Seeking Common Ground*, 133.
15 Ibid., 133–34.
16 Cai's words were quoted in Wang Xiuqing's July speech, "Denounce the American Imperialists That Are Controlling the YWCA of China to Implement a Policy of Cultural Invasion" [Kongsu meidi kongzhi Zhongguo nüqingnianhui zhixing qinlüe zhengce], trans. Erik Avasalu, *YWCA Magazine*, July 1957, 5, U121-0-61, SMA (hereafter *YWCA Magazine*/1957).

17 Liu Liangmo, "How to Hold a Successful Accusation Meeting, May 15, 1951," in Jones, *Documents of the Three-Self Movement,* 49–51.

18 This article also included the salutation "Chairman, comrades," further suggesting that it was delivered at the mass meeting.

19 Trans. Erik Avasalu, "YWCA News" [Xiehui xiaoxi], *YWCA Magazine*/1957, 18.

20 Garvie arrived back in England after her five-year assignment as a national student secretary in time to publish an article in the June issue of the British association's monthly magazine, the *Blue Triangle,* in which she described the Chinese people as courteous and kind. She praised her Chinese colleagues for their indomitable spirit in the face of unimaginable circumstances. She mentioned hyperinflation and the terror of the Guomindang secret police. Her references to the present were brief and positive: the Chinese association was preparing for a national convention and meeting YWCA representatives from all over the country. She did not comment on what duties she carried out during her final year at the national office. Miss Margaret E. Garvie, "Just Back from China," *Blue Triangle* 69, 6 (June 1951): 5, YWCA of Great Britain, Modern Records Centre, University of Warwick, Coventry, UK.

21 Trans. Erik Avasalu, "Denounce!" (Kongsu!), *YWCA Magazine,* July 1951, 1.

22 Deng Yuzhi, trans. Erik Avasalu, "American Imperialists' Criminal Invasion of Southeast Asia and China via the World YWCA and the Foreign Division of the YWCA of the USA" [Kongsu meidi tongguo Meiguo Nüqingnianxiehui guowaibu ji Shijie Nüqingnianhui jinxing dui dongnanya ji Zhongguode qinlüe zuixing], *YWCA Magazine,* July 1951, 2–5.

23 Liu Liangmo, "How to Hold a Successful Accusation Meeting," 50.

24 Ibid.

25 Ibid.

26 Deng Yuzhi, "American Imperialists' Criminal Invasion."

27 Wang Xiuqing, trans. Erik Avasalu, "Denounce the American Imperialists" [Kongsu Meidi kongzhi Zhongguo nü qingnian hui zhixing qinlüe zhengce], *YWCA Magazine,* July 1951, 5.

28 Ibid.

29 Ibid.

30 Untitled document, handwritten note "rough translation – unpolished" and "confidential," translation preceded by the name "Wang," Box 416, World/China. It can be assumed that Sui-May Kuo Ting also translated this document.

31 Helen Roberts to Inga-Brita Castrèn, April 16, 1956, 1–2, Box 416, World/China.

32 Francisca de Haan, "The Women's International Democratic Federation (WIDF): History, Main Agenda, and Contributions, 1945–1991," in *Women and Social Movements, 1840 to Present,* ed. Thomas Dublin and Kathryn Kish Sklar (2012), http://alexanderstreet.com/products/women-and-social-movements-international.

33 Zheng Wang, "Creating a Socialist Feminist Cultural Front: 'Women of China' (1949–1966)," *China Quarterly* 204 (2010): 834n21.

34 "A Report from the Women's Federation Concerning the YWCA" [Quanguo fulian guanyu Jidujiao n qingnian hui de baogao], 1953, 1031-1-6, Chongqing Municipal Archives. Dr. Kimberly Manning of Concordia University, Montreal, Canada, shared this document with me.

35 Helen Roberts to Inga-Brita Castrèn, April 16, 1956, 2.

36 "Summary of Conversations with Cora Deng and Some Impressions of the Congress," Loose-Leaf Binder China I – Visapää Visit 1957, World/China.

37 For the history of the magazine, see http://www.china.org.cn/english/PP-e/25471.htm.

38 "Christian Life and Activities," extracts from an article by Madame Teng Yu-Chih (Cora Deng), *China Reconstructs,* November–December 1953, Box 416, World/China.

39 "Note on Talk with Rev. Marcus James on His Return from a Visit to China July 18th, 1954," Box 416, World/China.

40 Lena Jeger to "Dear Madam" (The General Secretary), House of Commons, September 29, 1955, Box 416, World/China.

41 British Quaker Mission to the People's Republic of China, *Quakers Visit China* (London: Society of Friends, East-West Relations Committee and Peace Committee, 1956), https://www.pegasusbooks.biz/product/sku/6704.

42 W. Grigor McClelland, "Discussion with Christian Youth Leaders at the Community Church in Shanghai," marked "Strictly confidential: not to be published in any form," Circular Letters to the Executive 1955–1986, Loose-Leaf Binder China I, World/China; and "Grigor McClelland Obituary," *Guardian,* November 14, 2013, https://www.theguardian.com/education/2013/nov/14/grigor-mcclelland.

43 Details of Janet Rees's life come from her daughter's obituary: "In Memory of Dr. Katharine King," April 26, 2016, https://oxfordhigh.gdst.net/in-memory-of-dr-katharine-king. Her husband is listed in many directories of Christian missionaries in China; Janet W. Rees, "The YWCA of China Today," marked "Strictly confidential: not to be published in any form," Circular Letters to the Executive 1955–1986.

44 Mrs. George Wu, "Who Will Help Us Promote YWCA Work?," January excerpts, 3, World excerpts/1951.

45 "Transfer Lists of YWCA Industrial Nights Schools No. 1 and 2 to the Shanghai City Education Department upon Their Closing by the Department" [Shanghai shi jiaoyu ju guangan nü qingnian hui di yi er nügong yexiaoyijiao qingce], April 22, 1952, B-105-5-591, SMA.

46 YWCA Labor and Education Department, "An Overview of Labor and Education Work for the First Half of 1950" [Xiehui laogongji minjiao, yijiuwulingnian shangbannian laogongji minjiao gong zuo gaikuang], *YWCA Magazine*/1957, 4–8.

47 Yu Xiu'ai, trans. Erik Avasalu, "Beijing YWCA 40th Anniversary – My Impressions" [Wo dui Beijing Jidujiao nu qingnian hui sishi zhou nian dahui de ganxiang], *YWCA Magazine*/1957, 5.

48 Zhang Yuezhen, "Proactive in Our Work – Promoting Culture among Women to Serve Socialism" [Jija jiaqiang gongzou, bangzhu funü tigao wenhua, wei shehui zhuyi jianshe fuwu], *YWCA Magazine*/1957, 17–18.

49 For this discussion, see Zheng Wang, "State Feminism? Gender and Socialist State Formation in Maoist China," *Feminist Studies* 31, 3 (Fall 2005): 519–51.

50 Wang, *Women in the Chinese Enlightenment,* 142.

51 Castrèn was a member of the YWCA national committee of Finland. She served on the World YWCA staff from 1962 to 1969. Helen Roberts, "To Members of the Executive Committee," May 1956, 2, Loose-Leaf Binder China I – Visapää Visit, World/China; and Seymour-Jones, *Journey of Faith,* 502.

52 "Sylvi Visapää," *Wikipedia,* https://sv.wikipedia.org/wiki/Sylvi_Visap%C3%A4%C3%A4 (in Finnish).

53 Inga-Brita Castrèn to Helen Roberts, June 4, 1956, marked "confidential," Loose-Leaf Binder China I – Visapää Visit 1957, World/China.

54 Spence, *Search for Modern China*, 551–54. For a summary description of the Band-ung Conference, see United States Office of the Historian, "Bandung Conference (Asian-African Conference, 1955)," https://history.state.gov/milestones/1953-1960/bandung-conf.

55 "The YWCA of China" [Zhongguo Jidujiao nü qingnian hui 中国基督教女青年会], stamped "received 14 Dec. 1957," Box 416, World/China.

56 Spence, *Search for Modern China*, 567–68.

57 Excerpts from transcript of World Executive Committee meeting, July 1956, 1–4, Loose-Leaf Binder China I – Visapää Visit 1957, World/China.

58 Isabel C. Catto, President (of the World YWCA), to Miss Cora Deng, August 8, 1956, 2, Loose-Leaf Binder China I – Visapää Visit 1957, World/China.

59 Elizabeth Palmer to Miss Cora Deng, October 2, 1956, Box 416, World/China.

60 "Notes of Miss Visapää's First Talk to World YWCA Staff after Her Visit to China," November 6, 1957, Loose-Leaf Binder China I – Visapää Visit 1957, World/China.

61 Spence, *Search for Modern China*, 568–72.

62 Deng Yuzhi, trans. Erik Avasalu, "Three Thoughts on Christianity," edited version of speech delivered at the fourth meeting of the First National People's Congress [Youguan Jidujiao fangmiande sandian yijian], in *Deng Commemorative Volume*, 49–52.

63 China historians have raised the same question, and they disagree among themselves. Jonathan Spence, whose *Search for Modern China* has provided basic historical context for this book, believes it was "a muddled and inconclusive movement that grew out of conflicting attitudes within the CCP leadership" (574).

64 Gao Yuxin, trans. Erik Avasalu, "Studying Chairman Mao's 'On the Correct Handling of Con-tradictions among the People' – Excerpts of Discussion" [Xuexi Maozhuxi "quanyu zhengque chuli renmin neibu maodun de wenti" mantan zhailu], *YWCA Magazine*/1957, 11–13.

65 Wang, *Women in the Chinese Enlightenment*, 142.

66 A major landmark building in Shanghai built in 1954. It is now called the Shanghai Exhi-bition Center.

67 Chen Jieshi 陳介石, trans. Erik Avasalu, "I Saw the Respected and Beloved Chairman Mao" [Wo jiandaole zui jingaide Mao zhuxi], *YWCA Magazine* /1957, 12, December 1957, U121-0-61, SMA.

68 Garner, *Precious Fire*, 224.

69 Ibid., 210, 224; and "An American Woman in Shanghai," *People's Daily*, September 20, 1983, 6, Box 412, World/China. Gerlach's contract with the YWCA was not renewed, because of her outspoken support for the People's Republic of China and criticism of US foreign policy.

70 Talitha Gerlach to "Edith," December 11, 1975, Box 412, World/China. A second letter to Edith suggests that she worked for the national office of the YWCA of the USA. Her last name was pencilled in but is illegible.

71 Talitha Gerlach to "Lydia," June 5, 1979, Box 412, World/China. As this letter made its way into the World YWCA archives, this must be another YWCA secretary, pos-sibly Lydia Johnson, as she and Gerlach worked together at the national office in the late 1930s.

72 Ruth Sovik to Erica and Nita re: China visit, August 17 – September 9, 1980, "What We Learned about the YWCA of China," Loose-Leaf Binder China II – 1960s – Correspon-dence, World/China.

73 "Reflections of a Life-Long YWCA Leader in China," *Common Concerns,* December 1995, 20. *Common Concerns* is a publication of the World YWCA in Geneva, Switzerland.

CONCLUSION

1 Directory, Young Women's Association of China, December 1, 1934, and December 1, 1935, Microfilm 50, USA/China.

Bibliography

ARCHIVAL AND OTHER COLLECTIONS

Claremont University Graduate School Oral History Program
    China Missionaries Oral History Project, Special Collections, Honnold Library
        Lydia Johnson, YWCA Secretary
Shanghai Municipal Archives, Shanghai, People's Republic of China (SMA)
    Record Group U1-121-0-19-[2]
    Record Group U121-0-60-[4]
    Record Group B-105-5-591
Sophia Smith Collection of Women's History, Smith College, Northampton, MA
    Ruth Frances Woodsmall Papers
        Sophia Smith Collection MS175 Series V – Professional Activities
    Record Group 5 International Work, YWCA of the USA (USA/China)
        Sophia Smith Collection MS324, microfilms 152–53 (now missing)
World YWCA Archives, Geneva, Switzerland (World/China)
Note: Since my research trip in 2000, the following archives have been reorganized:
    Loose-Leaf Binders
        China I – Visapää Visit 1957 (includes 1950s correspondence)
        China II – 1960s – Correspondence
    Central Filing 1993–1997 B-C
    Box 368 – History of the Industrial Work of the World YWCA 1910–1932
    Box 371 – R. Porter, Study on "YWCAs of China Work with Industrial Girls"
    China files:
        Box 396 – 1899–1921/Correspondence
        Box 397 – 1919–1920/Minutes & Reports
        Box 398 – 1921–1922/Reports
        Box 399 – 1922–1923/Correspondence
        Box 400 – 1923/Minutes & Reports

Box 401 – 1924/Minutes & Reports
Box 402 – 1925–1926/Correspondence
Box 403 – 1925–1926/Minutes & Reports
Box 404 – 1927/Minutes & Reports
Box 405 – 1927/Correspondence
Box 406 – 1928–1929/Correspondence & Minutes
Box 407 – 1931/Reports
Box 408 – 1930–1931/Minutes & Correspondence
Box 409 – 1932–1933/Reports & Correspondence
Box 410 – 1934–1935–1936/Correspondence & Reports
Box 411 – 1937–1938–1939/Correspondence & Reports
Box 412 – Lydia Johnson, Talitha Gerlach, photos
Box 413 – 1890 (Miscellaneous documents)
Box 416 – 1947–1948–1949/Correspondence & Reports (+1951–1959)
Box 417 – 1944–1947/Correspondence & Reports
Box 418 – 1941–1942–1943/Correspondence & Reports
Box 419 – 1939/Minutes & Reports
Box 420 – 1940/Correspondence & Reports
Box 424 – 1911–1917/Reports (includes the 1930 Field Survey)
Yale Divinity School Library, New Haven, CT (YDSL)
  Microfilm Collection
  China Records Project (CRP)
    Record Group 8 – Miscellaneous Personal Papers (MPP)
    Boxes 36–38 Ruth White Carr
    Boxes 88–90 Sarah Boardman Goodrich
    Box 157   Florence Pierce
    Box 167, 9   folders Harriet Rietveld
    Record Group 11 – United Board for Higher Education in Asia (UBCHEA)
    Record Group 46 – World Student Christian Federation Collection (WSCF)
  Historical Records Collection (HRC)

SELECTED CONTEMPORARY NEWSPAPERS AND JOURNALS

Shenbao (Commercial Times), 1919–37
Xin qingnian (New Youth), 1917–19
Nü qingnian (YWCA Magazine), 1921–36, 1950, 1951, 1957
Chinese Recorder and Missionary Journal, 1900–36
"Green Year" Supplement (English supplement to *Nü qingnian*), 1919–29
International Quarterly (quarterly magazine of the World YWCA), 1911–30
North China Herald and Supreme Court and Consular Gazette, 1911–39

SELECTED SECONDARY SOURCES

Bays, Daniel H., ed. *Christianity in China from the Eighteenth Century to the Present.* Stanford, CA: Stanford University Press, 1996.
–. *A New History of Christianity in China.* Chichester, UK: Wiley-Blackwell, 2012.
Bergère, Marie-Claire. *The Golden Age of the Chinese Bourgeoisie 1911–1937.* Translated by Janet Lloyd. Cambridge: Cambridge University Press, 1989.

Boyd, Nancy. *Emissaries: The Overseas Work of the American YWCA 1895–1970*. New York: Women's Press, 1986.

Bradley, Anne-Marie. *Friend of China – The Myth of Rewi Alley*. London: Routledge, 2003.

Browder, Dorothea. "A 'Christian Solution of the Labour Situation': How Working-women Reshaped the YWCA's Religious Mission and Politics." *Journal of Women's History* 19, 2 (Summer 2007): 85–110. https://doi.org/10.1353/jowh.2007.0033.

Brown, Jeremy, and Paul G. Pickowicz. "The Early Years of the People's Republic of China: An Introduction." In *Dilemmas of Victory: The Early Years of the People's Republic of China*, edited by Jeremy Brown and Paul G. Pickowicz. Cambridge, MA: Harvard University Press, 2007.

Brownell, Susan. *Training the Body for China: Sports in the Moral Order of the People's Republic*. Chicago: University of Chicago Press, 1995.

Burchett, Wilfred, and Rewi Alley. *China: The Quality of Life*. Baltimore: Penguin, 1976.

Chang, Yü-fa. "Women – A New Social Force." *Chinese Studies in History* 11, 2 (1977–78): 29–55.

Chao, Jonathan. "Toward a Chinese Christianity: A Protestant Response to the Anti-Imperialist Movement." *Republican China* 17, 2 (April 1992): 95–109.

Ch'en, Jerome. *China and the West: Society and Culture 1815–1937*. Bloomington: Indiana University Press, 1979.

Chesneaux, Jean. *The Chinese Labor Movement 1919–1927*. Stanford, CA: Stanford University Press, 1968.

Chow, Tse-tsung. *The May Fourth Movement*. Cambridge, MA: Harvard University Press, 1960.

Clifford, Nicholas R. *Spoilt Children of Empire: Westerners in Shanghai and the Chinese Revolution of the 1920s*. Hanover, NH, and London: Middlebury College Press, published by University of New England Press, 1991.

Coble, Parks M. Jr. *The Shanghai Capitalists and the Nationalist Government, 1927–1937*. Cambridge, MA: Council of East Asian Studies, Harvard University Press, 1980.

Cohen, Paul A. *China and Christianity: The Missionary Movement and the Growth of Anti-foreignism, 1860–1870*. Cambridge, MA: Harvard University Press, 1963.

–. *History in Three Keys*. New York: Columbia University Press, 1998.

Cong, Xiaoping. *Teachers' Schools and the Making of the Modern Chinese Nation-State, 1897–1937*. Vancouver: UBC Press, 2007.

Cottrell, Debora Lynn. "Women's Minds, Women's Bodies: The Influence of the Sargent School for Physical Education." PhD diss., University of Texas at Austin, 1993.

Mr. Deng Yuzhi Commemorative Volume [Deng Yuzhi xiansheng jinian wenji 鄧裕志先生紀念文集]. Shanghai: National Committee of the Chinese YWCA, 2000.

Dju, Gioh-fang. *The YWCA of China, 1933–1947*. Shanghai: National Committee of the Young Women's Christian Association of China, 1947.

Drucker, Alison R. "The Role of the YWCA in the Development of the Chinese Women's Movement, 1890–1927." *Social Service Review* (September 1979): 421–40.

Eastman, Lloyd. *The Abortive Revolution: China under Nationalist Rule, 1927–37*. Cambridge, MA: Harvard University Press, 1974.

Esherick, Joseph W. *The Origins of the Boxer Uprising*. Berkeley: University of California Press, 1988.

Fairbank, John K., ed. *The Missionary Enterprise in China and America*. Cambridge, MA: Harvard University Press, 1974.

Fewsmith, Joseph. *Party, State, and Local Elites in Republican China: Merchant Organizations and Politics in Shanghai 1890–1930*. Honolulu: University of Hawaii Press, 1985.

Fitzgerald, John. *Awakening China: Politics, Culture and Class in the Nationalist Revolution*. Stanford, CA: Stanford University Press, 1998.

Foster, Carrie A. *The Women and the Warriors: The U.S. Section of the Women's International League for Peace and Freedom, 1915–1946*. Syracuse: Syracuse University Press, 1995.

Freedman, Estelle. "Separatism as Strategy: Female Institution Building and American Feminism, 1870–1930." *Feminist Studies* 5, 3 (Fall 1979): 512–29.

Gao, Wangzhi. "Y.T. Wu: A Christian Leader under Communism." In *Christianity in China from the Eighteenth Century to the Present*, edited by Daniel Bays. Stanford, CA: Stanford University Press, 1996.

Garner, Karen. "Global Feminism and Postwar Reconstruction: The World YWCA Visitation to Occupied Japan, 1947." *Journal of World History* 15, 2 (June 2004): 191–227.

—. *Precious Fire: Maud Russell and the Chinese Revolution*. Amherst: University of Massachusetts Press, 2003.

—. "Redefining Institutional Identity: The YWCA Challenge to Extraterritoriality in China, 1925–30." *Women's History Review* 10, 3 (2001): 409–40.

Garrett, Shirley S. *Social Reformers in Urban China: The Chinese YMCA, 1895–1926*. Cambridge, MA: Harvard University Press, 1970.

Gilkey, Langdon. *Shantung Compound: The Story of Men and Women under Pressure*. New York: Harper and Row, 1966.

Gilmartin, Christina K. *Engendering the Chinese Revolution: Radical Women, Communist Policies, and Mass Movements in the 1920s*. Berkeley: University of California Press, 1995.

—. "Gender in the Formation of a Communist Body Politic." *Modern China* 19, 3 (July 1993): 299–329.

Gipoulon, Catherine. "The Emergence of Women in Politics in China, 1898–1927." *Chinese Studies in History* 23, 2 (Winter 1989–90): 46–67.

—. "Integrating the Feminist and Worker's Movement: The Case of Xiang Jingyu." *Republican China* 10, 1 (1984): 29–41.

Hao, Yufan, and Zhihai Zhai. "China's Decision to Enter the Korean War: History Revisited." *International History Review* 19, 1 (February 1997): 94–115. https://www.jstor.org/stable/654064.

Henriot, Christian. *Shanghai, 1927–1937: Municipal Power, Locality, and Modernization*. Translated by Noël Castellino. Berkeley: University of California Press, 1993.

Hershatter, Gail. *Dangerous Pleasures: Prostitution and Modernity in Twentieth Century Shanghai*. Berkeley: University of California Press, 1997.

—. "Sexing Modern China." In *Remapping China: Fissures in Historical Times*, edited by Gail Hershatter, Emily Honig, Jonathan N. Lipman, and Randall Stross. Stanford, CA: Stanford University Press, 1996.

Hill, Patricia. *The World Is Their Household: American Women's Foreign Mission Movement and Cultural Transformation, 1870–1920*. Ann Arbor: University of Michigan Press, 1985.

Honig, Emily. "Christianity, Feminism, and Communism: The Life and Times of Deng Yuzhi (Cora Deng)." In *Christianity in China from the Eighteenth Century to the Present*, edited by Daniel Bays. Stanford, CA: Stanford University Press, 1996.

—. *Sisters and Strangers: Women in the Shanghai Cotton Mills, 1919–1949*. Stanford, CA: Stanford University Press, 1986.

Hu Pingsa (Hu Binxia). "The Women of China." *Chinese Students' Monthly*, January 10, 1914, 202–3.

Huang, Philip C.C., ed. "Symposium: 'Public Sphere'/'Civil Society' in China?" *Modern China* 19, 2 (April 1993): 107–240.

Hunter, Jane. *The Gospel of Gentility: American Women Missionaries in Turn-of-the-Century China*. New Haven, CT: Yale University Press, 1984.

—. "Introduction: 'Christianity, Gender, and the Language of the World.'" *Journal of American–East Asian Relations* 24 (2017): 305–20.

Israel, John. *Lianda: A Chinese University in War and Revolution*. Stanford, CA: Stanford University Press, 1998.

—. *Student Nationalism in China, 1927–1937*. Stanford, CA: Stanford University Press, 1966.

Johnsen-Rod, C. "The Catalyst Effect of the Y.W.C.A. on the Women's Movement in China: 1901–1927." Master's thesis, Florida Atlantic University, 1981.

Jones, Francis P., ed. *Documents of the Three-Self Movement: Source Materials for the Study of the Protestant Church in Communist China*. New York: National Council of the Churches of Christ in the USA, 1963.

Keller, Charles Andrew. "Making Model Citizens: The Chinese YWCA, Activism, and Internationalism in Republican China, 1919–1937." PhD diss., University of Kansas, 1996.

Kwok, Pui-lan. *Chinese Women and Christianity, 1860–1927*. Atlanta: Scholars Press, 1992.

Latourette, Kenneth Scott. *A History of Christian Missions in China*. London: Society for the Promotion of Christian Knowledge, 1929.

Li Yuning and Chang Yü-fa, eds. *Jindai Zhongguo nüquan yundong shiliao, 1842–1911* [Documents on the feminist movement in modern China, 1842–1911], vols. 1–2. Taipei: Biographical Literature, 1975.

Lin Yutang. *My Country and My People*. London: W. Heinemann, 1936.

Littell-Lamb, Elizabeth A. "Caught in the Crossfire: Women's Internationalism and the YWCA Child Labor Campaign in Shanghai, 1921–1925." *Frontiers: A Journal of Women's Studies* 32, 3 (December 2011): 134–66.

—. "Ding Shujing: The YWCA's Pathway for 'New' Women." In *Salt and Light: Lives of Faith That Shaped Modern China*, vol. 1, edited by Carol Lee Hamrin and Stacey Bieler. Eugene, OR: Pickwick Publications, 2008.

—. "Engendering a Class Revolution: The Chinese YWCA Industrial Reform Work in Shanghai, 1927–1939." *Women's History Review* 21, 2 (April 2012): 189–209.

—. "Going Public: The YWCA, 'New' Women and Social Feminism in Republican China." PhD diss., Carnegie Mellon University, 2002.

—. "Gospel of the Body, Temple of the Nation: The YWCA Movement and Women's Physical Culture in China, 1915–1925." *Research on Women in Modern Chinese History (Jindai zhongguo funü shi yanjiu)* 16 (December 2008): 168–206.

—. "Localizing the Global: The YWCA Movement in China, 1899 to 1939." In *Women and Transnational Activism in Historical Perspective*, edited by Erika K. Kuhlman and Kimberly Jensen. Dordrecht, The Netherlands: Republic of Letters, 2010.

Lu Xun. "What Happens after Nora Leaves Home?" In *Silent China: Selected Writings of Lu Xun,* edited and translated by Gladys Yang. London: Oxford University Press, 1973.

Lutz, Jessie Gregory. *China and the Christian Colleges, 1850–1950.* Ithaca, NY: Cornell University Press, 1971.

Ma, Li. *Christian Women and Modern China: Recovering a Women's History of Chinese Protestantism.* Lanham, MD: Lexington Books, 2021.

Mann, Susan. *Precious Records: Women in China's Long Eighteenth Century.* Stanford, CA: Stanford University Press, 1997.

McKinnon, Stephen R. *Wuhan, 1938: War, Refugees, and the Making of Modern China.* Berkeley: University of California Press, 2008.

Mohanty, Chandra Talpade. "Under Western Eyes: Feminist Scholarship and Colonial Discourses." In *Third World Women and the Politics of Feminism,* edited by C.T. Mohanty, A. Russo, and L. Torres. Bloomington: University of Indiana Press, 1991.

Morris, Andrew. "Cultivating the National Body: A History of Physical Culture in Republican China." PhD diss., University of California at San Diego, 1998.

Nivard, Jacqueline. "Women and the Women's Press: The Case of the *Ladies' Journal* (*Funü zazhi*)." *Republican China* 10, 1b (November 1984): 37–55.

Paddle, Sarah. "The Limits of Sympathy: International Feminists and the Chinese 'Slave Girl' Campaigns of the 1920s and 1930s." *Journal of Colonialism and Colonial History* 4, 3 (Winter 2003): 1–22.

Perry, Elizabeth. *Shanghai on Strike: The Politics of Shanghai Labor.* Stanford, CA: Stanford University Press, 1993.

Ponto, Cassandra. "The Search for Grace in China." Master's thesis, Southern Oregon State College, 1993.

Porter, Robin. *Industrial Reformers in Republican China.* New York: M.E. Sharpe, 1994.

Rice, Anna. *A History of the World's Young Women's Christian Association.* New York: Women's Press, 1947.

Sahlins, Marshall. *Islands of History.* Chicago: University of Chicago Press, 1985.

Schneider, Helen M. *Keeping the Nation's House: Domestic Management and the Making of Modern China.* Vancouver: UBC Press, 2012.

–. "The Women's Advisory Council, Resistance and Reconstruction during China's War with Japan." *European Journal of East Asia Studies* 11, 2 (2012): 213–36.

Schoppa, R. Keith. *Revolution and Its Past: Identities and Change in Modern Chinese History.* 3rd ed. New York: Routledge, 2011.

Schott, Linda A. *Reconstructing Women's Thoughts: The Women's International League for Peace and Freedom before World War II.* Stanford, CA: Stanford University Press, 1997.

Seymour-Jones, Carole. *Journey of Faith: The History of the World YWCA 1945–1994.* London: Allison and Bushby, 1994.

Shemo, Connie. "Shi Meiyu: An 'Army of Women' in Medicine." In *Salt and Light: Lives of Faith That Shaped Modern China,* vol. 1, edited by Carol Lee Hamrin and Stacey Bieler. Eugene, OR: Pickwick, 2008.

Sheridan, James E. *China in Disintegration: The Republican Era in Chinese History, 1912–1949.* New York: Free Press, 1975.

Shi, Xia. *At Home in the World: Women and Charity in Late Qing and Early Republican China.* New York: Columbia University Press, 2018.

Spence, Jonathan. *To Change China: Western Advisors in China, 1620–1960*. New York: Penguin Books, 2002.

—. *The Search for Modern China*. New York: W.W. Norton, 1990.

Stranahan, Patricia. *Underground: The Shanghai Communist Party and the Politics of Survival, 1927–1937*. Lanham, MD: Rowman and Littlefield, 1998.

Strauss, Julia. "Paternalist Terror: The Campaign to Suppress Counterrevolutionaries and Regime Consolidation in the People's Republic of China, 1950–1953." *Comparative Studies in Society and History* 44, 1 (2002): 80–105.

Tillman, Margaret Mih. "Mediating Modern Motherhood: The Shanghai YWCA's 'Women's Work for Women,' 1908–1949." In *Spreading Protestant Modernity: Global Perspectives on the Social Work of the YMCA and YWCA, 1889–1970*, edited by Harald Fishcher-Tiné, Stefan Huebner, and Ian Tyrell. Honolulu: University of Hawaii Press, 2021.

Tsai, Kwei (Cai Kui) and Lily K. Haass. "A Study of the Young Women's Christian Association of China: 1890–1930." YWCA of China, 1930. Reprinted in *Chinese Studies in History*: Part I – 10, 3 (1977): 73–88; Part II – 11, 1 (1977): 18–63; Part III – 11, 4 (1978): 48–71.

Varg, Paul. *Missionaries, Chinese, and Diplomats: The American Protestant Missionary Movement in China, 1890–1952*. Princeton, NJ: Princeton University Press, 1958.

Wakeman, Frederic Jr. *Policing Shanghai, 1927–1937*. Berkeley: University of California Press, 1995.

Wakeman, Frederic Jr., and Wen-hsin Yeh, eds. *Shanghai Sojourners*. Berkeley: University of California Press, 1992.

Wang, Zheng. "State Feminism? Gender and Socialist State Formation in Maoist China." *Feminist Studies* 31, 3 (Fall 2005): 519–51.

—. *Women in the Chinese Enlightenment: Oral and Textual Histories*. Berkeley: University of California Press, 1999.

Ward, Jane Shaw W. *Shanghai Sketches*. New York: Women's Press, 1917.

Who's Who in China: Biographies of Chinese Leaders. Shanghai: *China Weekly Review*, 1917–50. Reprint: Hong Kong: China Materials Center, 1982. 3 vols.

Wickeri, Philip L. *Seeking Common Ground: Protestant Christianity, the Three-Self Movement, and China's United Front*. Eugene, OR: Wipf and Stock, 2004.

Witke, Roxanne. *Comrade Chiang Ch'ing*. Boston: Little, Brown, 1977.

Wong, Christina Wai-yin. "Expanding Social Networks: A Case Study of Cora Deng and Y.T. Wu on Their Roles and Participation in the National Salvation Movement of 1930s China." In *Great Faiths of Our Times: Wu Yaozong and 20th Century Chinese Christianity* [Dashidai zongjiao xinyang: Wu Yaozong yu ershiji Zhonghua Jidujiao], edited by Na Fuzeng, 291–340. Hong Kong: Chinese Christian Religious Culture Research Centre [Jidujiao Zhonghua zongjiaowenhua yanjiushe], 2011.

Woodhead, H.G.W., ed. *The China Yearbook*. Tientsin and Shanghai: North China Daily News and Herald, 1912–36.

Xing, Jun. *Baptized in the Fire of Revolution: The American Social Gospel and the YMCA in China, 1919–1937*. Bethlehem, PA: Lehigh University Press, 1996.

Yang, Kuisong, "Reconsidering the Campaign to Suppress Counterrevolutionaries." *China Quarterly* 193 (2008): 102–21.

Ye, Weili. "'Nü Liuxuesheng': The Story of American-Educated Chinese Women, 1880s–1920s." *Modern China* 20, 3 (July 1994): 315–46.

Yeh, Wen-hsin. *The Alienated Academy: Culture and Politics in Republican China, 1910–1937*. Cambridge, MA: Harvard University Press, 1990.

Ying, Fuk-Tsang. "The CPC's Policy on Protestant Christianity, 1949–1957: An Overview and Assessment." *Journal of Contemporary China* 23, 89 (June 2014): 884–901.

Yip, Ka-che. *Religion, Nationalism and Chinese Students: The Anti-Christian Movement 1922–1927*. Bellingham: Center for East Asian Studies, Western Washington University, 1980.

Zhang, Aihua. *The Beijing Young Women's Christian Association, 1927–1937: Materializing a Gendered Modernity*. Lanham, MD: Lexington Books, 2021.

Index

Notes: The following abbreviations are used in subheadings: "ACDWF" for All-China Democratic Women's Federation, "CCP" for Chinese Communist Party, "CIC" for Chinese Industrial Cooperative, "GMD" for Guomindang, "NCC" for National Christian Council, "PRC" for People's Republic of China, and "WIDF" for Women's International Democratic Federation. "(f)" after a page number indicates a figure.

Abe, Bishop, 126
acting executive committee, 123
Addams, Jane, 70, 78, 211*n*8
ai guo (patriotism), 162, 163, 170, 185.
    See also nationalism
All-China Democratic Women's Federation
    (ACDWF): alternative name of,
    219*n*13; city associations join, 158;
    at conferences, 166, 177–78; name
    change of, 182; purpose of, 148;
    Wang Guoxiu on, 168
Alley, Rewi, 119–20, 213*n*60
Allied Powers' Far Eastern Commission, 141
American Board of Commissioners for
    Foreign Missions (ABCFM), 159
American diplomatic corps, 159
American imperialism, 141, 157, 165,
    168, 170–71, 172–76
"American Imperialists' Criminal Invasion of
    Southeast Asia" (Deng Yuzhi), 173
American secretaries: acknowledged
    at enlarged national executive

committee meeting, 153–54;
    associated with imperialism, 157;
    Berninger, 34; Brennecke, 151, 155–
    56, 157, 176; Chinese secretaries'
    animosity toward, 156; Christianity
    of, 192; denounced, 175–76; Dudley,
    Marion, 134; at first secretarial
    conference, 49; internment
    of, 127, 128; petition against
    extraterritoriality, 44; Sino-Japanese
    War and, 121, 123; sponsorship for,
    23. *See also* Coppock, Grace; Haass,
    Lily; Morrison, Esther; Paddock,
    Estelle; Palmer, Elizabeth
American Women's Club, 40
American YWCA. *See* YWCA of the USA
Anderson, Leila, 152
annual reports, 17, 25, 50–51, 117
anti-Christian movement, 20–21, 51,
    89, 161
Anti-Rightist Campaign, 186–88
Article Five of the Common Program, 161

associate general secretaries, 49, 190
associate national general secretaries, 64, 191
association histories: co-authored by Cai
	Kui and Haass, 67, 73, 89–90, 93;
	credit Joint Committee, 205n83;
	on Japanese secretaries at Chinese
	YWCA, 125; organizational chart
	in, 52
association way: Dingman on, 84;
	domestication of, 5, 12, 52, 87,
	192; Venable on, 51
At Home in the World (Xia Shi), 11
Australian secretaries, 34, 204n55. *See also*
	Hinder, Eleanor

Bagwell, May, 97–98, 102
Bai Juyi, 56
Bandung Conference (1955), 183, 225n54
Baoji, 120
Barnard College, 47
Bays, Daniel, 9, 20
Before Lunch (play), 96
Beijing, 19, 31, 111, 116, 140
Beijing city association: changes in programs
	at, 51; Chinese leadership at, 47;
	formed, 27; fortieth anniversary
	celebration, 182; Haass at, 44;
	Japanese YWCA members visit, 121,
	125; Jeger visits, 180; in occupied
	territory, 111. *See also* Ding Shujing:
	at Beijing city association
Beijing University, 20, 114
Beijing Young Women's Christian Association
	(Aihua Zhang), 7, 11–12
Berninger, Martha, 34
Blue Triangle (magazine), 223n22
Book of Rites, 71, 210n60
bourgeois-democratic revolution, 148
bourgeoisie, 149, 160, 188
Boxer Protocol, 19, 54
Boxer Rebellion, 54, 62
Boxer uprising, 19
Boyd, Nancy, 217n59
Bradley, Anne-Marie, 213n66, 216n34
Brennecke, Margaret, 151, 155–56,
	157, 176
Bridgman Academy, 59
Britain, 19, 118, 125, 165, 180, 181

British concession, 116, 118
British secretaries, 22, 45, 49. *See also*
	Garvie, Margaret
British Women's Club, 38, 40
British YWCA: Chinese YWCA requests
	workers from, 27, 34; defining
	influence of, 84; extends YWCA
	movement, 21–22; news of
	Chinese YWCA forwarded to,
	180; progressive agenda of, 5, 192;
	publishes article on Garvie's work
	in China, 172, 223n22; student
	YWCAs in, 202n23; war ends
	rivalry with American YWCA, 140;
	work with urban women, 28
Buddhism, 8–9, 55, 56, 61, 75, 193
Bureau of Social Welfare, 131
business department, 122
Butler, Esther H., 208n10

Cai Chang, 55–56, 148
Cai Hesen, 207n3
Cai Kui: appointed acting national general
	secretary, 67, 108–9; appointed
	national general secretary, 68, 116;
	approach to, 5, 15, 53, 54, 75, 195;
	Christian denunciation campaign
	and, 170–72, 173, 176; Christianity
	of, 54, 58, 61, 62, 73–75, 151, 176,
	193; co-authors association history,
	67, 73, 89–90, 93; on democracy in
	Chinese YWCA, 110, 116–17; with
	Deng Yuzhi and Ding Shujing at
	national office, 191; Ding Shujing's
	influence on, 191; early life and
	education of, 10, 54, 55, 56–57,
	58–59, 60–61, 63, 67, 74, 75; feels
	disillusioned, 193; feels hopeful,
	135, 143; in glossary, 196; health
	of, 46; and Japan's involvement
	with Shanghai committee, 126–27;
	Japanese YWCA and, 121–22, 141;
	lack of personal papers of, 13–14,
	62, 73; marriage, 59, 60–61, 63,
	208n17; mental and emotional
	challenges faced by, 101, 134; 1949
	letters to Helen Roberts, 145–46,
	150–52; overview of Chinese

YWCA career of, 4; pathway to leadership, 48, 64–65, 67–68, 116; personality of, 61; postwar plan authorized by, 132, 133, 136; rehabilitation budget developed by, 136; on relocating association headquarters, 123; resignation of, 142, 145, 151–52, 156, 193–94; travels during Sino-Japanese War, 61, 112, 113–15, 116, 117; vision for Chinese YWCA, 69, 73–75; at west China regional conference, 130; on Western secretaries, 68, 133; at Zhou EnLai's 1951 meeting, 170

Campaign to Suppress Counterrevolutionaries, 155

campuses-in-exile, 114, 138

Cao Yuanpei, 20

capitalism, 62, 67, 102–3, 148, 149

Castrèn, Inga-Brita, 183, 224n53

CCP. See Chinese Communist Party (CCP)

Central Committee (PRC), 155

Ceylon YWCA, 184

Chambéry resolutions, 35–36, 37, 39, 50, 70

Chang Lien-Hua, 218n80

Changsha, 55, 56, 147

Changsha city association, 47, 58

Chariots of Fire (movie), 217n59

Chen, Gideon, 94

Chen Duxiu, 20, 60

Chen Jieshi, 188

Chen Ruifu, 120

Chen Wangdao, 60–61, 198

Chen Zhenxin, 208n17

Cheng, Julia, 147

Cheng Wanzhen: as anti-imperialist voice, 194; in glossary, 196; hired for industrial work, 37; industrial work by, 38–39, 40–41, 42; resignation of, 45, 60

Chengdu, 114, 122–23, 134

Chengdu city association, 120, 134, 157–58

Chesneaux, Jean, 204n60

Chiang Kai-shek: bourgeois-democratic revolution and, 148; converts to Christianity, 90; foreign support of, 159; in glossary, 198; Hundred Regiments Campaign and, 124; and protection of Chinese YWCA, 107; resignation of, 145; United Front and, 77, 79, 111; wife of (see Song Meiling)

Child Labor Commission, 39–40, 41, 119

child labour campaign, 39–43; anti-imperialism and, 194; failure of, 43, 52, 80, 141; as joint effort, 40, 50; Normal School and, 33; Song Meiling's work on, 40, 119, 141; and statement on helping labour classes, 88

child labourers, 85

Child Welfare Institute, 189

China. See People's Republic of China (PRC)

China Centenary Missionary Conference (1907), 24, 27, 30

China Daily News (Shenbao), 37

China Reconstructs (magazine), 179–80

China Records Project, 13

Chinese characters, 14

Chinese Christian women: approach to, 5, 53, 192–93; scholarship on, 8–12. See also Cai Kui: Christianity of; Deng Yuzhi: Christianity of; Ding Shujing: Christianity of

Chinese Church, 89, 161, 162–63, 170

Chinese communist movement, 59

Chinese Communist Party (CCP): ACDWF incorporated into, 182; alliance with GMD, 20–21, 77, 111; Campaign to Suppress Counterrevolutionaries, 155; Chen Wangdao and, 60; on Cheng Wanzhen, 37; Christian beliefs aligned with, 150; Deng Yuzhi recognized as ally by, 148; Deng Yuzhi's first contacts with, 98; endorses Christian Manifesto, 162; Hundred Flowers Campaign and, 184, 186, 187, 225n65; Hundred Regiments Campaign by, 124; Marshall's attempts to unite GMD and, 135; national office studies literature of, 145, 147; party members working in YWCA, 96–97, 98, 107; peasant support

for, 79; private charity organizations
subsumed by, 151; and "reactionary"
YWCA members, 157; recruitment
at night schools by, 85; religious
freedom and, 161; victories in civil
war, 143, 144
Chinese Industrial Cooperative (CIC)
movement, 119–20
Chinese names, treatment of, 14
Chinese People's Political Consultative
Conferences, 98, 148, 149–50,
160–61, 180, 186
Chinese People's Volunteer Army (CPV
Army), 164
Chinese Recorder (magazine), 30, 106–7,
123–24
Chinese Red Cross, 166
Chinese secretaries and staff: approach
to, 144; become officers of
national committee, 49, 190;
difficulty recruiting and retaining,
49, 90, 131; "direct approach"
alters relationship with Western
secretaries, 86–87; education
required of, 45–46, 49; on
governing committees, 47–48;
international conferences and, 165;
lack of relationships with Western
women, 156; living in settlement
project, 78–79; number of Western
vs, 49–50, 90, 105, 192; in postwar
plan, 133–34; in rehabilitation
budget, 137–38; relationship with
World YWCA, 175; remaining
during first years of PRC, 147;
responsibilities given to, 154; risk
being arrested, 116; at second
industrial secretaries' conference,
91. *See also* Cai Kui; Deng Yuzhi;
Ding Shujing
Chinese Women and Christianity (Kwok), 9
Chinese Women's Christian Temperance
Union (WCTU), 40, 43, 100, 148,
187–88
Chinese Women's Club, 111
Chinese Women's League for the Promotion
of Women's Rights, 100, 118, 198
Chinese Women's Suffrage Association, 43

Chinese YMCA: Article Five of the
Common Program and, 161; vs
Chinese YWCA, 23–26; Christian
Manifesto and, 163; conservative
pastors' attack on, 158; cooperation
with Chinese YWCA during Sino-
Japanese War, 119; field survey
and, 93, 94; GMD and, 107;
headquarters, 33; James on, 180;
and marriage options for YWCA
women, 59; model industrial
village of, 83, 85; organizes first
YWCA national committee, 18;
place in Maoist state, 144; radical
Christians in, 157; Robbins Strong
at, 159; secretaries, 86, 94, 198;
serves elites, 24, 25, 30; sports and
physical education classes, 31; Tu
Yuqing's work with, 218n93. *See
also* Liu Liangmo; Wu Yaozong
Chinese YWCA: approach to, 3–7, 14–16,
18, 190–95; beginning date of,
201n7; Chinese name of, 146, 219n4;
vs Chinese YMCA, 23–26; historical
context to 1925, 19–21; intense life
of secretaries at, 46; membership
numbers, 24, 104, 181; number of
staff at, 181; purposes of, 39, 87,
104–5, 134; related scholarship,
8–12, 145, 201n7; sources for study
of, 12–14; staff lists, 98, 116, 147,
204n55. *See also* indigenization;
industrial work; Maoist state; national
general secretaries; national office;
Sinification
Chinese YWCA new women, 8
Chongqing: association headquarters
relocates to, 134; communists take,
147; competition in, 131; refugee
crisis in, 115; regional conference in,
116–17; as wartime capital, 112, 123
Chongqing city association, 134
Chongqing cooperative, 129–30
Christian colleges and universities, 55,
57, 59, 138, 207n6. *See also* Jinling
College
Christian denunciation campaign, 167,
169–77, 223n20

Christian economic and social order,
72–73, 82, 91, 109, 160
Christian humanism. *See* Cai Kui:
Christianity of
Christian identity, 146, 149, 150–51,
153, 154
"Christian Life and Activities" (Deng
Yuzhi), 180
Christian Literature Commission, 62
Christian literature project, 73
Christian Manifesto, 162–63, 164, 170
Christian new women, 7–8, 11, 192
Christian revolution, 158–64
Christian socialism, 58, 102. *See also*
Deng Yuzhi: Christianity of
Christian Weekly, 150, 155, 162
Christian Women and Modern China
(Li Ma), 12
Christianity
anti-Christian movement, 20–21, 51,
89, 161
approach to, 143
community preserved in Maoist
state: Anti-Rightist Campaign
and, 187; approach to, 144–45;
Christian Manifesto, 162–63,
164, 170; Deng Yuzhi's article
on, 180; discussed at enlarged national executive committee meeting, 153; Garvie's and Strong's
descriptions illuminate, 160;
scholarship and, 150; Visapää on,
185; Zhou Enlai's role, 161–62,
169, 170
Coppock's, 26–27, 33
Harrison's, 36, 102, 204n60
linked with democracy, 136–37
missionaries' conservative interpretation of, 156
in national office's postwar plan, 132, 133
physical education and, 32
radical Christians, 157
scholarship on history of, 8–12,
145, 150
second national convention's statement
on, 89
Three-Self Patriotic Movement and, 182
war as opportunity to actualize, 110

World YWCA Council on politics
and, 142. *See also* Chinese Christian
women; communism: Christian-
ity and; conversions; imperialism:
Christianity and; Jesus
churchgoing policy, 36, 105
CIC. *See* Chinese Industrial Cooperative
Movement (CIC)
city associations: affiliate with ACDWF,
148; autonomy given to, 105,
158; Changsha, 47, 58; Chengdu,
120, 134, 157–58; classification
during Sino-Japanese War, 117–18;
conference of, 50–51; difficulty
recruiting and retaining Chinese
secretaries, 49, 90, 131; direct
affiliations with World YWCA,
127, 217n53; expansion to, 27, 28,
124; field survey and, 93; general
secretaries of, 4, 25; girls' work
secretaries at, 138–39; Guiyang,
130; Hankou, 112, 113; industrial
work vs work with middle-class
women, 106; map of, 2(f);
Nanjing, 27, 182, 222n3; number
of, 24, 25, 181; number of Western
women in, 192; postwar plan for,
132, 133; rehabilitation budget
for, 137; represented on national
committee, 47, 122, 153; at third
national convention, 104; turnover
at, 131; Xian, 183. *See also* Beijing
city association; Haass, Lily: as
national city association secretary;
Shanghai city association; Tianjin
city association
civil war: approach to, 15; Brennecke
returns to China despite, 176;
end of, 147; fall of Nanjing, 146;
momentum shift in, 142–43; 1947
World YWCA Council meeting
and, 140; tests Chinese YWCA
women, 110, 138; United States
supports Nationalists during, 156
Clark-Kerr, Archibald, 120
class: Cai Kui on, 117; child labour
campaign and, 41, 88; class
boundaries ignored, 92;

New Democracy unites all classes,
149; upper-class women, 28–30,
202n23; working classes, 72, 81, 82,
88–89. *See also* middle-class women
class struggle, 103, 106
club work, 86, 97
Colonial Division (British YWCA), 21
Columbia University, 47, 67, 74
Comintern, 20–21, 77
Committee on the Church's Relation
　to Economic and Industrial
　Problems, 38
Committee on Culture and Education
　(State Council), 170
Common Concerns (World YWCA
　publication), 226n75
Common Program: Article Five in, 161;
　Christian Manifesto mentions,
　163; discussed at enlarged national
　executive committee meeting, 154,
　155; produced by Chinese People's
　Political Consultative Conference,
　149–50; Robbins Strong on, 160;
　Wang Guoxiu on, 168
communism: Christianity and, 62, 76,
　92, 102–3, 160; Garvie praises,
　158–59, 160. *See also* Chinese
　Communist Party (CCP)
Communist Manifesto, 60
Communist Party (Soviet Union), 184
community internationalists, 70
concession areas, 116, 118, 125
Confucianism: *Book of Rites,* 71, 210n60;
　Christian dogmas and, 58;
　Coppock on, 26; in Deng Yuzhi's
　family, 55; New Culture Movement
　rejects, 20; provisional constitution
　and, 30–31; women and, 9, 57
conversions: Cai Kui, 54, 56, 58, 75, 193;
　Chiang Kai-shek, 90; Deng Yuzhi
　and her family, 54, 56, 75, 193;
　Ding Shujing and her family, 54, 55,
　61, 75, 193
cooperation: Cai Kui's commitment to, 75,
　117; Chambéry resolutions suggest,
　37; Chinese staff lack understanding
　of, 50; Deng Yuzhi on, 180; Ding
　Shujing's commitment to, 70,

105; enlarged national executive
committee meeting promises, 154;
Haass on, 124; between organizations
during Sino-Japanese War, 119–20;
between YWCA and YMCA, 26
Coppock, Grace: approach to, 195; death,
33, 38, 63; foreign secretaries
invited by, 22; indigenization as
goal of, 18–19, 27–28, 45, 46, 47,
49–50; interest in industrial work,
34–36, 37–38; internationalism
promoted by, 70; mental and
emotional challenges faced by, 101;
overview of Chinese YWCA career
of, 4; physical education programs
promoted by, 31, 32–33; plans for
Ding Shujing to succeed her, 63–
64; plans for membership building,
25; Sinification process begins with,
190; sponsorship for, 23; vision for
Chinese YWCA, 26–28
Cotton, Eugénie, 165–66
cotton industry, 34, 203n52
counterrevolution, 155, 157
Cultural Revolution, 188–89
cultural transmission, 6–7

Dan Dexing, 45, 196
day nurseries, 130
de Mel, Mrs. F.B., 184
democracy: approach to, 15, 110, 143;
　Chinese YWCA as "people's
　organization," 110, 112–13, 116–17;
　in Chinese YWCA during Sino-
　Japanese War, 122, 124; at enlarged
　national executive committee meeting,
　153; linked with Christianity, 136–37;
　in Morrison's work with girls, 139;
　in national office's postwar plan,
　132, 133; at west China regional
　conference, 130; Wu Yaozong on, 129
demonstration projects, 94–95
Deng Shuci, 207n7
Deng Xiaoping, 184
Deng Yingchao, 113
Deng Yuzhi
　appointed national general secretary,
　　65, 73, 152, 189

approach to, 5, 15–16, 53, 54, 75, 109, 195

Christianity of: Cai Kui and, 151; Christian socialism, 56, 61–62, 66–67, 72–73, 75, 102, 105–7, 150, 176, 193; conversion, 54, 56, · 75, 193; marriage and, 57

democracy and, 137

Ding Shujing's influence on, 191

early life and education of, 10, 55–56, 63, 75, 139; at Jinling College, 57–58, 60, 65, 191, 207n7; at London School of Economics, 60, 66, 73, 84, 95

in glossary, 196

at Hankou city association, 112, 113

health of, 46

industrial secretaries' conferences and, 72, 80–82, 91

industrial work by, 58, 84–85, 90, 97, 98; influence of Christian social-ism on, 66–67, 73, 105–7; named national industrial secretary, 4, 60, 64–66, 81, 83, 95; report at 1947 setting-up conference, 139–40; takes over national industrial department, 92; vision for, 96

lack of personal papers of, 13–14

marriage, 56, 57–58, 60, 207n7

meets with Castrèn, 183

memorials to, 13, 207n7, 208n16

mental and emotional challenges faced by, 101

as national student secretary, 4, 60, 65, 191

1950 travels to conferences, 165–66

other scholarship on, 9–10, 215n8

overview of Chinese YWCA career of, 4

pathway to leadership, 48, 60, 64–67

personality, 61, 65–66

politics and, 6, 142, 153, 160, 186, 194; approach to, 166; arrest, 188–89; at Chinese People's Politi-cal Consultative Conferences, 98, 148, 150, 180, 186; contact with World YWCA at WIDF conference, 177–80; denunciations by, 172, 173–75, 176, 177, 223n20; May

Fourth Movement's influence on, 20, 55, 56, 63, 75; "Responsibility of the YWCA in the Reconstruction of China," 148–49; views founding of PRC, 147; on YWCA Magazine's political uses, 168–69; Zhou Enlai and, 113, 161–62, 163, 170

Rees visits, 181

sends Western secretaries home, 68, 156

vision for Chinese YWCA, 69, 72–73

Wang Guoxiu on, 156–57

and World YWCA's 1957 visit to China, 184–85

Deng Zhenying, 60

denunciation campaign, Christian, 167, 169–77, 223n20

departments: business, 122; Chinese staff lack understanding of, 50–51; girls' work, 138; industrial and mass education, 137; Nanjing YWCA educational, 182; national city, 115, 120, 137, 138; rural, 52, 88; student, 138. See also editorial department; national industrial department

devolution. See indigenization

Ding Ling, 55–56

Ding Mingyu, 27–28, 49, 202n21

Ding Shujing: advocates for Deng Yuzhi, 65–66; appointed national general secretary, 18, 21, 64, 191; approach to, 5, 15, 53, 54, 75, 195; at Beijing city association, 19, 49, 59, 62, 63, 191; on Cai Kui's marriage, 208n17; on Chinese women's lack of understanding of YWCA, 46; Christianity of, 54, 55, 61–62, 68, 71, 75, 193, 210n60; concrete programs preferred by, 83–84, 87, 192; death, 67, 108; decision to make Deng Yuzhi an industrial secretary, 81, 83, 95; democracy and, 137; early life and education of, 54–55, 56–57, 59, 62, 64, 70, 75; feels disillusioned, 193; on field survey, 92–93; foreign secretaries invited by, 22; in glossary, 196; as good

leader, 88; at industrial secretaries'
conferences, 80, 83–84, 91, 92,
117; on industrial work, 73;
internationalist agenda of, 62–63,
69–72, 75, 89, 193; on Japanese
aggression, 99, 100–1; lack of
personal papers of, 13–14; mental
and emotional challenges faced
by, 101; other scholarship on,
12; overview of Chinese YWCA
career of, 4; pathway to leadership,
48, 63–64, 67; personality, 61;
Venable promotes advancement
of, 33, 50, 64, 66, 69; on Western
secretaries, 62, 68–69, 105; years
of tenure as national general
secretary, 76
Dingman, Mary: child labour campaign
and, 40, 42, 43; first industrial
secretaries' conference report sent
to, 81; Haass's letters to, 66, 83–84;
Harrison's letter to, 38; recruits
Hinder, 77
Djeng, Beatrice (Zheng Ruquan), 126,
131, 198
Dongwu University, 114
Dudley, Marion, 134

East, YWCAs in the, 179
ecumenism, 26–27. See also Ding
Shujing: Christianity of
Eddy, George Sherwood, 24
editorial department: Cai Kui's work
at, 4, 60, 62, 67, 73, 191; Cheng
Wanzhen's work at, 37; Thoburn's
work at, 17
education, 25, 45–46, 49, 202n21,
208n16. See also Cai Kui: early
life and education of; Deng Yuzhi:
early life and education of; Ding
Shujing: early life and education of;
Jinling College
education work: approach to, 15; Deng
Yuzhi's vision for, 96; discussed at
industrial secretaries' conferences,
82, 92; field survey report on, 94;
Hinder's, 78; Jiang Qing's, 107;
mass education, 86, 124, 137, 139;

1910s–1920s courses and lectures,
29–30; mid-1930s lectures, 108;
1951, 181; Normal School, 23, 31–
33, 50; number of girls attending
classes, 106; during Sino-Japanese
War, 111, 120, 130. See also literacy
classes; night schools; schools
elites, 24, 25, 30
Empire of the Sun (movie), 217n56
Enemy Property Commission, 125
evangelism, 5, 18, 24, 192
Executive Order 9066, 127–28
"Expanding Social Networks" (Wong), 10
expansion, 21–22, 25, 27, 28, 124, 137
extraterritoriality, 18, 44

Fan Yu Jung, 34, 204n55
Far Eastern regional conference (1936), 74
Feng, Jin, 10
Feng Yuxiang, 166
Ferry Road Center, 94–95, 96
field survey (1930), 92–95, 105
finances and funding: Chinese YWCA's
reliance on, 5, 191; Christian
denunciation campaign and, 169,
175–76; CIC's, 120; fundraising
tours, 23; in national office's
postwar plan, 134; in national
office's rehabilitation budget, 137,
138; Western secretaries and,
71–72, 105
Finnish Missionary Society, 183
Finnish YWCA, 183, 224n53. See also
Visapää, Sylvi
first national convention (1923):
constitution passed at, 47; decision
on membership parameters, 70;
Ding Shujing and, 46, 49, 64, 191;
as major event, 21; as marker of
Sinification, 190–91; Venable on,
51; Woodsmall speaks at, 101
First World War, 34, 132, 203n52
Foreign Division (YWCA of the USA):
denounced, 173; Ding Shujing's
requests of, 68–69; field survey
and, 93; Forsyth's work at, 142,
165, 173; funding provided by, 23;
Sarah Lyon's work at, 127, 142; and

sources for study, 12; Wang Guoxiu and Deng Yuzhi's letter to, 157
foreign secretaries and staff. *See* Western secretaries and staff
Forsyth, Margaret, 142, 156–57, 165, 173
Foster, Carrie, 70
Fudan University, 60
Fujian Province, 147
funding. *See* finances and funding
Fuxiang Middle School for Girls, 56, 57, 60, 62
Fuzhou city association, 47

Gao Renying, 148, 196, 208n16
Gao Tao Yong, 187
Gao Yuxin, 172, 186–87, 196, 219n21
Garden Bridge, 126
Garner, Karen, 10
Garvie, Margaret: on Christian revolution, 158–59, 160, 162; last letter in World YWCA Archives, 220n51; leaves China, 13, 155, 172; on weekly study sessions, 147; writes article on her time in China, 172, 223n22
General Labour Union, 81
general secretaries, 4, 25, 102, 126. *See also* national general secretaries; Shanghai city association: Coppock's work at
general secretaries (World YWCA), 145–46, 150–52, 177, 183. *See also* Palmer, Elizabeth; Spencer, Clarissa; Woodsmall, Ruth
Gerlach, Talitha: on Ding Shujing's visit to Japanese YWCA, 72; employment with YWCA ends, 189, 225n71; industrial work by, 98; at national office, 225n73; rehabilitation budget and, 138; and YWCA jobs for Chinese students, 149
Germany, 20, 127, 136
girls' conferences, industrial, 97–98
girls' work, 91, 96–97, 135–36, 138–39; department, 138; secretaries, 139. *See also* education work; industrial work

glossary, 196–98
GMD. *See* Guomindang (GMD)
Goa, 217n60
"Going Public" (dissertation; Littell-Lamb), 8, 14, 199n10
Gong Hezhen, 44, 47–48, 196
Gong Peizhen, 78, 85–86, 98, 196
governing committees, 28, 47–48. *See also* national committee
government schools, 27, 30–31, 32
Great Revolution, 77, 85, 87, 90, 109
"Green Year" Supplement (magazine), 79, 85, 206n101
Guangzhou, 147
Guangzhou city association, 47, 181
Guiyang, 114–15
Guiyang city association, 130
Guizhou Province, 114–15
Guomindang (GMD): alliance with CCP, 20–21, 77, 111; Chinese YWCA escapes notice of, 98, 107–8; discussed at second industrial secretaries' conference, 91; estimates on number of refugees, 115; Garvie on, 159, 223n22; losses in civil war, 146; Marshall's attempts to unite CCP and, 135; missionaries and, 89; New Democracy dedicated to wiping out, 149; 1950 resistance by, 152, 157; progressive Christians on harm caused by, 160; seat on United Nations Security Council, 164; student protests against, 218n93; supports CIC movement, 120; suppresses General Labour Union, 81; United States supports, 156. *See also* Nationalist government

Haass, Lily: advocates for Deng Yu-zhi, 65–66; Cai Kui denounces, 171–72; on Cai Kui's personality, 61; co-authors association history, 67, 73, 89–90, 93; on Deng Yuzhi's personality, 61, 65, 66; departure of, 136; on field survey, 93; Forsyth's letter to, 165; at industrial secretaries' conferences, 80–81, 91; industrial work and,

82–84, 95–96, 98, 192; Laymen's
Foreign Missions Inquiry interview,
102–3; as national city association
secretary, 66, 67, 105, 171, 192;
as national personnel secretary, 66,
67, 171, 192; at NCC, 44–45, 65,
66, 78, 83, 171; on new trends and
Sino-Japanese War, 123–24; report
on personnel and training, 131–32;
settlement project of, 78–79; travels
during Sino-Japanese War, 112–13,
114, 115, 116, 117; on west China
regional conference, 128–29
Handbook of National YWCAs (World
YWCA), 169, 179
Hangzhou, 56, 140, 201n7
Hankou, 112
Hankou city association, 112, 113
Hanyang, 112
Harrison, Agatha: Christianity of, 36,
102, 204n60; first industrial
secretaries' conference report sent
to, 81; Haass describes Deng Yuzhi
to, 66; hired by Coppock, 19, 36;
industrial work by, 36–38, 40, 42,
204n60
health education work, 130
Hikaru, Miss, 125
Hilda Smith (Cai Kui's code name),
126, 142
Hinder, Eleanor: assists Deng Yuzhi,
96; at first industrial secretaries'
conference, 81; hired for industrial
work, 45, 78, 95; international
study tour by, 77–78; on
relationship between Western
and Chinese secretaries, 86–87;
settlement project of, 78–79, 85;
on social revolution, 79–80, 81
Hinkley, Leila, 127, 128, 156, 159,
217n59
Hirohito, Emperor, 126, 135
Hiroshima, 135
Hong Kong, 127
Hongkou, 85, 126
Honig, Emily, 9–10, 37, 97, 107, 113,
215n8
Hoople, Ruth, 80

hostels, 94–95
Hsueh, Mrs. S.Y., 125–26, 197
Hu Binxia, 47–48, 197
Hu Shi, 93
Huangpu River, 86
Hubei Province, 117
Hull House Settlement, 78, 211n8
Hunan Province, 147, 183
Hundred Flowers Campaign, 167, 184,
185–86, 187, 225n65
Hundred Regiments Campaign, 124
Hungarian revolt, 184, 185
Hunter, Jane, 7–8

identities: middle-class, 72, 81, 89, 103;
of new women, 25, 192; Sino-Japanese War and, 115, 118; of women
served by mass education, 124; of
women textile workers, 37. *See also*
Christian identity
imperialism: Christianity and, 19, 89,
102–3, 162–63, 169, 172–73, 186
(*see also* anti-Christian movement);
Deng Yuzhi on Chinese YWCA
and, 149; enlarged national
executive committee meeting and,
154; First United Front fights,
77; as impediment to China's
modernity, 194; Japanese, 48, 122;
May Thirtieth Incident protests
about, 43; Resist America and
Assist Korea movement and, 172;
Wang Guoxiu on, 153; Western,
40–41, 44, 89; Western secretaries
oppose, 18; World YWCA on, 179.
See also American imperialism
India, 217n60
indigenization: approach to, 15; Ding
Shujing's vision counters, 71–72;
disagreements on implementing,
134; discussed at enlarged national
executive committee meeting, 154;
in early years, 45–51; and number
of Western vs Chinese secretaries,
90; postwar plan and, 133; vs
Sinification, 5, 190; Spencer's goal
of, 3, 27, 45, 53; Thoburn on, 17–
18, 76; World YWCA promotes, 4,

5, 190. *See also* Cai Kui; Coppock,
   Grace: indigenization as goal
   of; Deng Yuzhi; Ding Shujing;
   Sinification
indigenous church movement, 89, 161,
   162–63, 171
industrial centres, 104, 106, 107–8, 124
industrial cooperatives, 120–21, 129–30,
   137, 139
industrial department (Shanghai), 78, 85,
   94, 96. *See also* national industrial
   department
industrial districts, 86, 94. *See also* Zhabei
industrial girls' clubs, 91, 96–97
industrial girls' conferences, 97–98
industrial justice, 35
industrial and mass education
   department, 137
industrial secretaries: Bagwell, 97–98,
   102; contacts with communist
   cadres, 107; disagreement
   with national committee, 84,
   192; Harrison on, 36; living
   in settlement project, 78–79;
   mass education work by, 124;
   national, 44–45, 76–77; need to
   be "labourized," 94; number of,
   106; relationship between Western
   and Chinese, 86–87; Shanghai
   radicals and, 76–77; in Tianjin city
   association, 120; at World YWCA,
   40, 81. *See also* Deng Yuzhi:
   industrial work by; Hinder, Eleanor
industrial secretaries' conferences: 1927,
   72, 80–84, 86, 88, 89, 91, 95;
   1930, 73, 90, 91–92, 95, 117;
   1933, 103, 106
industrial women: Bagwell on, 97; Deng
   Yuzhi on, 82; Ding Shujing on,
   92; direct work and, 91; national
   conventions and, 87, 88, 104
industrial work: approach to, 76,
   109, 195; Bagwell's, 97–98; in
   Changsha, 58; Coppock's interest
   in, 34–36, 37–38; Ferry Road
   Center, 94–95, 96; field survey
   report on, 93–94; goals for,
   82; Harrison's, 36–38, 40, 42,

204n60; Hinder's study tour of,
   77–78; Japanese invasion forces
   program closures, 213n55; levels
   off after 1934, 105–6; lost in
   Maoist state, 149; Normal School
   and, 33; related scholarship,
   213n60; settlement project,
   78–79, 80, 85; staffing for, 19, 36,
   37, 44–45. *See also* child labour
   campaign; Deng Yuzhi: industrial
   work by; education work; labour
   movement; national industrial
   department
intellectuals, 76–77, 83, 91–92
International Council of Women, 99
International Labour Organization,
   38, 78
internationalist agenda, 133–34. *See also*
   Ding Shujing: internationalist
   agenda of
internment, 125, 127–28, 159, 217n59,
   217nn56–57

James, Marcus, 180
Japan: aggression by, 99, 100–1, 104,
   105, 109, 121; Cai Kui's father
   in, 57; Christian denunciation
   campaign and, 174; investments
   in China during First World War,
   203n52; Paris Peace Conference
   and, 20; prisoner exchange with
   United States, 217n60; surrenders,
   135; at war with United
   States, 125, 127, 129. *See also*
   Manchurian invasion; Sino-
   Japanese War
Japanese: imperialism, 48, 122; internees,
   128; Methodist Church, 126; mills,
   108; national general secretaries,
   121, 125; YMCA, 126
Japanese YWCA: Ding Shujing at
   national convention of, 72; guests
   at third national convention, 104;
   helps secure national headquarters
   building, 127; 1947 World YWCA
   Council meeting and, 140, 141,
   174; visits during Sino-Japanese
   War, 121–22, 125

Jeger, Lena, 180
Jesus: Cai Kui and, 151; Deng Yuzhi
    and, 56, 72, 75, 153, 160, 193;
    and diversity of Christianity, 89,
    92; enlarged national executive
    committee meeting invokes, 154,
    155; social equality preached by,
    4, 62; social revolution and, 150;
    value placed on women in message
    of, 9; war as opportunity to live
    gospel of, 110; Yu Xiu'ai on, 182
Jiang Qing, 107
Jiangnan, 57
Jiangsu Province, 120, 126
Jiangxi Province, 117
Jin Longzhang, Mrs. (Mrs. L.C. King),
    76, 102–3, 197
Jinling College: Cai Kui at, 54, 56, 58,
    61; Chinese YWCA's association
    with, 33, 50; Deng Yuzhi at, 57–58,
    60, 65, 191, 207n7; language of
    instruction, 207n6; location and
    religious affiliation, 4; other Chinese
    YWCA women at, 208n16; relocates
    to Chengdu, 114, 123; scholarship
    on, 10; student protests at, 58–59
Johnson, Hewlett, 183
Johnson, Lydia, 127, 128, 225n73
Johnston, Edith, 45, 78
Joint Committee of Shanghai Women's
    Clubs, 38–40, 42, 43, 118–19,
    205n83
Journal of American–East Asian Relations, 7
justice, 74, 100–1. See also social justice

Kao, Jean, 149, 219n21
Kato (Japanese national general secretary),
    121
Khan, Ivy, 185
Khrushchev, Nikita, 184
Kim Il-Sung, 164
King, Mrs. L.C. (Mrs. Jin Longzhang),
    76, 102–3, 197
Korean Armistice Agreement, 183
Korean War: and conference of Christian
    leaders, 170; Deng Yuzhi on, 166,
    179; expert on, 221n77; PRC in,
    162, 164–65, 176

Korean Women's Democratic Union, 166
Kunming, 114–15, 129
Kunming city association, 134
Kwok, Pui-lan, 9

labour legislation, 39. See also child labour
    campaign
labour movement: club work and, 86;
    Deng Yuzhi on loss of momentum
    in, 106; in Deng Yuzhi's 1947
    report, 139; discussed at industrial
    secretaries' conferences, 81, 82–83,
    84, 89, 91–92, 103; Gideon Chen's
    suggestions for, 94; Hinder's plan
    to contact women labour leaders,
    78, 80; national committee and,
    84, 90–91, 192. See also industrial
    work; organizing labour
Labour Party (Britain), 180
Ladies' Journal, 39
Laymen's Foreign Missions Inquiry, 100,
    101–3
League of Left-Wing Educators, 98
League of Left-Wing Writers, 98
League of Nations, 89, 101
League of Nations Commission of
    Enquiry, 99–100, 118, 191, 194
Lewis, Robert, 23
Li Dazhao, 20
Li Dequan, 166
Li Zongren, 145, 146
Lianda, 114
Library of Congress, 13
Liddell, Eric, 217n59
Lien, Lingling, 221–22n25
Lin Yutang, 58
Linqing, 55
literacy classes: average attendance at
    night schools, 90–91; combined
    with courses in organizing, 103;
    first, 85, 86; girls' clubs and, 96;
    Hinder as driving force behind,
    95; Nanjing YWCA's, 182; during
    Sino-Japanese War, 124
Liu Liangmo: at Chinese People's Political
    Consultative Conferences, 150;
    in glossary, 198; instructions on
    accusatory sessions, 172, 173–75,

176; Robbins Strong and, 159; at Second World Peace Conference, 165, 166
Liu-Wang Liming, 148, 187–88
local YWCAs. *See* city associations
Lockhart, W. Bruce, 42
Loh, Mrs. Mason, 125, 197
London Mission Society, 85
London Missionaries Societies, 163
London Observer, 163
London School of Economics: Christian socialism and, 102; Deng Yuzhi at, 60, 66, 73, 84, 95; Haass at, 44, 83; Harrison at, 36
Lu Dingyu, 170
Lunghwa internment camp, 217*n*56
Lyon, D. Willard, 23
Lyon, Sarah, 62, 126–27, 142
Lytton Commission, 99–100, 118, 191, 194

Ma, Li, 9, 12
Ma Zhongjie, 187
MacArthur, Douglas, 164
MacGillivray, Mrs. D., 38
MacNeill, Ella, 34, 204*n*55
"making opinion," 36–37
Manchuria, 117, 143
Manchurian invasion: as catalyst for nationalism, 6; Chinese Women's League on, 100; delays third national convention, 104; Ding Shujing and, 72; forces closure of industrial programs, 213*n*55; influence on education work, 96; Mukden city association and, 127, 217*n*53; Shanghai War and, 99. *See also* Sino-Japanese War
Mao Zedong: announces creation of PRC, 142, 147, 150; bourgeois-democratic revolution and, 148; Chinese YWCA's adulation of, 188; Christians' loyalty to, 162; endorses Campaign to Suppress Counterrevolutionaries, 155; Hundred Flowers Campaign of, 184, 185–86; Korean War and, 164, 165; national committee declares support

for, 155, 191; New Democracy of, 145; policy of "leaning to the left," 146, 154, 165; wives of, 55, 107
Maoist state, 144–89; approach to, 3, 5, 6, 15–16, 144–45, 166, 167, 190; Cai Kui's 1949 letters to Helen Roberts, 145–46, 150–52; Castrèn meets with Deng Yuzhi, 183; Chinese YWCA severs ties with Western secretaries, 155–56, 157–58, 165, 177; Christian denunciation campaign in, 167, 169–77, 223*n*20; Christian revolution in, 158–64; Deng Yuzhi and World YWCA at WIDF conference, 177–80; Deng Yuzhi's arrest, 188–89; Deng Yuzhi's August 1949 article, 148–49; girls' work absorbed by, 139; Hundred Flowers Campaign, 167, 184, 185–86, 187, 225*n*65; meeting of enlarged national executive committee, 153–55, 156–57; World YWCA's 1957 visit to, 184–85, 186; *YWCA Magazine*'s description of work in, 169, 181–82
map of city associations, 2(f)
Marco Polo Bridge Incident, 110–11, 125
marriage: Cai Kui's, 59, 60–61, 63, 208*n*17; Deng Yuzhi and, 56, 57–58, 60, 207*n*7; Ding Shujing and, 59; during Sino-Japanese War, 131; slows indigenization, 46
Marshall, George C., 135
Marx, Karl, 62
Marxism, 160, 200*n*17. *See also* radicalism
Marxist-Leninist Study Group, 213*n*60
mass education, 86, 124, 137, 139
maternalism, 28, 62, 199*n*10
May Fourth Movement: description of, 20; influence on Cai Kui and Deng Yuzhi, 20, 55, 56, 57, 58–59, 63, 75; influence on Chinese YWCA secretaries generally, 117; political neutrality and, 194
May Thirtieth Incident, 18, 21, 78, 80. *See also* national committee: response to May Thirtieth Incident

Mayhew, Abby, 31–33, 37
McClelland, William Grigor, 181
"Mediating Modern Motherhood"
    (Tillman), 11
microfilms, 13, 14
middle-class identity, 72, 81, 89, 103
middle-class women: education work with,
    181; industrial districts outside
    domain of, 78; industrial secretaries
    as, 94; national committee members
    as, 63; number of secretaries
    working with, 106; programs for,
    28–30; work with urban women in
    Britain and United States, 202n23
Millett, Allan R., 221n77
mills, 34, 37, 108, 203n52
mission schools: China Inland, 202n21;
    Chinese YWCA's work with,
    29, 31; Deng Yuzhi at, 56; Ding
    Mingyu at, 202n21; Ding Shujing
    at, 55, 59; Paddock's work with, 30;
    student YWCAs in, 201n7
missionaries: attacks on, 19, 21, 161,
    171; Chinese YWCA grows
    out of "mission impulse," 17;
    Chinese YWCA's critique of, 103;
    Christians associated with foreign,
    157; conservative interpretations
    of Christianity, 156; flee from
    revolutionary armies, 89; Hunter
    on work by, 7–8; internment of,
    217n59; leave China, 159; Quaker,
    151; Rees's husband, 181, 224n45;
    role in World YWCA expansion, 22,
    25; as tool of foreign imperialism, 20;
    Wu Yaozong's critique of, 148
Morrison, Esther, 135–36, 138–39, 144,
    155, 156
Mother (Sarah Lyon's code name),
    126–27
mothers, old-style vs new-style, 29
Mott, John R., 24
Mount Holyoke College, 102
Mowill, Mrs. H.W.K., 184
Mukden city association, 127, 217n53
My Country and My People (Lin
    Yutang), 58

Nagasaki, 135
Naito, Miss, 125, 127
Nanjing, 111, 131, 146
Nanjing city association, 27, 182, 222n3
Nanjing Decade, 77
Nanjing government. See Nationalist
    government
Nanjing Massacre, 112
Nanjing University, 114, 207n6
national business secretaries, 125–26
National Christian Council (NCC): Article
    Five of the Common Program and,
    161; conference of, 80; cooperation
    with, 50; formed, 107; Gideon Chen
    at, 94; industrial work undertaken
    with, 38; list of secretaries, 204n55;
    Rees's husband's work at, 181. See also
    Haass, Lily: at NCC
national city association secretaries, 80.
    See also Haass, Lily: as national city
    association secretary
national city department, 115, 120,
    137, 138
national committee: accepts Cai Kui's
    resignation, 152; articulates
    association's Chineseness, 191; chair
    as part of personnel committee,
    154; Chinese women become
    officers of, 49, 190; choice of
    national general secretaries, 63–64,
    67–68; composition of, 47, 122,
    153; on cooperation with Chinese
    YMCA, 26; decision to send
    Western secretaries home, 156,
    157, 165; delays in hiring Deng
    Yuzhi and Cai Kui, 60; Deng Yuzhi
    defers to, 178; Deng Yuzhi's radical
    friends escape notice of, 98; enters
    CIC movement, 120; on field
    survey, 93; formed, 21, 23, 201n7;
    forms rural department, 88; goals
    for Normal School, 32; important
    role of, 48; industrial work and,
    34, 37, 38, 84, 90–91, 137, 192;
    Kunming YWCA not recognized
    by, 114; lends Haass to NCC, 83;
    promoting Deng Yuzhi and Cai

Kui, 64–65, 66, 67–68; resolves
not to accept foreign funding, 169;
response to May Thirtieth Incident,
43–44, 48, 88, 99, 191, 194; rules
for training Chinese secretaries,
45–46; as socially conservative, 92,
106; Sui-May Kuo Ting on, 222*n*3
national committee (Finland), 183, 224*n*53
national committee chairs, 44, 47–48, 74,
99, 154
national committee chairs (Japan), 125
National Conference on Christianizing
Economic Relations (1927), 80
national conventions, 134, 136, 142,
153, 223*n*22. *See also* first national
convention; second national
convention; third national convention
national conventions (United States), 34–35
National Council of Women, 100
national executive committee:
composition of, 47, 122, 153;
decision to relocate headquarters,
122–23; meeting of enlarged,
153–55, 156–57, 191, 194; power
invested in, 143; presidents of, 129;
reaction to Japan's involvement
with Shanghai committee, 126–27;
rehabilitation budget and, 136; role
of, 48; on Sinification, 3, 144
national general secretaries: emergency,
126–27, 131; Haass more powerful
than, 171–72; on personnel
committee, 154. *See also* Cai Kui;
Coppock, Grace; Deng Yuzhi; Ding
Shujing; Paddock, Estelle; Venable,
Rosalee
national general secretaries (Japan),
121, 125
national girls' work committee, 138
national headquarters building, 125–26,
127, 147, 189
national industrial department: accepts
Gideon Chen's recommendations,
94; closure, 37, 65; Ferry Road
Center and, 96; formed, 19, 39, 51;
Jiang Qing's work at, 107; reopening,
82, 84, 90; takes on mass education

and industrial cooperatives, 139.
See also Deng Yuzhi: industrial work
by; industrial work
national industrial secretaries, 44–45,
76–77. *See also* Deng Yuzhi:
industrial work by
National League for Defense, 100
national office, 110–43
approach to, 110, 143
Cai Kui joins, 60
Deng Yuzhi joins, 58, 60
and formation of Guangzhou city association, 47
Gao Renying's work at, 208*n*16
Garvie's work at, 223*n*22
Gerlach's work at, 225*n*73
lack of mid-1950s documents from, 167
1947 World YWCA Council meeting
and, 140–42
during 1949 battle for Shanghai, 146–47
number of Chinese vs Western staff
at, 192
position on Japanese aggression, 101
on progressiveness of their Christianity,
158
reaction to city associations' direct
affiliation with World YWCA, 127,
217*n*53
Rees visits, 181
rehabilitation budget of, 136–38
during Sino-Japanese War: feels
discouraged, 130–32; goal of maintaining autonomy and identity,
118; Japan declares war on Chinese
YWCA, 125–28; new trends noted
by Haass, 123–24; during 1937
battle for Shanghai, 111; postwar
plan of, 132–34, 136; relocates
headquarters, 114, 122–23, 134;
travels, 61, 112–15, 116, 117; and
visits by Japanese YWCA members,
121–22, 125; war-relief work,
119–21, 130, 131; west China
regional conference, 128–30
steadfast leadership of, 194
studies CCP literature, 145, 147
uneasiness about Maoist state, 149

National People's Congress, 186
national personnel secretaries, 66, 67, 171, 192
National Salvation Movement, 98, 108
National Southwestern Association University, 114
national student secretaries: Deng Yuzhi, 4, 60, 65, 191; Garvie, 223n22; Shi Baozhen, 208n16; Steel-Brooke, 66
National Training School (New York City), 23, 31, 64, 70
nationalism: approach to, 6, 110, 194; Cai Kui on "irrational," 74; China as "too nationalistic," 122; Deng Yuzhi's, 73, 149; Ding Shujing on negative influence of, 70; in statement to Lytton Commission, 99, 100, 191; as threat to Christianity, 51; in Wang Guoxiu's 1951 YWCA Magazine article, 168; at west China regional conference, 129. See also patriotism; politics
Nationalist army, 112, 145
Nationalist government, 77, 89, 90, 118, 123
Nationalist Party. See Guomindang
NCC. See National Christian Council (NCC)
Netherlands, 125, 136
new China: approach to, 143; Cai Kui on, 115, 117, 130; discussed at enlarged national executive committee meeting, 153; national office's lack of consensus on 1949, 147; in national office's postwar plan, 133; of 1928, 87, 88; as theme of west China regional conference, 129. See also Maoist state
New Culture Movement, 20, 199n5
New Democracy, 145, 149. See also Maoist state
New History of Christianity in China (Bays), 9
New Life Movement, 118
"New Trends in the Young Women's Christian Association" (Haass), 123–24
new women, 7–8, 11, 25, 192, 199n5

New York University, 139
New Youth (magazine), 20
night schools: average attendance at, 90–91; CCP cadres working in, 98; closure, 139, 151, 181, 213n55; courses in, 85, 86, 96; as prototype for mass education, 124; teacher kidnapped from, 136, 218n80
Normal School for Hygiene and Physical Education, 23, 31–33, 50
North China Herald, 13, 40, 41, 42, 44
North China Union Women's College, 55, 57, 59, 207n6
North Korea, 164, 175

Ohio Quakerism, 208n10
"On the Correct Handling of Contradictions among the People" (Mao Zedong), 185–86
"On the Cult of Personality and Its Consequences" (Khrushchev), 184
organizing labour: Chambéry resolutions and, 36; communism and, 85; discussed at second industrial secretaries' conference, 92; Gideon Chen on, 94; Harrison on, 37; Hinder's interest in, 80; training in, 86, 103, 108

Packard, Ruth, 120
Paddock, Estelle, 22, 26, 27, 30, 31
Pak Chong-ae, 166
Palmer, Elizabeth, 140–41, 158–59, 178, 179, 184–85
Paris Peace Conference (1919), 20
patriotism, 162, 163, 170, 185. See also nationalism
peace: American imperialism and Chinese YWCA's pursuit of, 141, 165; Cai Kui's pursuit of, 75; Deng Yuzhi on world, 179; Ding Shujing's pursuit of, 63, 70; Japanese aggression and Chinese YWCA's desire for, 99, 100–1; as women's issue, 35
Pearl Harbor attack, 125, 213n55
Peng Dehuai, 164
People's Daily, 162, 186
People's Representative Conference, 180

People's Republic of China (PRC):
    creation of, 142, 147, 150, 152;
    histories of Christianity in, 145;
    in Korean War, 162, 164–65, 176;
    magazine allowed in United States,
    179; open and conciliatory era in,
    183–84, 185; Russell supports,
    200*n*17. *See also* Maoist state
personnel committee, 154
pictorial brochure, 183–84
Pierce, Florence, 152, 157
political neutrality, 146, 158, 194
politics: in enlarged national executive
    committee meeting, 154–55; May
    Fourth Movement's influence on Cai
    Kui's, 55, 57, 58–59, 63, 75; World
    YWCA Council on Christianity
    and, 142; in *YWCA Magazine*'s
    1957 issues, 182. *See also* Deng
    Yuzhi: politics and; nationalism
Polk, Margaret, 40
Porter, Robin, 102, 204*n*60, 205*n*83
PRC. *See* People's Republic of China (PRC)
Precious Fire (Garner), 10
"Present-Day Tragedy of Christianity"
    (Wu Yaozong), 147–48
press bylaw, 41–42
Principles of Foreign Policy, 154
prisoner exchange, 128, 159, 217*n*60
private schools, 30, 31
professional women, 87–88
programs. *See* education work;
    industrial work
progressiveness: of American, British,
    and World YWCAs, 5, 18, 192;
    American imperialism's use of,
    173; of Chinese YWCA, 149,
    154, 158; in Ding Shujing's and
    Deng Yuzhi's families, 55, 56, 59;
    Jiangnan as region of, 57; Robbins
    Strong on some Christians', 160
Protestant church. *See* indigenous church
    movement
Protestants, 5, 101, 192–93. *See also*
    Society of Friends
protests, 20, 56, 59, 135, 218*n*93. *See also*
    May Thirtieth Incident
Pudong, 83, 85, 147

Qian Cuige, 78, 197
Qing dynasty, 19–20, 30, 57
Qinghua University, 114
Quakers. *See* Society of Friends

radicalism: Cai Kui's, 59; Deng Yuzhi
    and, 56, 66, 95, 98; in mid-1930s,
    105–8; radical Christians in
    Chinese YMCA and YWCA, 157;
    Russell's, 62, 98, 200*n*17; Shanghai
    intellectuals', 76–77, 83; and vocal
    attacks on the United States, 135
ratepayers, 40, 41, 42–43
reconstruction, 116, 132, 134
Rees, Janet W., 181, 182, 224*n*45
refugees, 111, 115, 117, 120–21, 159
regional conferences, 116–17, 128–30
Regulations Governing All Organizations
    Subsidized with Foreign Funds
    (State Council), 169
religion. *See* Buddhism; Christianity;
    Confucianism
religious freedom, 30, 160, 161, 178
Republican government, 20
Resist America and Assist Korea movement,
    166, 167, 169, 170–71, 172
Resolution 83, 164
"Responsibility of the YWCA in the
    Reconstruction of China" (Deng
    Yuzhi), 148–49
Roberts, Helen, 145–46, 150–52, 177, 183
romanization, 14
Roosevelt, Franklin, 127
rural associations, 153
rural department, 52, 88
rural women, 87, 88, 103, 104, 124
Russell, Maud: Christian socialism of,
    58, 102; friendship with Deng
    Yuzhi, 10, 65, 189; promotes CIC
    movement, 120; radicalism of, 62,
    98, 200*n*17
Russian Communist International
    (Comintern), 20–21, 77

Sahlins, Marshall, 6
schools: Fuxiang Middle School for Girls,
    56, 57, 60, 62; government, 27,
    30–31, 32; Shanghai Municipal

Council and, 40; Zhounan Girls'
     Middle School, 55, 148. *See also*
     education; mission schools; night
     schools
Search for Modern China (Spence),
     225*n*65
Second International Congress of
     Working Women, 39
second national convention (1928), 6,
     87–89, 93, 117, 194
Second World Peace Conference (1950),
     165–66, 175
secretarial conferences, 21, 28, 46, 49,
     87. *See also* industrial secretaries'
     conferences
self-governance, 89
setting-up conference (1947), 139–40
settlement projects, 78–79, 80, 85, 211*n*8
Severin, Theresa, 63, 69
Shaanxi Province, 120
Shandong Province, 19, 55, 127, 159
Shanghai: Chiang Kai-shek's army reaches,
     77, 79; fall of, 111, 144; Garvie on
     her experience in, 159; internment
     camps in, 127, 217*n*56; McClelland
     visits pastors in, 181; mills in, 34,
     37, 203*n*52; mission schools in,
     202*n*21; national headquarters
     relocates from, 122–23; radical
     intellectuals in, 76–77, 83
Shanghai Baptist College, 85
Shanghai city association: Chen Jieshi's
     work at, 188; Coppock's work at,
     4, 18, 26, 27–28, 47, 190; Deng
     Yuzhi's work at, 58; Ding Mingyu's
     work at, 49; Jeger visits, 180;
     Johnston's work at, 45; location,
     116; Mrs. L.C. King's work at, 102;
     during 1949 battle for Shanghai,
     147; Normal School and, 33; in
     occupied territory, 111; scholarship
     on, 11; Shanghai radicals and,
     76–77; Social Service Institute at,
     29. *See also* industrial work
Shanghai committee of the national
     committee, 123, 125, 126–27
Shanghai International Settlement:
     bombing of, 111; city association's

location in, 116; extraterritoriality
     in, 44; Garden Bridge as boundary
     of, 126; hostility toward Japanese
     community in, 99; industrial
     work and, 35, 38–40, 94–95,
     96; Japanese occupy, 125, 139,
     213*n*55; May Thirtieth Incident
     in, 18, 21, 43; press bylaw and, 41;
     YWCA headquarters in, 23
Shanghai Municipal Archives, 12, 13
Shanghai Municipal Council, 39–40, 41,
     43, 119
Shanghai Volunteer Corps, 126
Shanghai War, 72, 99–100, 103–4, 110
Shanghai Women's Club, 38
Shantou, 117
Sheng Zuxin, 47–48, 99, 100, 125,
     126–27, 197
Shi, Xia, 11
Shi Baozhen, 181, 197, 208*n*16
Shi Meiyu, 40
Shi Ruzhang, 181, 197
Shu Houren, Mrs., 113
Sichuan Province, 157–58
silk filature factories, 84–85
Sinification: approach to, 3–5, 53,
     190–95; completion of, 167; vs
     indigenization, 5, 190; Mrs. Shu
     Houren on, 113; national executive
     committee on, 3, 144; Wang
     Guoxiu and Deng Yuzhi on, 157;
     war necessitates, 114. *See also* Cai
     Kui; Deng Yuzhi; Ding Shujing;
     indigenization; Maoist state
Sino-American Treaty for the
     Relinquishment of Extraterritorial
     Rights in China, 44
Sino-Japanese War: approach to, 15;
     beginning of, 110–11, 125; as
     catalyst for Chinese nationalism,
     194; end of, 135; Hundred
     Regiments Campaign, 124; Japan
     declares war on Chinese YWCA,
     125–28; Japanese-occupied territory
     in 1939, 117; Nanjing Massacre,
     112; Pacific War and, 116; Shanghai
     International Settlement occupied,
     125, 139, 213*n*55; as spiritualizing

experience, 110, 193; tests Chinese YWCA women, 110; Tianjin Incident, 118. *See also* national office: during Sino-Japanese War

Sino-Western hybrid, 5, 18, 114, 191

Sisters and Strangers (Honig), 10

Smedley, Agnes, 98

Smith, Harriet, 80

Smith College, 13, 37

Snow, Edgar, 98, 120

Snow, Helen Foster, 98, 120

social equality, 4, 62, 74

social feminism, 199n10

social gospel movement, 62, 102

social justice, 4, 35, 56, 109, 160. *See also* industrial work

Social Service Institute, 29

Society of Friends (Quakers): Cai Kui as member of, 54, 58, 62, 75, 151, 193; Harrison as member of, 204n60; Nanjing Fellowship and Ohio Quakerism, 208n10; 1955 delegation visits China, 181

Song Meiling, 40, 107, 118–19, 120, 141, 197

Song Qingling, 179, 189

Songshu, 120

Sophia Smith Collection of Women's History, 13

South Korea, 164

Soviet Union, 164, 165, 176, 184, 185

Spence, Jonathan, 225n65

Spencer, Clarissa: indigenization as goal of, 3, 27, 45, 53; industrial work and, 34; negotiates with NCC, 107; vision for Chinese YWCA, 27, 28; work assigned by, 11

Spielberg, Steven, 217n56

Spreading Protestant Modernity (book), 11

St. John's University, 141, 156, 218n93

St. Mary's Episcopal Church, 202n21

Stalin, Joseph, 146, 184, 185

State Council, 169, 185

Steel-Brooke, Gertrude, 66

Stockholm Appeal, 175

strikes, 108

Strong, Anna Louise, 98

Strong, Robbins, 159–60, 162

student department, 138

student secretaries, 31. *See also* national student secretaries

student work, 27, 30–31, 138

student YWCAs: in Britain and United States, 202n23; Deng Yuzhi's work at, 56, 60, 62, 65; in 1890, 201n7; at enlarged national executive committee meeting, 153; field survey and, 93; number of, 24; Paddock establishes, 31; rehabilitation budget and, 138; at third national convention, 104

students, 87, 131, 149

study groups, 98, 145, 147, 171, 186–87, 213n60

"Study of the YWCA of China 1891–1930" (report), 93–94

"Studying Chairman Mao's 'On the Correct Handling of Contradictions'" (*YWCA Magazine*), 186–87

Su Shi, 56

"Summary of Conversations with Cora Deng" (World YWCA), 178

Sun Dayu, 187

Sun Yat-sen, 20, 77, 210n60

Supreme Commander for the Allied Powers (SCAP), 141

Suyekane, Mr., 126

Suzhou University, 114

Taiwan, 156, 164

Tao Zhixing, 98

Taylor, Harriet, 27

Theological College (Nanjing), 222n3

third national convention (1933): churchgoing policy changed at, 36; CIC movement fulfills promises of, 120; Ding Shujing at, 72, 193; nationalism and, 6; overview of, 103–5; west China regional conference and, 130

Thoburn, Helen, 17–18, 26, 50–51, 63, 76

Thompson, Paul, 217n59

"Thousand Characters" (literacy texts), 86

Three-Self Patriotic Movement, 163, 182, 222n3

Three-Self reform movement, 169–71
Thurston, Matilda, 58, 65
Tian Han, 96–97, 98
Tianjin, 106, 111, 126, 131, 159
Tianjin city association, 111, 116, 120,
     126, 208n16
Tianjin Incident, 118
Tillman, Margaret Mih, 11
Ting, K.H., 222n3
Ting, Sui-May Kuo, 181, 197, 222n3,
     223n32
Tong Xing mill, 108
treaty ports, 27, 116
Truman, Harry, 146
Tu Yuqing, 141, 218n93

unions, 78, 81, 85, 91, 95, 106. See also
     labour movement
United Front: First, 21, 77, 79, 88, 89;
     Second, 111, 112, 113
united front policy, 161
United Nations, 173, 175
United Nations Security Council, 164
United States: atomic bombs dropped by,
     135; Cai Kui's time in, 67, 74; civil
     war and, 146, 156; Deng Yuzhi's
     time in, 139; as destination for
     refugees, 159; Ding Shujing's time
     in, 63, 64, 68–69, 70, 191; Gerlach
     criticizes, 225n71; internees from,
     125; investments in China during
     First World War, 203n52; jobs for
     Chinese students returning from,
     149; Mao on, 154; PRC magazine
     allowed in, 179; PRC supporters
     in, 200n17; prisoner exchange with
     Japan, 217n60; refusal to enter
     Sino-Japanese War, 118; at war
     with Japan, 125, 127, 129. See also
     American imperialism; American
     secretaries; YWCA of the USA
University of Nebraska, 23
upper-class women, 28–30, 202n23
urban women, 27–30, 202n23. See also
     industrial work
"US Imperialists' Criminal Invasion of
     China via the YWCA" (Deng
     Yuzhi), 172, 223n20
US State Department, 44, 123, 173

Venable, Rosalee: appointed national gen-
     eral secretary, 33, 64; Ding Shujing
     confides intention to resign to, 108;
     lends Haass to NCC, 44; promotes
     Ding Shujing's advancement, 33,
     50, 64, 66, 69
Visapää, Sylvi, 140, 141, 183, 184–85

Wang, Zheng, 177–78
Wang Cunyi, 183
Wang Guoxiu: article in 1951 YWCA
     Magazine, 168–69; Christian
     Manifesto and, 162; on Deng
     Yuzhi, 156–57; at enlarged national
     executive committee meeting, 153;
     in glossary, 197; name appears
     on post-1949 documents, 147;
     as national committee chair, 48,
     74; in pictorial brochure, 184;
     relationships with Western women,
     156; steadfast leadership of, 194
Wang Xiuqing, 170, 172, 175–77, 197,
     223n32
Wang Zhijin, 85–86, 97, 98, 197
war-relief work, 119–21, 130, 131
War of Resistance against Japan. See Sino-
     Japanese War
Ward, Jane, 102–3
Weimura, Mrs., 125
Weixian Civilian Assembly Center, 127,
     159, 217n57, 217n59
Wellesley College, 47, 119
Wen Yiduo, 135
West, Ruth, 155–56, 157–58
west China regional conference (1942),
     128–30
West China Union College, 114
Western imperialism, 40–41, 44, 89
Western secretaries and staff: acknowledged
     at enlarged national executive
     committee meeting, 153–54;
     approach to, 15, 144; Australian, 34,
     204n55 (see also Hinder, Eleanor);
     British, 22, 45, 49 (see also Garvie,
     Margaret); Cai Kui's attitude toward,
     68, 133; Chinese YWCA depends
     on, 31; Chinese YWCA severs
     ties with, 68, 155–56, 157–58,
     165, 177, 191–92; on Christian

revolution, 158–59, 160, 162; cultural transmission experienced by, 7; decreasing number of, 71–72, 105; difficulty with indigenization, 46, 51, 53, 133; Ding Shujing's attitude toward, 62, 68–69, 105; "direct approach" alters relationship with Chinese secretaries, 86–87; and Jiang Qing, 107; leave China after Maoist revolution, 139; limitations on role in industrial work, 82; living in settlement project, 78–79; meeting style of, 47; necessary for setting up YWCAs, 22; number of Chinese vs, 49–50, 90, 105, 192; oppose imperialism, 18; promote Deng Yuzhi's and Cai Kui's advancement, 65–66; qualifications required of, 48–49, 68–69; role in democratization of Chinese YWCA, 143; at second industrial secretaries' conference, 91; sent to city associations, 25; Sino-Japanese War and, 114, 116, 121; third national convention and, 193. *See also* American secretaries

Where to Go? (skit), 96

WIDF. *See* Women's International Democratic Federation (WIDF)

Witke, Roxanne, 107

wives, old-style vs new-style, 29

women in the home, 87

women labour leaders. *See* labour movement

women of leisure, 27, 28–30, 87

Women's Advisory Council, 118–19, 131

Women's Christian Temperance Union. *See* Chinese Women's Christian Temperance Union

Women's International Democratic Federation (WIDF), 166, 177–80

Women's International League for Peace and Freedom, 70, 89, 99

Women's Rights Association, 100

Women's Suffrage Association, 100

Wong, Christina Wai-yin, 10

Woodsmall, Ruth: Cai Kui's letters to, 121, 127, 135; Deng Yuzhi denounces, 174; desire to hire Ding

Shujing, 108; Dudley's letter to, 134; on Lytton Commission, 100; at 1947 World YWCA Council meeting, 140–41; resignation of, 142; work on Laymen's Foreign Missions Inquiry, 101–3

working classes, 72, 81, 82, 88–89. *See also* industrial women; industrial work

world conferences and conventions (YWCA), 22, 34, 70

World Court, 89

World Federation of Democratic Youth (WFDY), 183

World Student Christian Federation, 20, 222n3

World YWCA: agreement with YWCA of the USA, 23; annual reports to, 50; attempts to find newsworthy items from China, 169, 181; Castrèn at, 224n53; Chinese YWCA as full constituent of, 64; Christian denunciation campaign and, 173–75, 176; *Common Concerns* publication, 226n75; contact with Deng Yuzhi at WIDF conference, 177–80; on cooperation with YMCA, 26; direct affiliations with, 127, 217n53; and enlarged national executive committee meeting, 154, 155; Far Eastern regional conference, 74; formed, 21–22; funds Deng Yuzhi's 1950 travels to conferences, 165; indigenization policy of, 4, 5, 190; industrial secretaries at, 40, 81; interest in industrial work, 34, 35–36, 39; job offer to Ding Shujing, 108; maintenance of relationship with Chinese YWCA, 154, 157, 167, 177; missionaries' role in expansion of, 22, 25; 1950s attempts to visit China, 183; 1957 visit to China, 184–85, 186; position on Sino-Japanese War, 121; progressive agenda of, 5, 18, 192; relocates headquarters, 140; and sources for study, 12, 13; women's internationalism embraced by, 70, 75; *YWCA Magazine* and, 168–69

World YWCA Archives, 12, 14, 220n51
World YWCA Committee, 90
World YWCA Council: Ding Shujing as
    member of, 72, 108; meetings of,
    35, 70, 140–42, 174, 177
World YWCA executive committee:
    meetings of, 136, 165, 166; news
    of Chinese YWCA forwarded to,
    180–81; and 1947 World YWCA
    Council meeting, 140; on 1957
    visit to China, 184–85; on Sino-
    Japanese War, 121; Visapää on, 183
World YWCA general secretaries,
    145–46, 150–52, 177, 183. See also
    Palmer, Elizabeth; Spencer, Clarissa;
    Woodsmall, Ruth
Wu Yaozong: at Chinese People's Political
    Consultative Conference, 150;
    Christian Manifesto and, 162;
    on communism as solution for
    China's problems, 160; Deng
    Yuzhi's friendship with, 98; in
    glossary, 198; meeting with Zhou
    Enlai, 161; "Present-Day Tragedy
    of Christianity," 147–48; Robbins
    Strong and, 159; scholarship
    on, 10; social gospel movement
    promoted by, 62, 102; "state of
    Chinese Christianity" speech by,
    169–71; at west China regional
    conference, 129
Wu Yifang, 10–11, 12, 123, 129, 130, 197
Wuchang city association, 112
Wuhan, 77, 112, 115
Wuxi, 106

Xiamen, 147
Xian city association, 183
Xiang Jingyu, 55–56, 207n3
Xinhai Revolution, 20, 54–55, 57, 62
Xu Peiling, 98, 197

Yale Divinity Library, 13
Yale-in-China Hospital, 56
Yan, James, 86
Yang Kaihui, 55–56
Yang Shuyin, 197
Yangshupu, 85

Yangtze River, 146
Yanjing University, 114, 207n6
Yantai, 116, 176
YMCA of the USA, 25, 92
YMCAs, 126. See also Chinese YMCA
Yong An mill, 108
Yu Xiu'ai, 182
Yuan Shikai, 20, 55
Yugoslavia, 164, 176
Yunnan Province, 114–15
YWCA of India, 185
YWCA Leadership Training Institute,
    165, 166
YWCA Magazine: on association's 1951
    work, 181; ceases and resumes
    publication, 168; Chen Jieshi's
    article in, 188; Cheng Wanzhen's
    articles in, 39, 40–41; Deng Yuzhi's
    articles in, 148–49, 165–66,
    168–69, 172; "Denounce!," 167,
    172–73; "Green Year" Supplement,
    79, 85, 206n101; 1957 issues, 182;
    as source for study, 13; "Studying
    Chairman Mao's 'On the Correct
    Handling of Contradictions,'"
    186–87
YWCA Record Group 5, 13, 14
"YWCA Seeks Its Place in a Social
    Revolution" (Hinder), 79–80, 81
YWCA of the USA: annual reports
    to, 50; archives, 156; Chinese
    YWCA requests workers from,
    27, 31, 34; defining influence of,
    84; denounced, 174, 175; Ding
    Shujing's vision for cooperation
    with, 71; extends YWCA
    movement, 21–22; field survey by,
    92; first secretaries sent to China,
    26; funding provided by, 23, 64;
    Gerlach's work at, 149; national
    conventions of, 34–35; Pierce
    and Anderson at, 152; progressive
    agenda of, 5, 192; Sarah Lyon at, 62;
    secretaries sent to city associations,
    25; Sino-Japanese War and, 117,
    121; Song Meiling speaks at
    convention of, 119; and sources
    for study, 13, 14; student YWCAs

in, 202*n*23; war ends rivalry with
British YWCA, 140; Woodsmall
as member of, 101; work with
urban women, 28. *See also*
Foreign Division
YWCAs, 183, 184, 185, 224*n*83. *See also*
British YWCA; Chinese YWCA;
Japanese YWCA; World YWCA

Zeng Baosun, 12
Zeng Guofan, 12
Zhabei, 20, 78–79, 84–85, 111, 126
Zhabei Civilian Assembly Center,
127–28
Zhang, Aihua, 7–8, 11–12, 199*n*5
Zhang Bojun, 187

Zhang Dabing, 207*n*7
Zhang Xueyan, 150
Zhang Yuezhen, 197
Zhao Zichen, 150, 198
Zhejiang Province, 56–57, 117
Zheng Ruquan (Beatrice Djeng), 126,
131, 198
Zhou Enlai: on broad support for socialist
system, 160; on Christianity's
future in China, 163–64; meetings
with Christian representatives, 113,
161–62, 169, 170; remakes PRC's
image, 183
Zhou Shao Yirong, 120
Zhounan Girls' Middle School, 55, 148
Zhu De, 184

Printed and bound in Canada by Friesens
Set in Garamond by Apex CoVantage, LLC
Copy editor: Frank Chow
Proofreader and indexer: Marnie Lamb
Cartographer: Eric Leinberger
Cover designer: George Kirkpatrick
Cover images: *Bottom left:* "Singkiang Conference 1919"; *top left:*
  "Training Class for Leaders"; *bottom right:* "YWCA Group Photo."
  Courtesy of the Anderson photograph collection of YWCA in China,
  1920s–40s, East Asia Library Special Collections, Stanford University.